By the Same Author

Renegades: Hitler's Englishmen
Science and the Swastika

Patriot Traitors

Roger Casement, John Amery and the Real Meaning of Treason

ADRIAN WEALE

VIKING

VIKING

Published by the Penguin Group
Penguin Books Ltd, 27 Wrights Lane, London W 8 5 T Z, England
Penguin Putnam Inc., 375 Hudson Street, New York, New York 10014, USA
Penguin Books Australia Ltd, Ringwood, Victoria, Australia
Penguin Books Canada Ltd, 10 Alcorn Avenue, Toronto, Ontario, Canada M 4 V 3 B 2
Penguin Books India (P) Ltd, 11 Community Centre,
Panchsheel Park, New Delhi – 110 017, India
Penguin Books (NZ) Ltd, Cnr Rosedale and Airborne Roads,
Albany, Auckland, New Zealand
Penguin Books (South Africa) (Pty) Ltd, 5 Watkins Street,
Denver Ext 4, Johannesburg 2094, South Africa

Penguin Books Ltd, Registered Offices: Harmondsworth, Middlesex, England

First published 2001
1

Copyright © Adrian Weale, 2001

The moral right of the author has been asserted

Set in 12/14.75pt Monotype Bembo
Typeset by Rowland Phototypesetting Ltd,
Bury St Edmunds, Suffolk
Printed in Great Britain by Clays Ltd, St Ives plc

A CIP catalogue record for this book is available from the British Library

ISBN 0-670-88498-7

Contents

List of Illustrations

Illustration Acknowledgements

1, 7, 36: Mansell/Time Pix/Katz; 2, 6, 16: courtesy of the National Library of Ireland – 2 (Ref: R10131), 6 (Ref: t101 green), 16 (Ref: t176 Casement); 3: Anti-Slavery International; 4, 38: © Bettmann/CORBIS; 5, 9: Mary Evans Picture Library; 8, 19, 21, 28: Hulton Getty; 10, 27, 29, 30, 31, 32, 39: Public Records Office; 11, 12: National Maritime Museum of Ireland; 13, 18, 22: Topham; 14, 15: Camera Press; 17: Press Association/Topham; 20: Associated Press/Topham; 23: London Metropolitan Archives; 24: reproduced by courtesy of the keepers and governors of Harrow School; 25: Popperfoto; 26: © Underwood & Underwood/CORBIS; 33: Popperfoto/UPI; 34: Author; 35: AKG, London; 37: Syndication International

Acknowledgements

In writing this book I am indebted to the following institutions: The Public Records Office, London; the National Library of Ireland, Dublin; The Bundesarchiv, Koblenz; The United States National Archives, Washington; the Imperial War Museum, London; Harrow School; Kensington Public Library; the Haldane Library of the Imperial College of Science and Technology.

Much of the material in this book has been derived from personal files compiled by the Security Service (MI5) and recently released to the Public Records Office. Whilst I can't claim credit for having these documents released, I have found the Security Service a surprisingly helpful and responsive organization and I would like to place on record my gratitude to the Director General and his officers.

I have sought information, advice and guidance from individuals too numerous to mention but I must particularly cite my long-suffering – and immensely patient – editor Eleo Gordon and her team; Helen MacLeod Campbell who meticulously and considerately copy-edited an embarrassingly raw manuscript; and, as always, my agent, Andrew Lownie for his encouragement.

Finally, my personal thanks are due to Elizabeth Anne and Michael Wainwright, in whose house I was staying when much of the book was written; Diane Vilquin, Anne Grosset and my mother, Carole Weale, who looked after the children and kept everything running while I was tearing my hair out trying to string sentences together; and of course my wife Mary for her great patience, support and ruthless criticism of my grammar.

Introduction

'Hegel says somewhere that all great events and personalities in history reappear in one fashion or another. He forgot to add: the first time as tragedy, the second as farce.'[1]

On 3 August 1916 the executioner Albert Ellis led Roger Casement the short distance from the death cell in Pentonville Prison, north London, to the gallows. Until four days previously Casement had been a knight bachelor and Companion of the Order of St Michael and St George, but now, stripped of his Imperial honours and convicted of high treason, he was to be hanged.

Ellis remembered:

The impression will ever remain on my mind of the composure of his noble countenance, the smile of contentment and happiness, as he willingly helped my assistant. . . . The steady martial tread of his six feet four inches and soldierly appearance adding to the solemn echo of his prompt and coherent answers to the Roman Catholic chaplain . . . Roger Casement appeared to me the bravest man it fell to my unhappy lot to execute.

Hooded, and with the noose about his neck, Casement's last words were 'Lord Jesus receive my soul.' 'He may have been a traitor,' recalled Ellis, 'but he died like a soldier.'[2]

A little less than thirty years later, on 19 December 1945, a similar scene was enacted across the Thames at Wandsworth Prison. Ellis's eventual successor as 'number one' on the Prison Commissioner's list of approved executioners, Albert Pierrepoint, entered the death cell to lead John Amery to the scaffold. By this time Pierrepoint had officiated at well over 100 hangings in Britain and Ireland (and in the course of the next ten years would carry out 400 more) and they had become more or less routine for him, yet he was surprised when his victim turned to meet him as he entered the death cell and held out his hand. Pierrepoint took it. 'Mr Pierrepoint,' Amery told him, 'I've always wanted to meet you, although not, of course, under these circumstances.' Pierrepoint shook his hand, then gently turned him about, pinioned his arms and propelled him through to the death chamber. A few seconds later he was dead. 'He was', concluded Pierrepoint, 'the bravest man I ever hanged.'[3]

Why have I chosen to compare Roger Casement and John Amery? There is a simple answer to this and also a complex one. The simple answer is that after I researched and wrote a book about British traitors in the Second World War,★ a friend suggested I should read Brian Inglis's masterly biography of Casement. The complex answer is that I was struck then, and remain struck, by how closely their careers *as traitors* paralleled each other. Their crimes, and the outcome of their crimes, were as identical as two separate and unrelated events in history can possibly be. As a conscientious historian of the modern school I can only conclude that this is the result of coincidence.

Despite what is probably only a superficial – if striking – similarity between the details of the two cases, it did seem to me that a more extended and general pursuit of the parallels between these examples of treason was worthwhile. Treason, as we shall see, has always held a place as a special crime – not only in Britain – and traitors have usually been held in particular contempt, not just by the group or people they betray, but often also by those who employ them. It is worth noting, for example, that the traitor and spy Kim Philby was not permitted to enter the headquarters of the KGB, for whom he had been an important agent for nearly thirty years, for many years after he finally defected to Moscow. Leaders of indigenous collaborationist groups in German-occupied Europe were kept, as a rule, as far from the real levers of power as their

★ *Renegades: Hitler's Englishmen*, Weidenfeld and Nicolson, 1994.

German rulers could tactfully manage, whilst they were still encouraged to provide Germany with military and industrial manpower. Ideas of loyalty are evidently widespread, instinctive and deep-rooted. To become a traitor is to break a very powerful and long-standing social and cultural taboo: stronger, if we make a simple numerical comparison, than those against murder, rape and a whole realm of crimes which would appear to have consequences which are at least as serious.

In so far as nobody has published a full-length biography of John Amery and research into his life has been limited, he does not pose any great problems of interpretation for modern historians, but the opposite is true of Casement. Since his execution in 1916 he has been the subject of a considerable number of historical and biographical investigations, many of which have been of great value, but few of which have concentrated on the reason for which he is remembered now: although he was correctly convicted of high treason on the plainest evidence one could imagine, the British Government took great pains to ensure that he was hanged for it through their disgraceful use of Casement's private diaries, the so-called 'Black Diaries', which revealed him to be, *inter alia*, a predatory and unrepentant pederast.

Amery was the victim of a similar circumstance. He had pleaded guilty to high treason – the only person recorded as having done so – on the basis that he had no possible defence in law (neither had Casement, although his lawyers essayed one), but his lifelong history of personality disorder might well have led his lawyers and family to hope that the Government might grant him clemency. This turned out to be a forlorn hope.

The similarities between the courses of action which led Casement and Amery to the scaffold are striking: both men found themselves outside the country when the United Kingdom, of which they were native citizens, went to war with Germany; both had strong political convictions opposed to the existing British constitution; both understood that they were faced with a choice between acquiescence in a war with which they strongly disagreed – and treason.

Nor do the parallels end there. One of the most striking points of comparison between the two men is how ineffectual they were. For all their fervour, Casement's recruiting efforts for his Irish Brigade and Amery's for the British Free Corps raised only a handful of recruits, and both men were miserable propagandists. How then could the British Government see their actions as such a threat to the state that it needed to liquidate them, and in Casement's case to mount a disreputable propaganda campaign in a largely successful attempt to forestall criticism and protest? The answer lies in the special nature of the crime of high treason.

'If a man do levy war against our Lord the King in his realm or be adherent to the King's enemies in his realm, giving them aid and comfort in the realm or elsewhere', he has committed high treason. Until 1998, a guilty verdict on such a charge would have led to an automatic death sentence, which would have been carried out — since the abolition of the death penalty for murder — at the country's last operational gallows at Wandsworth Prison.

Had the conviction occurred prior to 1820, the means of execution would have been somewhat more savage than the brisk and almost clinical hangings which took place in the twentieth century. Albert Pierrepoint, who conducted the executions of traitors at the end of the Second World War, would take a last puff on his trademark cigar and then place it in the ashtray in the executioners' room before going to the death cell entrance a few seconds before the appointed time. He timed his routine so that he arrived there just ahead of the High Sheriff's party and would be instantly ready for action. Once the signal was given he was generally confident that he could have his victim pinioned, hooded and dead at the end of the rope within approximately fifteen seconds of first entering the death cell, dropping the prisoner between six and eight feet, depending on height, weight and build, to ensure instantaneous death; on occasion he achieved this in considerably less time. To the amazement of his younger assistants, and the macabre amusement of the older ones, his cigar would generally still be alight when he returned to retrieve it a few minutes later.

When the Cato Street conspirators, who had plotted to assassinate members of the Cabinet, went to the Newgate gallows in the last public executions for high treason, on 1 May 1820 in front of a large crowd, their deaths were evidently less quick. At that time, hanging was by means of a short drop of a couple of feet or so, insufficient to kill the prisoner outright or even induce unconsciousness: 'Brunt [one of the conspirators] kicked and choked for five minutes on his noose, until the executioner pulled his legs.'[4]

An hour after the five conspirators had been hanged, they were removed from their nooses and placed in coffins, still in full view of the public. At this point, a masked man took each body in turn and decapitated it with an anatomist's knife before handing the heads to the assistant executioner who lifted each and loudly informed the crowd that 'This is the head of the traitor . . .' – for example – '. . . Thistlewood.' The decapitations enraged the crowd who greeted each with 'howls, groans and hisses'.[5] 'The rush of blood was so great . . . that the end of the scaffold had the aspect of a slaughterhouse.'[6] The heads were stuffed back into the coffins and the bodies were taken away for burial in quicklime within the prison grounds.

Even this horrific scene was mild in comparison to the sentence handed down to Colonel Despard, who had determined to attempt to bring down the Government after being unjustly suspended from military duty, and six fellow conspirators in 1803. They were to be 'severally drawn on an hurdle to the place of execution, and there be severally hanged by the neck, but not until you are dead, but that you be severally taken down again, and that whilst you are yet alive, your bowels be taken out and burned before your faces, and that your bodies be divided each into four quarters, and your heads and quarters be at the King's disposal'.[7]

In fact in this case, as had become the practice since the wave of executions following the Jacobite rising of 1745, the more extreme elements of the execution were conducted symbolically: Despard and his followers were briefly dragged round the courtyard of Horsemonger Lane Prison on the hurdle before being hanged and mutilated *after* death; the last actual evisceration of a convicted traitor – again post-mortem – had taken place in 1783 when the French spy La Motte was sentenced to be hanged, drawn and quartered.

Perhaps this pantomime barbarity of post-mortem mutilation was significant in suggesting, at least, that although the mob that attended public executions had lost its stomach for the Grand-Guignol spectacle of treason executions by the end of the eighteenth century, the state had not, and was still determined to hand down condign punishment to malefactors.

In passing judgment after the Gunpowder Plot in 1606, Sir Edward Coke detailed not only the punishment to be faced by the traitors, but the symbolic reasoning behind it. Traitors were to be dragged to their executions across bare ground because they were 'not worthy any more to tread upon the face of the earth'; they were to be dragged backwards because their behaviour was 'retrograde to nature'; they must be strangled 'hanged up by the neck between heaven and earth, as deemed unworthy of both, or either'; their sexual organs were to be cut off and burnt in front of them 'as being . . . unfit to leave any generation after [them]'; their 'bowels and inlay'd parts taken out and burnt, who inwardly had conceived and harboured in their hearts such horrible treason'.[8]

As Coke makes perfectly clear, traitors were the object of particular loathing – at least with the judiciary – and the survival of the aggravated death sentence into the early nineteenth century, as well as the capital sentence itself to the very end of the twentieth, suggests that this was true of the executive as well. The British establishment has retained a special detestation of the crime of treason which has endured into modern times.

Or has it? Today, the idea of a prosecution for high treason seems almost inconceivable. The last treason trials in the United Kingdom took place in the immediate aftermath of the Second World War, and although nearly 200 British subjects were investigated as 'renegades or persons suspected of assisting the enemy', only four – John Amery, William Joyce, Thomas Cooper and Walter Purdy

– were actually prosecuted as traitors. The great majority of those who were prosecuted for helping the Germans – about 140 of them – were tried under the Emergency Defence Regulations of 1939 for 'assisting the enemy' or for the military offence of 'aiding the enemy whilst a POW'. But since the war, almost all cases of treason have been dealt with using Official Secrets legislation; when, that is, the Government has gone so far as to prosecute.

This is an important point. In the post-Second World War era there were a number of cases in which British citizens were convicted of espionage on behalf of foreign powers, and several of these cases were at least as damaging to British interests as anything that Roger Casement or John Amery ever did. Most took place in the context of the Cold War, the confrontation between the Western democratic powers on the one side and the Soviet Bloc on the other. War was never declared – the legal reason why charges for high treason could not be brought – but the stakes were just as high: the espionage activities of Klaus Fuchs and Alan Nunn May, for example, undoubtedly allowed the Stalinist Soviet Union to catch up with the West in vital areas of nuclear research at a point when nuclear weapons were the only significant qualitative advantage that Allied – in reality American – forces had over the highly experienced Soviet army.

So was there something special about the treason of Roger Casement and John Amery that caused them to be executed when others were not, or was there something special about the traitors themselves?

In one very real sense, both men were representatives of a type that the evidence suggests was particular anathema to the British state – the borderline establishment figure who rejects, for whatever reasons, the values that he is supposed to hold dear. How else can we interpret the data? Unfortunately there are no convenient contemporary parallels for Casement, but in Amery's case we can make a judgment: in the aftermath of the Second World War the two men, out of approximately 140 cases, who were hanged for treason (as opposed to 'treachery', which covered wartime

espionage), were John Amery and William Joyce, both of whom
were essentially propagandists. Of the many who suffered lesser
penalties were the forty or so active members of the British Free
Corps of the Waffen-SS and other units of the German armed
forces, including at least one who had been deeply involved in
some of the most grotesque crimes of the Jewish holocaust; and a
smaller number who had acted as informers in POW camps for
their own reward. When one understands what John Amery did,
and what kind of man he was, it is difficult to conclude that he was
worse than any of them, except that his family background should
have made more of him.

Without a comparable set of renegades providing a context in
which to place him, it is difficult to make comparisons with Casement. Yet there are also real problems in interpreting Roger Casement and his place in history. Although he had a distinguished
record as a Consular official – in which role he performed two
significant humanitarian investigations – and a meteoric career as
an Irish Nationalist activist, he is primarily remembered now
because of the continuing controversy over the three diaries which
the Metropolitan Police Special Branch discovered in his baggage
after his arrest in 1916. In these, Casement is shown to be an actively
– compulsively, almost – promiscuous homosexual, finding his
sexual partners amongst the lowest strata of the societies, primarily
in the Third World, in which he lived at the time the 'Black
Diaries' were written. These diaries were used by British police
and Intelligence officials around the time of Casement's trial to
influence opinion on both sides of the Atlantic, with the aim of
counteracting any protest movement against his execution.

This was a gross and ghoulish abuse of what was, in effect,
privileged information, and has resulted in a controversy which has
continued for more than eighty years over whether the diaries are
genuine or not. For the most part the controversy has derived from
the difficulty that many Irish Republican sympathizers, largely
conservative Catholics, have in accepting that it is possible to be
both an ardent Republican and a homosexual. Casement's real

place in history has been lost in a sterile and ultimately morbid controversy over whether he was able to conceal his sexuality – which was then effectively criminal – from his friends, and in speculation about how far such sinister bodies as the British Government and British Intelligence would go to ensure that Casement hanged. Clearly the answer was 'as far as they needed to go', but as Casement was fairly convicted of high treason according to the law of his own country, the diaries have been given more prominence in this matter than they deserve.

As we will see, the acts that led to the treason for which Casement and Amery both died were rooted strongly in their pasts: to understand the nature of their crimes we need to examine what they did and what led them to do it.

PART I
Roger Casement

1. The Casements of County Antrim

The Casement family have lived in Antrim, in the heartland of Ulster, since the mid-eighteenth century.[1] They arrived there from the Isle of Man as a result of the British Government's ongoing policy of subduing rebellious Catholic Ireland by settling it with, and granting land to, loyal Protestants. Family tradition had it that the Casements were descended from French roots,[2] their name supposedly corrupted from 'Caissement', but the reality appears to be that their antecedents were Norsemen, descendants of the Viking pirates who settled islands and coastal areas from Spain to Canada during the latter half of the first millennium. The earliest Manx forms of the name seem to be 'Casmyn' and 'Mac Casmund',[3] which strongly suggest that their supposed Norman origins were a harmless fantasy of the Casements, of a sort indulged in by many well-to-do families in the nineteenth century.

The Casements occupied a position of some standing in Ulster: they did not belong to the highest echelons of the Protestant ascendancy but they owned land and a large house at Magherin-temple near Ballycastle in Antrim, and in the eighteenth and nine-teenth centuries produced a number of distinguished servants of the rapidly expanding British Empire: lawyers, soldiers, sailors, doctors and civil servants.

One such was Roger Casement, the son of Hugh Casement, a well-to-do ship owner. His father purchased Roger a commission after he completed the grand tour of Europe, and he began a career as an army officer in India in 1840, serving as a Cornet★ in the Third Light Dragoons.[4] He remained in India for eight years, taking part in campaigns against the Afghans and the Sikhs and being

★ Second lieutenant.

promoted to lieutenant before selling out his commission and returning to Europe in November 1848.

Soon after leaving the army, Roger Casement became embroiled in a strange episode involving the attempt by Lajos Kossuth and his Hungarian nationalist followers to gain independence from Austria. In 1849, having fought in the Sikh war the previous year, Casement took himself to the Balkans to offer his services to Kossuth. He was nearly too late: when he arrived in the region, Kossuth's remaining 5,000 or so rebels had been forced to cross the border into Turkey at Widdin where they were petitioning the Ottoman Empire for sanctuary. Naturally, the Austrian Government was exerting strong pressure to have the rebels expelled, and Kossuth was contemplating the prospect of being returned with his men to face Austrian retribution. His hope was that Britain might intervene, and soon after his arrival at Widdin, Casement was despatched back to London, carrying a personal letter from Kossuth to the Prime Minister, Lord Palmerston. This had the desired effect: Britain did intervene and the Hungarians survived.

This romantic adventure did not, however, give much shape to a seemingly aimless existence. Casement spent the next few years travelling, visiting North America (where he encountered Kossuth again) and continental Europe where, in Paris, he met and married a young Irishwoman, Anne Jephson.

Despite being distantly related to one of the great Anglo-Irish Protestant families, the Jephsons of Mallow — descendants of William Jephson who had sat in the Long Parliament and supported the Puritan cause in England, to the extent that he was a supporter of the proposal to make Cromwell king in 1656 — Anne Jephson was in fact a Catholic, and in the nineteenth century, marriages between Catholics and Protestants in Ireland were certainly unusual, though by no means unheard of. It may well have been that his marriage caused a certain coolness between Casement and his family because, after a short period of service as a captain in the North Antrim Militia and the birth of his first child, Agnes (known as Nina), in 1856, Roger Casement began a peripatetic life around Britain, Ireland and Europe with his wife and daughter.

After a gap of five years, three further children were born: the eldest, Charlie (later to emigrate to Australia), in 1861; next Tom, in 1863; and finally Roger David, on 1 September 1864 at Kingstown (now Dun Laoghaire) near Dublin.

Little reliable information is available about the early childhood of Roger David Casement. It is known that he was raised as an Anglican Protestant of the established Church of Ireland but that, at his mother's instigation, he was also secretly and conditionally baptized as a Catholic when he was four years old, during a holiday in North Wales. With hindsight, this incident has probably assumed a much greater significance for biographers of Casement than it merits. In later life he certainly liked to identify with the Catholic majority in Ireland, but this was for cultural and political reasons, not for religious ones, and to suggest that there was a 'Catholic part of Roger's nature' that 'lay dormant within him'[5] is to exceed the mark. Even if there was some kind of subliminal religious conflict in the Casement family, it is also clear that Roger and his siblings were happy and their parents' slightly unconventional relationship was based on a deep mutual love, but this came to an end in 1873 when Anne Casement died in childbirth.

Anne's death led to a dramatic change in the family's circumstances. Roger Casement senior had by now exhausted much of his capital and, rather than attempt to keep the family together, he sent his four children to live at Magherintemple House while he resided in Ballymena, some twenty-five miles away. It has been suggested that following his wife's death Roger Casement turned to spiritualism[6] – his motives are not difficult to fathom – and began holding seances in a hotel at Ballymena. In the meantime, his children lived in the 'physically more spacious, but emotionally less free'[7] atmosphere of Magherintemple as they continued their education.

The loss of Anne Casement was followed, just three years later, by the demise of Roger, apparently at the hotel in Ballymena where

he had taken up residence. By this time, Roger David Casement
had entered the Church of Ireland Diocesan School at Ballymena
as a boarder; now orphans, he and the other children were made
wards in Chancery, in the care of their uncle, John Casement, at
Magherintemple. By and large, Roger's school holidays were spent
with his Aunt Grace – his mother's sister – in Liverpool, where her
husband Edward Bannister specialized in West African interests for
a local trading company.

Roger and his sister Nina spent a great deal of time with the
Bannisters and came to be looked on by the Bannister children
almost as siblings:

> He spent many of his holidays with us, and we came to look on him
> more as an elder brother than a cousin. He was devoted to my mother,
> who, unlike his own mother, was very small. He always spoke and wrote
> of her as 'Dear Wee Auntie'. During his holidays he would play games
> with us and entertain us for hours . . . He was always fond of painting
> and of inventing stories . . .[8]

In fact their family circumstances were, coincidentally, similar: like
her sister, Grace Bannister was a Roman Catholic married to a
Protestant and ostensibly raised her children in the Anglican faith,
but there do appear to have been strong Catholic undercurrents in
the household, and at least one of the Bannister children subsequently
came to embrace Catholicism fully. Then, perhaps even more so
than now, this was an important factor for Irish people: in the 1870s,
the rebellion of 1798 and the subsequent Act of Union were still just
within living memory; the famine and the events of 1848 were much
closer. The history of the relationship between Ireland and the rest
of the British Isles has been, in part at least, a story of struggle between
different ethnic, cultural and religious groups; in order to understand
the singularity of the political position which Roger Casement later
came to occupy, it is important to look in some detail at the central
tenets of this aspect of Irish history.

★

The popularly accepted view of the relationship between Ireland and Britain during the latter part of the twentieth century and the beginning of the twenty-first holds that for more than 800 years, the indigenous Gaelic population of Ireland were cruelly oppressed by Anglo-Saxon invaders. The evils that befell Ireland were the result of the exploitation of the native Irish by an unsympathetic and greedy colonial power. It is a view which is not entirely consistent with historical reality.

In fact the earliest known inhabitants of the island of Ireland were a people called the Finbolg. Several centuries before the birth of Christ they were supplanted by Gaelic tribes which had migrated northwards from the Iberian peninsula. The Gaels brought with them a complex social structure and legal system, together with their own language, but their tenure of Ireland was by no means exclusive. During the succeeding centuries, they were followed by, and absorbed, a range of different peoples, who, although the Gaelic language and culture remained pre-eminent, nevertheless left their mark.

Gaelic rule in Ireland, however, was irrevocably changed by the arrival in the twelfth century of Norman invaders from England. Robert Kee, the historian of Irish Nationalism, has made the point that 'Invaders like Robert Fitzstephen and Richard, 2nd Earl of Pembroke, known as Strongbow . . . were Norman adventurers, speaking Norman French. They came not in England's interest but their own, in search of land, power and wealth.'[9] Moreover, they had come at the invitation of an Irish chief to help him in a dispute he was having with rivals. The arrival of the Normans – and a grant of authority over Ireland from Pope Adrian IV, the only English Pope, to Henry II – established the concept that the King of England was also King of Ireland, although this had little practical effect at that time. In fact the idea of theoretical submission to the English king does not appear to have been objectionable to the Gaelic chiefs, provided he did not interfere with their traditional way of life, and this remained largely the case until the accession in England of the Tudor dynasty.

The most forceful of the Tudor kings, Henry VIII, was determined to substitute a strong new administrative control from England for the comparatively loose feudal link which had hitherto
existed, and his mechanism for doing this was to demand that the
Gaelic chiefs of Ireland surrendered their land to him so that he
could, in turn, regrant it to them, thus symbolically demonstrating
that their position in Gaelic society was within the gift of the king.

In many ways this was a neat solution from Henry's point of
view: without depriving the chiefs of any of their actual authority,
surrender and regrant would clearly demonstrate to whom they
owed their position. But it completely ignored the traditional
Gaelic view of land ownership: that lands were owned by the tribe
collectively and not by the chiefs as individuals. In fact many of the
major chiefs welcomed the change, in so far as it secured their own
position and that of their families, but others opposed this attempt
by the monarch directly to control their affairs. There were also
divisions among lesser chiefs and the common people; attempts to
resist the new Tudor system of government by the greater chiefs
inevitably dragged them into conflicts that they would rather have
avoided, whilst acquiescence by their 'betters' deprived them of
their traditional rights under the old system. Inevitably, the arrival
of the new system caused deep rifts in Gaelic society, and Irish and
'Old English' (the descendants of the Norman settlers of the twelfth
century and afterwards) were to be found on both sides. The
greatest of the Irish chieftains to oppose Henry – Shane O'Neill –
was finally defeated in battle not by the English but by an Irish
rival, the O'Donnell, and there was no real sense in which the
conflict was seen as a struggle between England and Ireland: 'it was
a conflict between an old system of government and a new one'.[10]

One of the interesting outcomes of the Tudor wars in Ireland
was the system of 'plantation', the resettling of confiscated lands by
farmers from England and Scotland. The first of the plantations
took place during the reign of Queen Mary (elder daughter of
Henry VIII) and Philip of Spain, but they were followed by many
more. The Reformation of the Church had had little effect in

Ireland, partly for cultural reasons – the native Gaelic-speaking Irish could not be proselytized by English-speaking priests – and partly for political ones: the Tudors were anxious not to provoke a religious conflict which could be parlayed by England's Catholic enemies, France and Spain, into the use of Ireland as a base for attacks against England. But the plantations brought a significant population of Protestants into Ireland – on a basis that was naturally antagonistic to the indigenous people – and set in place the cultural and sectarian schism in Irish society which has persisted to this day.

Indeed, it was the plantation of Protestants in Ulster which was to provoke the next significant crisis in Irish history in 1641. Driven to desperation by their insecure status and hold on their lands in the face of the Protestant settlers, the surviving Irish Catholic (both Gaelic and Old English) land-holding gentry of Ulster descended upon their Protestant neighbours in a wave of violence. This essentially conservative rebellion, which continued for eleven years, was only finally brought to a conclusion by the end of the English Civil War which had taken place alongside it. In August 1649, Oliver Cromwell arrived in Ireland as Commander-in-Chief of the parliamentary forces; on 2 September he stormed the town of Drogheda and massacred the civilian population; on 2 October he did the same thing at Wexford. By 1652, when the fighting finally ended, more than one-third of the Irish Catholic population had died, and their lands, which they had been fighting to protect, had largely passed into the hands of the Protestant minority: prior to the rebellion, about two-thirds of cultivable land in Ireland was owned by Catholics; afterwards, less than one-quarter remained in Catholic ownership.

Part of the reason for this large-scale expropriation of Catholic lands lay with the necessity to pay Cromwell's soldiers. In lieu of cash, many of them were granted confiscated lands in Ireland on which to settle and also, the English Government hoped, to form a Protestant militia of ex-soldiers who would garrison the country, thus increasing the numbers of Protestants in Ireland and exacerbating the alienation between Protestant and Catholic. Even the

Restoration, after which a Catholic Lord Deputy for Ireland (Richard Talbot, Earl of Tyrconnell) was briefly appointed, failed to improve the lot of Irish Catholics; and the arrival of William of Orange and the defeat of the Jacobites at the Boyne and Aughrim (1690 and 1691 respectively) simply confirmed their second-class status.

But the century following the Battle of the Boyne brought about a change in Ireland: the birth, for the first time, of a genuine Irish national self-consciousness. Oddly enough, many of those who now embraced the concept of an Irish nationality were from the relatively newly arrived Protestant families: people who were sufficiently cosmopolitan to recognize how one-sided the relationship between Ireland and England was. Ireland had had an independent parliament under the Crown since before the reign of Henry VIII, fulfilling much the same role as the English parliament across the sea, but the tendency of the great Old English families to use it as a means of opposition to the wishes of the English Crown had led to its powers being curtailed and subjugated to the English parliament. This had led the English parliament to take advantage of its position to impose protectionist measures designed to bolster English trade at the expense of Ireland.

In the years following William of Orange's victory at the Boyne, a body of legislation known as the Penal Laws came to be enacted, explicitly intended to separate Protestant from Catholic. These prevented Catholics from owning land, holding public office, attending Mass, being educated in their faith and so forth. Although much of this was tacitly ignored, it did crystallize the difference between the two faiths as one between rich and poor, privileged and dispossessed. By depriving Catholics of the ability to own land or acquire security of tenure as tenants, the law effectively relegated them to the status of slaves: landlords could charge extortionate rents for land; and competition for land was so great that if tenants could not pay they would be evicted, and new tenants found. Not surprisingly, conditions like this, amounting to a form of forced labour, stirred enormous resentments against landlords, and in response, rural areas saw a growth in oath-bound secret societies which handed out rough justice to the more vulnerable of the rapacious landlords and agents, thereby creating, one might argue, an enduring tradition in Irish politics.

Meanwhile, the response of the political classes, who were, of course, almost entirely Protestant, was more muted but at least as significant. In the early part of the eighteenth century the idea began to achieve acceptance that the commercial restrictions imposed by England upon Ireland were untenable (and in fact by disadvantaging Protestant commercial interests were part of the cause of the miserable conditions that the Catholic Irish had to endure). This resentment grew and culminated, in 1783, in the Irish parliament passing a Declaration of Independence from the parliament of England. By then, feeling was so strong and widespread in Ireland that the Act was accepted by the English Government who, for its part, passed an Act renouncing its legislative interests in Ireland. In theory at least, this created two independent countries, united under a joint Crown.

In practice, however, this was not the case: the unreformed electoral system actually gave the 'Crown' – the English Government – *more* power through patronage and straightforward political corruption. More than half the seats in the Irish parliament were 'rotten' or pocket boroughs, which the Crown could buy with titles, jobs and cash, and this guaranteed a compliant legislature.

It is difficult now to see how events might otherwise have turned out, but from 1789 onwards, European politics was galvanized by the outbreak of the French Revolution. The most lasting effect of this was to encourage the educated to begin to consider alternative forms of government beyond the old autocratic certainties. In Ireland, this was manifested by the first stirrings of the group that was to become known as the United Irishmen.

The ideas that underpinned the United Irishmen were that England and the English Crown were an inimical influence on Ireland which should be removed; that the best way to reform Ireland was by reform of its parliament; and that the best way to secure the reform of Parliament was to unite Protestant and

Catholic as Irishmen. To this end, the largely Protestant, middle-class and radical United Irishmen sought to ally themselves with the Defenders, an agglomeration of violent, anti-landlord, rural Catholic secret societies. Over the next eight years they and their allies strove to achieve their ends by open political agitation, rural violence, alliance with revolutionary France and finally, in 1798, open rebellion.

The details of 1798 are not important here, except in relation to the situation that Ireland was left with. The English response to the rebellion culminated in the Act of Union of January 1801, an Act designed to integrate Ireland and its institutions into mainstream British political life and to snuff out thoughts of independence amongst the middle-class élite by removing inequalities between the two countries. In this it was in some small respects successful: opinion was divided within Ireland's Protestant ruling class over whether full union was a good idea or not. But the Act of Union entirely failed to address the needs of Ireland's majority: the Catholics. Their grievances were more fundamental than the political radicalism of the United Irishmen: in an overwhelmingly rural, agricultural economy they were denied, by the system of land ownership and tenure, the means to make a secure living for themselves and their families. By integrating the Irish and British parliaments, Irish legislative priorities would inevitably slide well down the list of overall British political imperatives, and thus slow down or even prevent reform entirely.

It was therefore the pressure for land reform, exacerbated by the potato famine of the late 1840s, that was to do most to raise Irish Catholic political consciousness. And it was this new consciousness, translated into a range of different types of agitation, from respectful and essentially 'loyalist' appeals for reform from Ireland's Catholic hierarchy to terrorism and violence by the Fenian Brotherhood, supported by Irish exiles in America, that led William Gladstone to declare, on taking office as British Prime Minister in 1868, that his 'mission [was] to pacify Ireland'.

★

Thus the young Roger Casement was growing into adulthood at a time when he cannot have failed to notice the awakening of a distinct and Irish sense of national identity – albeit very much within the context of the British Empire – and to observe that issues concerning Ireland had achieved a high priority. But it is also the case that by birth and by upbringing, at least after the death of his parents, Roger belonged firmly to the tradition of the Northern Protestant Unionists who had always benefited from England's control over Ireland and in particular from the Act of Union itself.

Having left school at the age of fifteen, Roger was finally able to leave Magherintemple behind and go to stay permanently with the Bannisters in Liverpool in a family atmosphere that was secure, loving and congenial. By now he was a striking individual: 'He was over six feet . . . his eyes were grey and deep set, his face rather thin; and his hair nearly black and curly. He had good teeth, and a very clear skin. . . His speaking voice was beautiful – he never lost a very slight Irish accent, but his English was that of a cultured gentleman.'[11]

The original intention appears to have been to launch Roger on a career in the Civil Service but instead his family managed to secure him a place as a clerk in a Liverpool-based shipping line and thus set him on a path that would eventually take him, via West Africa, South America and Germany, to the execution shed at Pentonville Prison. Roger gained his place with his new employer, the Elder–Dempster Line, partly at least as a result of family influence: Hugh Casement was a director of the line, whilst the company chairman, Sir Alfred Jones, who was also later President of the Liverpool Chamber of Commerce, was a friend of the Bannisters. The life of an office clerk did not hold much appeal for the young man, however, and in 1883, after an incident in which he had refused to run an errand for Jones, resulting in his near dismissal, he was transferred instead to the SS *Bonny*, an Elder–Dempster steamer on the West Africa run, where he was to serve as purser.

Roger Casement made three round trips to West Africa before

his employment with Elder–Dempster was terminated, but it is clear that whatever he saw there had, to some extent at least, enthralled him, and in 1884 he returned to West Africa on an entirely different basis.

2. A Good Man in Africa

Roger Casement's unusual career and its extraordinary outcome were the direct result of his participation in the pioneering and development of one of the more peculiar colonial adventures of the nineteenth century: the attempt by King Leopold II of the Belgians to establish and maintain a large African colony for his own, almost exclusive, financial benefit. The part that Casement played in establishing Leopold's colony has usually been overlooked by his biographers, even though it was the major activity of his early life, in favour of his much better-documented reforming activities there, but there is sufficient evidence of what was happening at this time for us to infer that Casement's role was probably not quite as it has generally been presented.

Systematic exploration of the coastline of sub-Saharan Africa only really got under way in the fifteenth century, as a by-product of the development, in Portugal, of the caravel, a small, sturdy sailing vessel which was 'particularly good at sailing into the wind'.[1] Thus equipped, European sailors slowly pushed south the boundaries of the known world until, in 1482, a Portuguese sea captain, Diogo Cão, made an astonishing discovery.

Sailing close into the coastline, Cão crossed the Equator and then, a few days later, observed something extraordinary. Approaching a wide coastal inlet, he noticed the water change colour and then found his ship fighting against a strong current flowing out to sea. Tasting the water surrounding his vessel revealed that it was fresh rather than salt, and he soon realized that he had stumbled across the mouth of a vast, fast-flowing river. Cão landed, erected a small monument claiming the 'newly discovered' land for the King of Portugal, and continued with his explorations.

Of course, this part of West Africa around the mouth of the

Congo river was hardly 'newly discovered' to the population that had inhabited the area for thousands of years and built up a thriving and sophisticated civilization based on a form of Imperial federalism. But being black Africans – savages – they were beneath the new arrivals' notice except, perhaps, as slaves.

The discovery that the indigenous rulers of Western Central Africa themselves practised slavery and were prepared to sell slaves to the Europeans very quickly created a thriving trade in human lives. The new colonies being pioneered in the Americas at the beginning of the eighteenth century were desperately short of labour, and African slaves seemed an ideal way to overcome the problem. Moreover, finding slaves did not present any great problems for the Europeans: there were plenty of Africans prepared to do this for them for profit, and soon much of the west coast of Africa was being ravaged by the slave trade.

The Europeans rarely penetrated further inland from the coastline of Central Africa, for two important reasons. First, they did not need to: African slave-traders brought slaves directly to them. Second, they could not: not far inland, the Congo river was too fast-flowing to allow navigation in sailing vessels and soon turned into a series of cataracts, rapids and waterfalls. The only way to follow its course was on foot, and that involved travelling through dangerous, uncharted lands where malaria and other unknown tropical diseases were rife; supplies were limited to those that could be carried by native bearers. As a result, until the middle of the nineteenth century Central Africa and the Congo basin were represented on maps by a big blank: no European knew what was there, or where the great river's source lay.

By the 1860s, this situation was beginning to change. The growth around the world of the European colonial empires brought with it an enthusiasm for exploration. This was partly because Europe was in need of raw materials to drive forward the industrial revolution, and partly also because exploration could be depicted as interesting and exciting in the new era of mass media; furthermore, it could be cloaked with the high moral purposes of bringing 'civilization' and a Christian God to the benighted heathens and of combating slavery, which was still present with Afro-Arab traders supplying African slaves for Arabia and the Persian Gulf.

One of the most celebrated explorers of this era was Dr David Livingstone, a Scottish physician who combined exploration with Christian evangelism. Having become the first European to cross Africa from coast to coast, and been hailed as a national hero in the process, he disappeared into the Central African interior again in 1866 with the intention of finding the source of the Nile. Years passed and he failed to reappear, until Henry Morton Stanley, a Welsh-born journalist working for a New York newspaper, who had a talent for self-publicization, emerged from the jungle in the spring of 1872 to announce that he had found Dr Livingstone.

This dramatic exploit set off a wave of exploration in the area, despite the fact that Stanley had not brought Livingstone back with him (after the two men had spent some weeks together, Livingstone continued on his lonely travels and died in the bush in May 1873). At this stage, although the British had substantial colonies in South Africa and several European countries claimed territories on the east and west coasts, about 80 per cent of the African land mass was still under the control of the indigenous population – in other words ripe, from the colonialists' point of view, for seizure and exploitation (or 'civilization' as they would no doubt have preferred to put it). When one of Livingstone's successors, Lovett Cameron, emerged from the interior at Luanda in November 1875, he brought with him stories 'of healthy climates, beautiful scenery, and of deposits of coal, iron, gold and copper',[2] and at least one man in Europe immediately began to take an extremely close interest in the area.

Leopold II, King of the Belgians, ascended the throne in 1865 at the age of thirty. He was the product of a profoundly unhappy marriage between Leopold I, Belgium's first king, and Louise-Marie, daughter of Louis-Philippe of France. Leopold I, the eighth son of the Duke of Saxe-Coburg-Gotha, had acquired the Belgian throne by invitation, after an unplanned, spontaneous rebellion had thrown the shackles of Protestant Dutch rule off the Catholic provinces of Flanders and Wallonia. Having made a name for himself during the Napoleonic wars, and married Princess Charlotte of England, daughter of the Prince Regent, Leopold might have expected to become Prince Consort to the Queen of England, but Charlotte died young and, having remarried, he settled for Belgium instead.

Leopold was related by blood and marriage to most of the royal dynasties of Europe, but unlike them he was king of a new country, and his powers were closely bound by its constitution. This does not seem to have concerned him too much, but it certainly preyed on the mind of his elder son. Having been brought up in a rigidly formal atmosphere in which he and his younger brother were obliged to apply for an audience 'as if they were ordinary clients on state business'[3] when they wanted to talk to their father, Leopold II had withdrawn from an early age into a world of study, substituting personal relationships with books, maps and state documents as he sought to understand the world around him. In some respects this paid off: Leopold developed a profound understanding of the mechanics of government and business which were to make him fabulously wealthy in later life; but at the same time his emotional retardation was to impact on him, leaving him callous, resentful, selfish, misanthropic and deeply cynical.

One thing that greatly bothered Leopold II was the unwillingness of Belgium's democratic politicians to spend money on projects that would increase their country's grandeur, prestige and, above all, his personal wealth. Looking at his European royal cousins, Leopold could hardly help but notice that almost all of them were rulers of substantial and very prestigious colonial empires. By contrast, the Belgian Government showed every sign of being opposed to overseas adventurism. This view was not shared by Leopold, who became utterly obsessed with the idea of acquiring an overseas colony, by stealth if necessary, even if it meant doing so as a personal venture and then handing his acquisitions over to the nation. In 1864 and 1865 he made a long journey to the Far

East, where he observed the workings of the British, French and Dutch colonial systems: 'administration, the problems of colonial strategy, the proper relationship of metropolitan power to native ruler, did not attract him so much as the very limited science of using backward populations to produce wealth from the natural resources of their own country'.[4] On his return, he presented the Belgian Finance Minister, Frère-Orban, with a piece of marble taken from the Acropolis, engraved with a portrait of himself and the inscription: *Il faut à la Belgique une Colonie* ('Belgium must have a Colony').

Leopold spent the next ten years scouring the world in his efforts to fulfil his self-appointed mission. In the mid-1870s, as the explorers started to probe the secrets of Central Africa and the Congo basin, he began to think that an opportunity might be imminent.

Leopold's manoeuvres to acquire an African colony were, by any stretch of the imagination, astonishing, both in their scale and their sheer unscrupulous cynicism. Strangely enough, Roger Casement was to have a significant part to play in both their early and later stages.

The first steps in Leopold's lengthy scheme to seize personal control of the Congo basin were taken in 1876 when he issued invitations to several of the most noted and distinguished geographers and explorers of the day to attend an international conference in Brussels. The aim of the conference was to examine the question of Central Africa and, particularly, to consider the 'location of routes to be successively opened into the interior, of hospitable, scientific, and pacification bases to be set up as a means of abolishing the slave trade, establishing peace amongst the chiefs, and procuring them just and impartial arbitration'.[5] The conference was a masterpiece of *schmooze*, strongly reminiscent of the hoop-la which surrounds the bidding process for staging the modern-day Olympic Games and soccer World Cups: all of Leopold's twenty-four foreign guests were housed in the Royal Palace in Brussels; all were entertained sumptuously; each received the Cross of Leopold from the king.

Together, Leopold and the delegates discussed the location of the bases, which were to be manned by unarmed scientists, linguists and artisans who would be able to teach the natives various useful techniques while studying the geography, flora and fauna of the area. More importantly for Leopold, they also resolved to establish an African International Association (AIA) to oversee these developments. The ostensible purpose of this Association was to be a high-minded, altruistic body which would establish national committees in every interested European country. The committees would work in turn to raise awareness, interest and funds for the development of Central Africa, and answer to a central international committee. By overseeing the work of the outposts in Africa, the AIA would naturally assume the role of an authority, but because the chairmanship would revolve on an annual basis, control over the area would remain in international hands instead of being dominated by any one country. In grateful appreciation, the delegates elected Leopold as the AIA's first chairman.

It was critical for Leopold to keep his true intentions not only from the governments of the major colonial powers, who might not take kindly to his attempt to grab his own place in the sun, but also from his own government, which had no intention of allowing their king to saddle them with an expensive and potentially ruinous colony. Consequently, as he methodically continued with his scheme, now focusing exclusively on Central Africa, he worked, wherever possible, through proxies, cut-outs and dupes, the most important of whom was the greatest explorer of the day, Henry Morton Stanley.

As we have seen, Stanley had burst upon the African scene with his successful expedition to find Livingstone but he was no scientific explorer or geographer. In reality he was a journalist for the *New York Herald* who had led a somewhat varied life. Born in Denbigh, Wales, in 1841, Stanley had grown up in a workhouse before running away to sea and fetching up in the United States. There he had managed to see combat on both sides in the Civil War before taking up journalism, writing exciting despatches from the

American West, covering the Indian wars and eventually a British punitive expedition against the Emperor of Abyssinia, during which he bribed a telegraph clerk to ensure that his copy was the first home. In 1874, two years after his return from finding Livingstone, Stanley had led a vast expedition of nearly 400 African men (and some women and children) inland from Zanzibar on the east coast, with the intention of crossing the continent from east to west.

Stanley had a savage and barbaric idea of exploration, and even in his own time he was regarded as profoundly racist: Sir Richard Burton observed that 'he shoots Negroes as if they were monkeys'.[6] His expedition lasted more than two years and left a trail of destruction, attacking more than twenty-eight large towns and three or four score villages on the way; more than two-thirds of his own manpower, including the three Europeans who had accompanied him, died as well. Stanley's reaction to frightened Africans gesticulating at him with spears from the riverbanks was to shoot them with his repeating rifle; his response to indiscipline and slackness among his porters was flogging.

In August 1877, Stanley and the surviving members of his expedition emerged from the jungle near the mouth of the Congo having achieved their leader's aim: they had indeed crossed Africa from east to west; moreover, they had done so largely by following the course of the Congo river. Reading the accounts of the expedition that appeared in the London *Daily Telegraph*, which had partly financed it, Leopold now knew that the Congo would make a viable colony, if only he could get possession of it. He was sure that he could use Stanley to front up his takeover of the region.

After a year of careful cultivation by Leopold, Stanley did agree to return to Africa on the king's behalf. Stanley had been piqued that the British Government was unenthusiastic about opening up the Central African hinterland for the British Empire. For all his racism and brutality, he was an idealist: he believed in the civilizing mission of the white man and he genuinely wanted to bring order to the heathen chaos, as he saw it, of Africa. In return for a salary that was the equivalent of about £175,000 per annum in today's values, he agreed to set up a base near the mouth of the Congo and then to build a road through the Crystal Mountains, where the Congo river descended from the central plateau through more than 100 miles of cataracts and rapids, before establishing a chain of stations along the Congo river itself.

It was around this time that Leopold pulled the 'Big Switcheroo', to use P. G. Wodehouse's phrase. Throughout his wooing of Stanley, Leopold had given the impression that he was acting on behalf of the philanthropic and apparently respectable AIA, but Stanley's contract was actually with the Committee for the Study of the Upper Congo. Leopold gave Stanley to understand that the Committee was a dependent organization of the AIA, funded by a small group of Dutch, British and Belgian businesses. The story was put about that the Committee would supervise the foundation of a Confederation of Free Negro Republics, not unlike Liberia. In fact the Committee was another smokescreen, furnishing Leopold with the mechanism by which he could translate the apparently lofty ideals of the AIA into a commercial business.

Stanley had departed for Africa at the beginning of 1879, to recruit Zanzibari porters and begin work. He had some idea, through conversations with Leopold, of what the king's actual intentions on the Congo were – namely, the purchase from local chiefs of as much land as possible for commercial exploitation – but he was still under the impression that his work had an ultimately humanitarian and progressive objective. While he was in Zanzibar, however, the next stage of Leopold's scheme unfolded when the Dutch investor in the Committee, the Afrikaansche Handels-vereeniging, went bankrupt. Leopold used this opportunity to buy up the Dutch company's stock in the Committee, making himself overwhelmingly the largest shareholder, and when the board of the Committee met in November 1879, the other shareholders were told that as three-quarters of the start-up capital had been spent and the rest was required for payment of creditors and the liquidation of contracts, the whole enterprise was in dire straits.

As the shocked shareholders digested this prospect, Leopold's nominee came up with an alternative outcome: if they agreed to dissolve the Committee, the king would return their original investments to them. The investors would have been mad to refuse this offer – which they did not – and thus the work of the Committee, which had itself inherited the goodwill, prestige and reputation accrued by the AIA (which in any case had never in any legitimate way licensed the activities of the Committee), passed entirely under the personal control of Leopold II.

The time was by no means ripe for Leopold to show his hand, however. Instead, he created the Association Internationale du Congo (AIC) as yet another layer of cover. The name was deliberately selected to create confusion with the AIA which now simply disappeared into obscurity. Meanwhile, Leopold appropriated the AIA's flag – a gold star on a blue ground – and continued to consolidate his growing toehold in Africa. The switch had worked: even Stanley believed that the AIA, the Committee and the AIC were much the same thing: 'the Committee at a later period, having satisfied itself that progress and stability were secured, assumed the title of "Association Internationale du Congo", which, be it remembered, was originally started with the philanthropic motive of opening up the Congo basin . . .'[7]

However philanthropic the original motives had been, however, Stanley can have had few illusions about the way things were turning out in the Congo basin. Part of his work, aside from the construction of the physical infrastructure of the proto-colony, was to persuade the tribal chieftains to agree to treaties with the AIC, ceding in perpetuity land and trading rights in return for such marvels as bolts of cloth. Few of the chiefs had ever seen the written word, let alone grasped the nuances of what Stanley and his assistants were demanding of them, and although some 450 chiefs from the Congo basin did agree to treaties with the AIC, it is impossible to believe that they fully understood what they were signing up to. In addition, Leopold was already urging Stanley to buy up any ivory he could lay his hands on, and to place tolls and barriers on the roads he was carving out. In short, Leopold, with Stanley as his willing and highly paid accomplice, was creating by stealth a sovereign state, in the name of an entirely bogus entity which he, in fact, wholly owned.

With Stanley on the ground in Africa, building the infrastructure of Leopold's colony, the king began to use his network of contacts to push towards wider acceptance of the AIC's activities. One of his most important proxies in this was a wealthy American, 'General'★ Henry Shelton Sanford, who had been for a short period the United States' Minister in Belgium. Sanford had inherited great wealth which he was steadily losing in a series of ill-judged business ventures – he was a terrific snob who greatly enjoyed Leopold's patronage. In fact Leopold trusted him enough to have sent him as one of the two emissaries who had made the initial approach to Stanley, but now he had an even more important task for Sanford – to use his connections with the Republican Party in the United States to attempt to get the US to recognize the AIC's sovereignty over the Congo basin.

For two years Sanford carefully and deceitfully outlined the aims and intentions of the AIC, carefully cultivating in the minds of President Chester Arthur and his Government the idea that the Association was the same philanthropic body set up with such fanfare in 1876. In many ways Sanford, and other Leopold-funded propagandists elsewhere, were successful. Even Roger Casement's most recent biographer was misled, referring in 1984, fully 100 years after the event, to 'the uncertainties of Leopold's International Association, which had been seen to go into a decline under its first constitution, and had only started its new lease of life in 1883',[8] unaware that he was talking about two completely different entities, connected only by the fact that they were set up and controlled by Leopold entirely for his own ends.

Sanford's first major success was to persuade President Arthur to incorporate a positive mention of the AIA's work in the Congo

★ A courtesy title he received for funding an artillery battery during the American Civil War.

basin into his annual message to Congress in 1873. Arthur praised the Association for offering 'freedom to commerce', not realizing that that was the last thing Leopold intended, and for its prohibition of the slave trade (which by now, in any case, was only a fringe activity). The next stage involved persuading newspaper editors and Congressmen to lobby on Leopold's behalf. This was achieved partly by flattery and deceit, partly by outright bribery, but by April 1884 Sanford had created such a favourable climate that the US Secretary of State could happily issue an official statement:

The Government of the United States announces its sympathy with and approval of the humane and benevolent purposes of the International Association of the Congo, administering, as it does, the interests of the Free States there established, and will order the officers of the United States, both on land and sea, to recognize the flag of the International African Association as the flag of a friendly Government.[9]

Even this announcement shows the effectiveness of Leopold's obfuscations: Secretary Freylinghuysen managed to use the names of the active AIC – entirely controlled by Leopold – and the long extinct AIA to describe the same organization. Over the next year, Leopold strengthened his grip on the colony by means of a series of bilateral agreements and secret deals, thereby contriving either to dupe his potential rivals into acquiescence or to buy them off. Thus French recognition was secured by offering the Government of France 'first refusal' on the colony; Germany was offered guarantees of free trade.

It was during this period that Roger Casement became involved in the machinations. After his three trips to West Africa as purser of the SS *Bonny*, he returned in 1884 to work for Stanley and the AIC.

Biographers have tended to gloss over this period of Casement's life, not least because there is only fragmentary evidence about what he was doing for Stanley, but this is surely a great mistake.

The picture that history paints of Casement is of a naïve and slightly unworldly idealist who gradually transcended his Ulster Protestant, British Imperialist background to become a political, religious and sexual rebel, and a scourge of Imperialism in all its many forms. In later life, Casement was instrumental in publicizing the atrocities that resulted from Leopold's administrative system in the Congo, but as one of Stanley's functionaries, he was himself involved in setting it up. It would be easy to gain the impression that Stanley and his men were dupes of Leopold, but this is only loosely true, in so far as Stanley probably did not appreciate the full scope of Leopold's deceptions. Nevertheless, Stanley and his subordinates were the men who negotiated the treaties with the chiefs, and they certainly knew about the restrictive trade agreements that they contained, which were the key to later exploitation: their contracts of employment in fact specifically forbade them from publicizing this. Stanley also knew, and one can assume that his small group of European employees did as well, of the nature of Leopold's owner-ship of the AIC, even if he did not quite appreciate what Leopold's final objective was. To portray Casement as an innocent working in the midst of all this is to stretch credulity. Stanley and his men, Casement included, did what they did because they believed that by introducing the Africans to European methods of trade, agricul-ture and manufacture, they would ultimately benefit. They may not have realized that Leopold's intention was to extract as much profit as possible from the Congo for the least possible outlay, but they certainly enabled him to do so.

Stanley left the Congo later in 1884 to attend a conference in Berlin called by the German Chancellor Bismarck in order to settle various questions relating to the colonization of Central Africa. The AIC could not attend, as it was not a *de jure* government, whatever its *de facto* status, but Leopold was none too bothered: the chief of the US delegation was Henry Shelton Sanford (Stanley was technical advisor); the Belgian delegation of course consisted of his own men; whilst the British position was compromised because the Foreign Secretary's personal assistant owed money to one of Leopold's henchmen, and the legal advisor to the British delegation had previously been employed by Leopold to help draw up his treaties with the Congo chiefs. When the conference drew to a close in February 1885 with the signature of the Treaty of Berlin, which carved up responsibility for Central Africa between the colonial powers, Leopold had nearly everything he wanted: widespread international recognition of the AIC's role in Central Africa, and acceptance of his own imposture as a benign father figure to the region. The Europeans in the Congo, who were taking Leopold's shilling, can have had no doubt whatsoever from whom they derived their livelihood.★

Casement worked directly for the AIC for the two years after his arrival in the Congo in 1884. That he was popular and good at his job is evident from the close friendships he formed with his fellow Europeans. One of them, Fred Puleston, subsequently described the Casement he knew in Africa:

[His] disposition and make-up was the gentlest imaginable; he was always sweet-tempered, ready to help, condemning cruelty and injustice in any form. Indeed he was so emotional, tender and sympathetic that, when his fox terrier . . . got at cross-purposes with a wild hog and had his stomach ripped open, Casement was unable to control his feeling and wept like a girl.[10]

In 1886, Roger Casement left Leopold's direct employment to work for Henry Shelton Sanford. Sanford had importuned Leopold to give him a job as a colonial administrator based in Brussels, but Leopold turned him down, probably because he knew Sanford had little talent for administration and none of the ruthlessness that would be required. Instead, he gave him permission to begin the commercial collection of ivory and trade in other goods on the

★ Inglis claims that Stanley's European assistants were unpaid volunteers. This seems most implausible. Casement, for example, had very little money of his own and would have been extremely hard pressed at this time.

Congo river; the name given to this venture was yet another smokescreen– the Sanford Exploring Expedition.

Once again, this title has tended to confuse Casement's biographers. Sanford intended the expedition to be a purely commercial venture, which he planned to manage from Brussels; exploration in the form of opening up new territories played no part in it. Casement was given the job of supervising the supply base at Matadi, a task he fulfilled effectively enough to be transferred to a posting up country to manage Sanford's trading post at Equator.

It was during this period that a crisis developed in Sudan, where an uprising of Islamic fundamentalist Mahdists had led to the temporary overthrow of the joint Anglo-Egyptian suzerainty over the country. The Governor of the southernmost province of the country was Emin Pasha, a German Jew by birth who had trained as a physician. As the Mahdists took control of more and more of the country, Emin Pasha had appealed to Britain for help in resisting them; alas, none could be provided because the British Government was then stretched by its commitments to a wide range of colonial skirmishes. Instead, a clamour arose for a private expedition to go to Emin Pasha's relief, and the obvious choice of leader was Stanley.

Stanley approached this task with his usual vigour. Having secured the agreement of his employer, Leopold, that he could go (provided his expedition travelled via a hitherto unexplored part of the Congo basin) and acquired the latest model of Maxim gun, which had an impressive 600-rounds-per-minute rate of fire and would be 'of valuable service in helping civilization to overcome barbarism',[11] he recruited a large taskforce and set out, blazing his usual trail of destruction, burning villages which seemed hostile and taking women and children hostage to secure food from the local inhabitants. Whether or not Stanley was a genuine idealist, his behaviour in the field cannot possibly have escaped the attention of anyone working for him.

Casement was evidently not a success at running Sanford's trading post. Part of the problem was that there was as yet little trade to be had on the upper reaches of the Congo. It was certainly possible to buy ivory from the indigenous population, but the natives were not much interested in gathering it: European money had no real meaning for them and their normal way of life met most of their material needs. In writing to Sanford to explain his decision to resign from the expedition, Casement told him: 'The difficulty here is not that the country is not fertile, but that people do not work.'[12] Instead, Casement returned to Leopold's fold, helping to organize a survey of the trail between Matadi and the Stanley Pool to facilitate the eventual construction of a railway.

Survey work occupied Roger Casement for several months, but by November 1887 his part in it was finished and he found himself unemployed, with no immediate prospect of finding more work in Leopold's service. This resulted in a strange interlude during which he worked for several months as the salaried manager of a British mission station. The depredations of disease and climate had led to a temporary shortage of Europeans suited to this kind of work and when the Revd W. Holman Bentley, who ran an Anglican mission station on the Congo, heard that Casement might be available, he sought him out with a view to offering him the job.

The educational work of the mission probably strongly appealed to Roger: there is no question that throughout his life he was a man of strong and sincere ideals, even though these were subject to considerable change. Certainly the idea of civilizing and westernizing the natives was central to the motivation of those who, like Roger, had not gone to the Congo simply with the aim of getting rich quickly. His tasks at the mission centred largely around its administration – accounts, correspondence, building projects and so forth; although not actually taking part in teaching or evangelism, nevertheless it is likely that he found it satisfying to be part of this work.

What is odd about this period is not so much the work that Casement was doing as the fact that to get the job he persuaded Bentley 'of his conversion and faith in Christ'.[13] This seems strange because Casement was never a particularly religious man. Although he embraced the Catholic faith in the days leading up to his execution (as did William Joyce some thirty years later), before then he never demonstrated much interest in religion except in terms of the political dimension which it assumed in Ireland. He also gave Bentley assurances about his private life that were probably untrue: there is considerable evidence from later in his career that he was a promiscuous – and arguably predatory – homosexual. Most of his known sexual partners were young African and South American men and it seems likely that the relative sexual freedom he could enjoy – because of his isolation – during the pioneer days of this newly emerging colony was one of the reasons why Roger Casement found life there attractive.

Is it likely that he lied to Bentley? We cannot be sure: apart from the notorious 'Black Diaries', which are discussed in more detail later, evidence of Casement's homosexuality is largely confined to much later in his life. There is certainly no indication of when he became an active participant in homosexual intercourse, although one can infer, from the descriptions in his 1903 diary, that he was not new to the practice then. In any case, admitting to being a practising homosexual would, in the late nineteenth century, have been an act of folly that would have led, at the very least, to ostracism from the European community in the Congo and further afield. His claim to have undergone a religious conversion is perhaps less understandable, even though he was a humanitarian of broadly Christian outlook: if he did have a religious experience in the Congo, its effects seem to have been short-lived. One should certainly not condemn him on the grounds of this curious episode, however, for if he did lie, it was on the basis of expediency, but it serves as a warning that Casement was a considerably more contradictory and complex character than the saintly patriot he is often portrayed as.

At the end of the Congo rainy season in 1889, Casement left the mission to go elephant shooting and several months later was once again in the direct employment of Leopold. Having overseen part of the survey for the railway between Matadi and the Stanley Pool, Roger was to supervise its construction. The building of the railway has been cited as a significant step down the path towards forcible exploitation of the natives which ended up with the atrocities of the rubber trade only a few years later, and Casement's involvement in this cannot be shrugged off.

Leopold originally turned to Britain to provide his colony with its railway, and in 1885 a Royal Congo Railway Company was founded in Manchester by a syndicate which included Stanley, but protests in Belgium led to the establishment of a Compagnie du Chemin de Fer which eventually carried out the work.

Perhaps the most vivid description of the conditions that pertained to the construction of the railway while Casement was responsible for part of it at least is to be found in Joseph Conrad's *Heart of Darkness*:

A heavy and dull detonation shook the ground, a puff of smoke came out of the cliff, and that was all. No change appeared on the face of the rock. They were building a railway. The cliff was not in the way or anything; but this objectless blasting was all the work going on.

A slight clanking behind me made me turn my head. Six black men advanced in a file, toiling up the path. They walked erect and slow, balancing small baskets full of earth on their heads, and the clink kept time with their footsteps. Black rags were wound around their loins, and the short ends behind waggled to and fro like tails. I could see every rib, the joints of their limbs were like knots in a rope: each had an iron collar on his neck, and all were connected together with a chain whose bights swung between them, rhythmically clanking. Another report from the cliff made me think suddenly of that ship of war I had seen firing into a continent. It was the same kind of ominous voice: but these men could by no stretch of the imagination be called enemies. They were called criminals, and the outraged law, like the bursting shells, had come to them, an insoluble mystery from the sea.[14]

Although this was fiction, Conrad's journal makes clear that he saw scenes of this nature marking the early stages of work on the Congo railway. Casement's work on the project means that he was undoubtedly connected with the supervision of, if not participation in, violent and brutal forced labour. The treaties that Stanley had made with the local chiefs on Leopold's behalf usually stipulated that the tribe would 'assist by labour or otherwise, any works, improvements or expeditions which the said Association shall cause at any time to be carried out in any part of these territories'.[15] This amounted to the conscription of the entire indigenous population of the territory as forced labour – precisely as Leopold intended – to construct the infrastructure which would be used to oppress and enslave them more efficiently.

Casement's contract with the railway expired after a year and he decided not to renew it. Some years later he claimed that this was because he had become disenchanted with the increasingly Belgian nature of the enterprise and there is no reason to doubt this: many of the British pioneers of the Congo, from Stanley downwards, had hoped that the British Government would take a closer interest, perhaps even stepping in to take control of the country as they developed it, but Leopold had matters so neatly tied up, following the Treaty of Berlin, that this would not have been possible, even had there been any interest in Britain in doing so. Instead, Roger went home.

At this point it is worth taking stock of Roger Casement's life so far. He was twenty-eight when he finished his stint in the Congo and had come a long way from the orphaned clerk in Liverpool chafing at the routine of office work. He had been associated at close hand with Henry Morton Stanley, one of the great figures of the Imperial age, and had almost certainly seen many unpleasant sights as a relatively small cog in King Leopold's audacious and cynical scheme to bring the Congo under his own personal weal. He had also, we must assume, come to terms with his homosexuality, an area of his life that he would have to conceal rigorously if he was to achieve any measure of success. He may well have come to the conclusion that in the remoter parts of the world, where Europeans were much thinner on the ground, he would be far more able to give outward expression to his sexuality without the risk of compromise which attached to such activities in London, Dublin or Belfast.

The impression that Casement made on others was of a sympathetic, cheerful character, ready to help, self-sufficient and proud of his Irish roots. His employers on the railway described him as an '*agent exceptionnel*' when he left them. He was clearly in his element in the harsh environment of the Congo. Joseph Conrad saw him: 'start off into an unspeakable wilderness swinging a crook-handled stick for all weapons, with two bulldogs . . . at his heels, and a Loanda boy carrying a bundle for all company. A few months afterwards it so happened that I saw him come out again, a little leaner, a little browner, with his stick, dogs and Loanda boy, and quietly serene as though he had been for a stroll in a park.'[16] Casement's attitude towards the indigenous population was probably typical of the average European colonial pioneer of the time: he regarded them as lazy and indolent, and in need of re-education to European values. It is unquestionably true that the native Africans were being abused as forced labourers by the time that Casement left, and as part of projects for which he bore a degree of responsibility, but not to the extent that was later to cause such outrage across Europe. In so far as it is possible to make such a generalization, it is fair to say that Roger Casement was typical of the young and idealistic colonial pioneers then opening up the continent of Africa for European domination.

3. Her Majesty's Consul Casement

In 1892, Roger Casement moved from the employment of a foreign Imperialist monarch to that of his own and embarked on a career that was to endure for twenty years, bringing him professional success, celebrity, honour and public esteem, as well as ensuring that he could expect no mercy from a British establishment which eventually came to regard him, with considerable justification, as a treacherous renegade.

The job he took up, after a short period of home leave and a visit to the United States,* was as an employee, although not at this time a member, of Her Majesty's Consular Service in the Oil Rivers Protectorate† on the west coast of Africa. The task he was given was one for which he had demonstrable aptitude and experience: he was to survey areas of the Protectorate which had yet to be visited by Europeans, other than the occasional trader.

His work in West Africa was much closer to the Victorian ideal of enlightened, progressive exploration and colonial pioneering than anything he had done in the Congo. Unlike Stanley's, Casement's exploration did not involve the burning of towns, taking of hostages and use of Maxim guns against spear-armed natives. Two of Casement's forays into the relatively unknown hinterland of what is now Nigeria are well documented.

In March 1894 he set off from Itu, on the Cross river, with the aim of pioneering and opening a route to the Opobo river. Although accompanied by forty-three Africans, Casement had no European

---

* Although probably not to lecture on behalf of Sanford, as Inglis has suggested, since Sanford had died the previous year, having expended a good part of his fortune in various failed business enterprises, including his Congo venture.
† Now Nigeria.

companion and the expedition was unarmed. On only the second day they ran into difficulties: Casement noted 'a certain surliness and dislike to the white man',[1] and when they entered a village they were surrounded by aggressive and hostile locals, shouting, gesticulating and dancing, waving weapons and working themselves into a fury. Casement attempted to placate the leaders of the mob with cloth and tobacco, but this failed; when he attempted to move his caravan onwards, his party was attacked and many of his porters and much of their baggage were carried away.

This situation was resolved by the arrival of the King of the Inokun people who lived in the next village; through his intervention most of Casement's bearers and supplies were returned. In the following two weeks, Casement negotiated with the local rulers, discovering that both the main local tribes were cannibalistic and practised slavery, and learning that he could not hope to pass through the region for at least three months.

This expedition was followed, a month later, by a similar trip, although this time Roger Casement was accompanied by another European, Arthur Bourchier. This was more successful, in so far as Casement was able to travel between Esene, on the Opobu, and Ikorasan, on the Kwo Ibo. Even so, despite successfully reaching their destination, the bearers refused to return through the newly pioneered territory and they were obliged to return on a steamboat which they met on the river.

These were not great journeys of exploration but the nuts and bolts of Imperialism: the newly arrived Europeans introduced themselves to the local population and attempted to convince them (wrongly, but in good faith) that they were not necessarily a threat to the natives' way of life. It was a task that Casement performed well.

In addition to exploration, Roger Casement's work in Nigeria for the Consular Service included customs and excise tasks in Old Calabar, as well as normal Consular duties in the Protectorate, attending to the needs of British subjects who happened to find themselves there. After three years' hard work, which had greatly impressed both the local members of the Service and the Foreign Office in London, he returned to the United Kingdom for a period of well-deserved leave.

On his return to Ireland Casement found that his years of work in Africa were beginning to pay off. While he was staying in Magherintemple, he was contacted by the Foreign Office and told that his next assignment would be in Uganda where, with Leopold's effective seizure of the Congo, European interest in Central and Eastern Africa was beginning to focus. But everything changed in June 1895. A new Conservative Government under Lord Salisbury was elected at Westminster and its African foreign policy objectives were somewhat different, centred instead on growing unrest in the Transvaal. It would be preferable, therefore, to send an experienced Africa hand like Roger Casement to somewhere where he could be of real use; he was accordingly inducted straight into the Consular Service without having to sit the examination, and despatched to become Her Majesty's Consul at Lourenço Marques in Portuguese East Africa (now Mozambique).

The Consular Service exams were waived for no other reason than that Casement was needed at short notice and would not have had time to prepare himself thoroughly for them. It is certainly worth remembering that Roger had only been educated up to the age of fifteen and would have been at a disadvantage in any open, competitive examination. He was neither ignorant nor stupid, but he was to a great extent an autodidact and had spent a considerably larger part of his adult life than most people isolated from the company of his peers. It is hardly surprising, therefore, that whilst he showed considerable practical acumen in spheres of life with which he was familiar, he had a strong tendency towards intellectually naïve, romantic sentimentalism. This was most strongly evident during this period of his life in his execrable poetry,* and in

---

* Casement would have liked to have been a writer but his poetry, which he churned out relentlessly while in Africa, was clumsy and boring. A selection of it was eventually collected and published after his death.

somewhat gushing letters he wrote to members of t
family he encountered in his search for clues to hi
connection with the celebrated ascendancy family: a
continues to defeat scholars today as the result of the d(
during the Irish Rebellion and Civil War, of many ge   ...g.cai
records.

Casement's principal duties in Lourenço Marques involved the day-to-day running of the Consulate, a task which required a good deal of hard grind and mundane routine, but which Casement actually enjoyed: he had a 'love of all things clerical', according to one of his biographers. He was also required to protect the interests of British subjects in the Portuguese colony, a not altogether simple task, as he soon realized, because in many cases the Portuguese traders with whom Britons were attempting to compete also held positions of authority, such as magistracies, in the colonial government. The result of this was frequent instances of unfair and arbitrary impositions and restrictions on Britons and British companies, which Roger Casement soon realized were best solved by local low-level negotiations rather than threats and diplomatic *démarches*.

More important to Casement's employers in London, however, was his role in monitoring the freight being sent to the Boers on the new Lourenço Marques–Transvaal railway, which bypassed British controlled territory. The so-called Jameson raid in December 1895 had provided Kruger and the Boers with the perfect excuse to begin the importation of firearms for 'self-defence', and even before then the Boers had imported significant quantities of war *matériel*, recorded by Casement as including over four million rounds of ammunition, sixty-five cases of rifles and 100 Maxim guns. More weaponry was to follow.

Equally worrying to Lord Salisbury's Government was the potential threat of Germany making a deal with the Boers and perhaps seizing control of the Portuguese colony. Casement was tasked to discuss this with the acting Governor General of Mozambique and came away sympathetic to Portuguese fears of takeover plans by the major colonial powers, despite the reality that their

investment in the colony was severely inadequate and their treatment of the African population cruel. In fact, although discussions
did take place between Kruger and German representatives in the
region, Mozambique was not their target and this was an aspect of
the situation on which Casement had little to report.

After two years in Lourenço Marques, Casement found that the
climate was getting him down, his health was beginning to fail and
the petty irritations of a Consul's life – having drunken British
sailors and destitute British civilians bothering him for help at all
hours – were starting to wear on his nerves. He therefore applied
for a period of home leave, which was granted, and at the beginning
of 1898 he arrived in Britain to begin two months' rest and recuper-
ation. Ill health and family problems – his sister and brothers lived
even less stable lives than he did and were regularly importuning
him for financial and emotional support – caused him to stay in
London until July 1898, by which time the Foreign Office had
found a different post for him: he was to transfer across Africa to
Portuguese West Africa (now Angola) to be the British Consul in
St Paul de Loanda.

The Loanda posting was in all respects a promotion. As British
Consul, Casement's actual territorial responsibilities covered the
French Congo, to the north of the river, and Leopold's Congo Free
State, in addition to Angola. The reason underlying his reassignment
was that the French appeared to be encroaching into Sudan, via their
part of the Congo, taking advantage of continuing unrest among
the Mahdists, and the Foreign Office was understandably keen to
discover what was going on. With his deep knowledge of the region,
Casement was the obvious candidate for the job. By the time he
reached West Africa, however, Kitchener had defeated the dervishes
at Omdurman and turned south to confront the French. Bowing to
the inevitable, they had left the Sudan and the crisis had passed.

In addition to the Sudan problem, however, there was growing
disquiet in Britain about King Leopold's activities in the Congo.
Almost as soon as the Treaty of Berlin had been signed, Leopold
had begun using the exclusive trade deals made with the tribal

chiefs to close out foreign – that is, non–Belgian – competitors who were attempting to trade in ivory. Ivory was a useful commodity in the days before plastics, and there were considerable profits to be garnered from policing up the tusks of dead elephants, as well as slaughtering live ones, to acquire it, but the commodity which was to bring massive profits to Leopold, and years of subjugation, cruelty and atrocity to the Africans of the Congo basin and elsewhere, was rubber.

Rubber had been known about and collected for many years but it was the invention of pneumatic tyres, together with the discovery that rubber could be vulcanized and used to make durable pipes, tubes, hoses and gaskets, which caused the boom of the 1890s. More than half of the Congo Free State was covered by forest and jungle, and much of it harboured wild rubber vines, winding through the canopy like so much ivy. Cultivated rubber, in the form of rubber trees, would take some years to come on stream, as plantations needed time to grow and mature, so tapped wild rubber was the only serious source and Leopold now knew that his colony, which had hitherto been a drain on his resources, would actually make him fabulously wealthy. The only real difficulty in converting this tremendous natural resource into hard cash was finding the manpower to do it.

Again, this was not an insuperable problem. The collection of wild rubber was an arduous, dangerous and difficult job, and it was a problem for the concessionaires and the State to persuade local Africans to do it in exchange for the valueless lengths of brass rod and copper wire which Leopold had introduced as currency in the State (and which could be exchanged for goods at State-controlled shops and trading posts, although its international convertibility was nothing to write home about). But in the treaties which Stanley had made with the chiefs of the Congo Free State were clauses regarding the provision of labour for projects of improvement for the region, and what could be more improving than for the State to start showing a profit? Any reluctance by the natives to cooperate on these grounds could be swiftly overcome.

By now Leopold had constituted a militia, staffed by Belgian officers and African mercenaries, called the Force Publique. This had the ostensible purpose of protecting rubber gatherers as they went about their work; in reality it was an instrument of oppression for the traders and the agents of the State to extract as much rubber as possible for the least possible cost. The process was usually simple: a detachment of the Force Publique would arrive at an African village, loot it and seize the women. The women would then be held as hostages until the chief had persuaded his men to bring in a certain weight of rubber. When this was done, the Force Publique (or possibly members of a privatized company militia who operated in exactly the same way) would sell the women back to the village in exchange for livestock or other supplies and move on to continue collecting their quota. If a chief or headman refused to cooperate even after this, his people would be put to death and, appropriately in the ever cost-conscious Congo, the right hand would normally be taken from each corpse so that the African mercenaries could prove that they had used their ammunition for the purpose for which it was intended and had not wasted it on hunting or put it to some other frivolous use.

But the quotas for rubber collection demanded by the State and its concessionaires were so high that where they could be met, they represented almost full-time work for the great majority of the population, which had therefore become enslaved.

Evidence of this new form of slavery had been trickling into the public domain for some time, but the three most reliable European witnesses were all friends of Casement – indeed the first was his uncle, Edward Bannister. In 1892 Bannister had been appointed to a Vice-Consulship in Loanda, though with the Congo as his area of responsibility. He had discovered then that the Free State was illegally employing British West African subjects as soldiers and that any misdemeanours they committed were being punished by flogging. Bannister's persistence in uncovering this situation and protesting against it eventually caused enough trouble for the Belgians to take steps to have him removed from the Congo, but he had been followed by others, including Alfred Parminter and Edward Glave, who had both worked with Casement for Stanley in the early days of the colony and who were equally credible. Their reports were supported by some of the many missionaries who were present.

At this time, Casement was unable to penetrate inland much further than Boma, near the mouth of the Congo, because the Foreign Office had already despatched a member of the Consular Service, Major Pulteney, to investigate and were unwilling to have two Consuls covering the same ground at the same time. Instead, waiting in the port for Pulteney's return, Casement made a brief study of the freight traffic that was passing through. What he found led him to a surprising conclusion: large quantities of rubber were coming out, but virtually the only serious commodity going into the Upper Congo was weaponry and ammunition. In other words, the rubber was not being paid for and the guns could only be part of a system which extracted it by force: slavery.

Oddly enough, this was the same conclusion that had been reached by Edmund Morel, a clerk in the Elder–Dempster line, Casement's former employer, whose job involved visiting Belgium to ensure the smooth operation of the line's Congo business. Morel noticed that Elder–Dempster ships rarely carried anything other than armaments and goods for the Congo's European community and deduced that this could only be because the Congo's exports were being extracted without payment. Taking this further, he saw that while the declared value of the Congo Free State's exports was being published at a certain level, the actual trade value it reached was almost double the declared value, meaning that a vast tax-free profit was being skimmed off the top. Morel's deduction was that the only person or organization in a position to do this would be the Government of the Congo Free State and thus, in effect, King Leopold himself.

Thoughts of this kind were now interrupted by other events on the African continent. The outbreak of the Boer War led to Casement being summoned to Cape Town from where he was despatched back to Lourenço Marques to resume his previous task of monitoring shipments of weapons into the Transvaal along the railway. Returning – supposedly on holiday – Casement bribed the customs chief with £500 to discover that very little war *matériel* had come in; evidently the Boers could no longer afford German arms.

Returning from Lourenço Marques to Cape Town, Casement came up with the suggestion that a raiding party be sent from Natal to cut the railway anyway and offered both to take part in person and to recruit helpers in Mozambique. This idea, like many such 'Commando' actions, was most attractive to the British command in South Africa as it promised to reap a significant reward for relatively little outlay, and in March 1900 Lord Roberts, the British Commander-in-Chief, gave his agreement for it to go ahead. Preparations took several more months and in May Casement set out with an advance element before being recalled: other matters had by then become more pressing for the military authorities and anyway, it was realized, any breach in the line would have been repaired in a couple of weeks. Instead, Roger Casement returned to Britain in order to prepare to resume his Consulship in West Africa.

He had probably anticipated that he would be returning to Loanda but the Foreign Office had determined that the time had come to constitute a separate Consulate in the Belgian Congo. With this in mind, Casement read himself into the latest journalism from the Congo, much of it the result of Morel's investigations, and then set out for Brussels to meet King Leopold.

Casement and Leopold had two meetings, on 18 and 19 October 1900. Casement was of course chiefly interested in the Congo and the system of government that Leopold had instituted in the Free State but he soon realized that Leopold was more preoccupied by Anglo-Belgian relations. The king appeared anxious that the atrocity reports emanating from Central Africa should not sour relations between Britain and Belgium at a time when Kaiser Wilhelm's Germany was becoming increasingly bellicose and assertive. Casement pressed Leopold on the atrocities and was assured by the Belgian monarch that these had been maliciously exaggerated, although he admitted that there had been some cases of misconduct. The main outcome of the meetings appears to have been a determination on Casement's part to decide on the truth of the atrocity stories for himself. There is no particular evidence to support the observation by Constantine Phipps, the British Minister in Brussels, that Casement had been 'impressed' by the king.

Casement returned to the Congo in the new year of 1901 and set about establishing his Consulate in Boma, the seat of the Free State Government. Soon afterwards, however, he set out for Kinchasa on the Stanley Pool and began informally to investigate his territory. What he found shocked and disturbed him and confirmed the authenticity of the atrocity stories that had been emanating from Central Africa for more than ten years.

In June, Casement sent Lord Lansdowne, the British Foreign Secretary, a memorandum describing what he called 'the system' which Leopold had set in place since the Treaty of Berlin. Underpinning it was a clever scheme the king had instituted whereby he laid claim to 'protect' lands not already occupied by the tribes of the interior. In effect, alongside the treaties, this gave Leopold direct personal control over the whole country: he had exclusive trade deals with the tribes and owned the rest; in only a small number of relatively worthless areas was there any access for foreign traders.

This was complemented by the king's financial arrangements. The colony was extremely cheap for Leopold to run because his administrators were largely paid out of the commission which they earned from collecting rubber. This was of course illegal under the Treaty of Berlin, which had supposedly ensured that the Congo Free State was a non-profit-making body, but naturally the agents making their commissions were also the police and magistrates of the colony and were hardly likely to prosecute themselves for their infractions.

The involvement of the administrators in the commercial aspects of the colony also guaranteed a certain level of brutality. They demanded high productivity from the forced labourers in order to maximize their personal profits, and this translated into violence by the overseers towards the workers. This practice was of course illegal but was only going to be stopped by the administrators, and they relied on the violence to ensure their profit, as did everyone in the chain up to and including Leopold himself. Not surprisingly, Casement was disgusted and depressed by the system, and this may have been exacerbated by feelings of guilt that in his own small way he had been responsible for some aspects of setting it in motion. His memorandum was passed by Lansdowne to the Prime Minister, Lord Salisbury, who directed that for the time being no action need be taken.

It was at about this time that Edmund Morel threw himself full-time into exposing the iniquities of Leopold's rule in the Congo. He gave up his position with Elder–Dempster for good and took a job as a journalist on a newspaper dealing with African affairs. He turned out to be a highly effective propagandist, and over several years he was able to mobilize and manipulate public opinion to an extraordinary extent. Throughout 1902 and 1903, he bombarded his readers with well-researched, credible accounts of the horrors of the Congo, drawn from his correspondence with missionaries, traders and other eye-witnesses. Attempts by Leopold to intimidate and bribe Morel failed and in May 1903, Morel succeeded in persuading his parliamentary allies to stage a major debate on the Congo Question which was followed by a unanimous resolution of the House of Commons that the natives of the Congo should be governed with 'humanity'. Under this pressure, instructions were despatched to Casement that he should go to the interior as soon as possible and send back reports at the earliest opportunity.

The instructions from London came at a time when Casement had just concluded a period of leave spent in Ireland and Britain. In fact he had been all set to make an exploration of the upper Congo some months before, but had suddenly and capriciously changed his mind, telegraphing for permission to return to Europe and then, having received this, making no move to leave the Congo for several months. This had caused some speculation in the Foreign Office that Casement might have had a breakdown or gone off his head, but it was recognized that the harsh conditions under which he had to live and work meant that he must be granted some leeway and so permission had been given.

Casement's journey back to Africa, and his subsequent activities there, are recorded in the first of the notorious 'Black Diaries', covering the period from 14 February 1903 to 7 January 1904 (the first six weeks' worth of entries were torn out in 1916 to show to journalists). The early entries record the last few days of his leave in London, followed by a sea voyage to the Canary Islands and Madeira, where he spent a further three weeks in a fairly hectic social round.

Rather oddly, several of the entries covering his time in Madeira reveal Casement to have been somewhat title-struck, carefully recording the details of the aristocratic acquaintances he made during his stay, but he was also scrupulous in writing up his sexual encounters with local youths. It is hard in many cases to decide whether Casement is recording actual acts of sexual intimacy or fantasizing about what might have been, and part of the reason for this is the speed with which these transactions seem to have been embarked upon and consummated. If, indeed, they are a record of actual events, Casement was evidently practised at identifying and picking up like-minded young men, many of whom were paid for their services.

If the record of Casement's homosexual encounters is accurate, however, it does jar somewhat with the entry he made on 17 April when his ship put into the port of Kabinda, near the mouth of the Congo. There he learned that a distinguished British soldier, Major General Sir Hector Macdonald, had recently killed himself rather than face court martial as a homosexual. Casement seems to have been upset by what had happened as he returned to it several times during diary entries for the next few days, but the original entry has suggested to many that Casement himself was not a homosexual and that the sexual material in the diaries may have been interpolated at a later date by a forger. The entry for 17 April reads:

News of Sir Hector Macdonald's suicide in Paris! The reasons given are pitiably sad. The most distressing case this, surely, of its kind, and one that may awake the national mind to saner methods of curing a terrible disease than by criminal legislation . . .'[2]

Could someone who was a practising homosexual have written in these terms that homosexuality was a 'terrible disease'? An entry two days later goes on to mention that Casement was still 'very sad at Hector Macdonald's terrible end' and, almost two weeks after he first heard the news, Macdonald's death was still helping to keep him awake at night. Casement's biographer Brian Inglis has argued that 'To Casement, a man was a homosexual in the same way he was a diabetic. It was his misfortune, not his fault.'[3] This may well have summed up his attitude: there is no suggestion in the 1903 diary or the two later 'Black Diaries' that Casement felt any guilt or particular concern over his sexuality. As a homosexual in an era when such behaviour was strictly illegal, he had to learn to compartmentalize his life to an extraordinary degree in order to maintain his façade of normality and he showed considerable facility in doing this. The writer of the 'Black Diaries' is clearly someone who has accepted his sexuality for what it is and is keen to express it when the opportunity arises.

The entries concerning Macdonald also raise the intriguing possibility that Casement may have been acquainted with him. In the absence of any kind of confirmation this is purely speculation, but Casement's diary refers to Macdonald as 'Hector Macdonald' rather than 'Sir Hector' or 'General Macdonald' and this might appear to be indicative of some acquaintance, according to the usage of the time.

Casement did not at first show any great urgency as he began to pursue his investigation in Central Africa. He travelled first to

Matadi and waited for more than a month as a steamboat he had chartered was prepared for him, filling his time with a tour of the Stanley Pool and the area around it. He finally started out upriver in July, calling at the main trading posts and mission stations where he could talk with both Europeans and Africans about the situation. At first he heard complaints about the arbitrariness of Leopold's rule, how Africans would be beaten or imprisoned for failure to obey orders, but before long he began to come across evidence of the real horrors of the Congo.

The most obvious sign of this was the depopulation of the interior in comparison with Casement's previous stay in the Congo at the end of the 1880s. Lukolela, for example, had had a population of around 5,000 in 1887; in 1903 this had fallen to 352 of whom only 82 were men of working age. The official explanation for this was sleeping sickness, which was endemic in the region, but it was evident to Casement and the missionaries who were assisting him that this could not be true. The reality was that many of the Africans had fled to the relative safety of French-controlled territory, whilst many others had died of a portfolio of diseases brought on by forced labour, malnutrition and fear.

Then came the appalling tales of mistreatment from victims and eye-witnesses. By and large, sentries and Force Publique militia would cut the hands from corpses only to prove that they had been killed, but now Casement began to meet natives who had survived the process, some of whom were as young as eleven. In other cases, he collected evidence of the removal and collection of penises from the corpses of Africans killed when the demand had been made that only men were to be subjected to punishment.

By the end of September, Casement had seen all he could stomach and after sending a series of letters to the Free State authorities protesting at specific instances of cruelty and mistreatment, he retreated to Loanda in Portuguese West Africa to begin work on his report and to await instructions from London.

There is no question but that Casement was profoundly affected and disturbed by what he had seen. One slightly odd characteristic of the 1903 diary is that he records his concerns over the health of his bulldog John in almost obsessive detail. In Kinchasa, however, as he prepared to leave, he worked himself up into such a temper that he broke his walking stick over the unfortunate beast – an extraordinary fit of irritation from a man who was at heart as gentle as Roger Casement. As a result of his long years in the tropics, Casement's health was fragile and he was in any case something of a hypochondriac, but there is no doubt that 1903 marked a watershed in his physical and psychological state. This is not to suggest that he went mad, but that his experiences seem to have induced in him a sense of moral despair which would eventually lead him to accept the conclusion that the English presence in Ireland was no different to Leopold's misrule in the Congo.

Casement spent about a month in Angola and then returned home, on Foreign Office orders, to write up his report. He arrived in London on 1 December. Again, he found the experience deeply depressing: his Foreign Office superiors simply could not comprehend the horrors he had seen, but he did receive permission to talk to Edmund Morel and tell him of his experiences. Their meeting on 10 December would have a profound effect on both men. In his memoirs, Morel described his first impressions of His Majesty's Consul in the Congo Free State:

I saw before me a man, my own height, very lithe and sinewy, chest thrown out, head held high – suggestive of one who lived in the vast open spaces. Black hair and beard covering cheeks hollowed by the tropical sun. Strongly marked features. A dark blue penetrating eye sunken in the socket. A long, lean, swarthy Vandyck type of face, graven with power and withal of great gentleness. An extraordinarily handsome and arresting face. From the moment our hands gripped and our eyes met, mutual trust and confidence were bred and the feeling of isolation slipped from me like a mantle. Here was a man indeed. One who would convince those in high places of the foulness of the crime committed upon a helpless race . . .

Until now, Morel had been a lone crusader but with Casement's encouragement at this and subsequent meetings during the next few weeks, and with some financial backing, he was to found the Congo Reform Association, the key instrument in the campaign to wrest personal control of the Congo away from Leopold.

4. From Imperialist Jingo to Republican Rebel

The two years following Casement's return from the Congo were crucial in his life. It was then that he transformed himself from a convinced, if cranky, British Imperialist with a romantic interest in Irish history into an increasingly fierce critic of Imperialism and a thoroughgoing Irish Nationalist with strongly separatist sentiments. Much of this is attributable to the way in which the Foreign Office dealt with him and his report in the period directly after his return.

The report was completed on 8 January 1904 after which Casement left London to enter a nursing home in Belfast for an unspecified operation. As the report was being prepared for the printer, a debate arose within the Foreign Office over certain questions of style. This stemmed in part from Casement's concern that the report should not appear as an attack on the low-level agents of the Congo Free State. Although these individuals were at the forefront of the exploitation of the indigenous people, Casement did not believe them to be truly responsible: they were implementing a system that had been devised by others who were much more highly placed: in any case, Casement had accepted the agents' hospitality during his investigation and actually liked some of them. He therefore requested that their names be deleted from the report and this was agreed by his superiors. At this point, however, Lord Salisbury, the former Prime Minister, intervened, pointing out that the only aspect of the report that made him uncomfortable was the idea that the Africans who had given information to Casement would as a result be subjected to worse treatment than they had been receiving already. Consequently, while Casement was in Ireland receiving his medical treatment, the report was edited so that almost all names of people and places were replaced with meaningless initials.

This might well have been the best course from the safety point of view, but its effect was to depersonalize Casement's findings to such an extent that when it was finally published on 15 February 1904 the report did not make nearly as much impact with the press or the public as Casement and his colleagues had hoped for. Even so, digests of the report appeared on the news pages of the serious London daily newspapers and King Leopold immediately set about organizing rebuttals in the Belgian press with the firm intention of discrediting Casement.

The Belgian riposte to Casement was swift. In a response entitled 'Notes on Mr Casement's Report', Leopold argued that Casement had not been in the interior of the Congo long enough to have formed a realistic impression of what was going on; that much of his 'evidence' was hearsay; and that he had been misled by lying natives and disgruntled missionaries. For example, in the one specific case of mutilation cited by Casement and brought to the attention of the authorities at the time, that of a fifteen-year-old boy named Epondo who had had his hand cut off by a plantation sentry, Leopold claimed that Epondo had actually been badly bitten by a wild boar and that his hand had then become gangrenous. Epondo was produced to say that he had originally lied to Casement and an American missionary supposedly backed up this story.

The Belgian version of the Epondo story was clearly bogus: when they had first met, the boy had shown Casement a bullet wound in the same arm that had been mutilated by the sentry and he had only retracted his story after being taken alone to a Free State post where he was kept for some time. The missionary who had supposedly backed the story reported that he had simply witnessed Epondo giving the revised version of events in a confused and listless fashion.

Despite this, there was a certain amount of truth in some elements of the Belgian response, most notably in their claim that many of Casement's findings were based on hearsay. In fact this was not Casement's fault and had in any case been anticipated by him: he had assumed that his report would be used in conjunction with the many accounts of atrocities that had been filtering back from the Congo since the beginning of the rubber boom and even before. The Foreign Office had in its possession a substantial file of high-quality testimony on the atrocities, sent in by Casement's predecessors as Consul, by missionaries, traders and others who had witnessed at first hand the horrors of the Congo system. It did not occur to Casement that this material was politically double-edged: if the Foreign Office produced it now to accompany the Casement report, it would be shown to have been sitting on knowledge of what was happening in the Congo for many years without doing anything about it. This was a sensitive time politically: the ruling Conservatives had just lost a safe seat to the Liberals at a by-election, whilst a general election was due within the year. Lord Lansdowne, the Conservative Foreign Secretary, had no intention of giving any ammunition to the Liberals and was not prepared to deploy the Foreign Office's knowledge of what had really been happening if this would occasion any political embarrassment. Consequently, while Casement faced overt attacks from Brussels together with sly briefings from Leopold's various agents and front men about his bias and lack of objectivity, the Foreign Office sat on its hands and declined to come to the aid of its servant. No doubt depressed by his experiences, in poor physical health, piqued by the refusal of the Foreign Office to act in the way that he thought most effective, and despite the knowledge that he was due to be promoted to become Consul in Lisbon, one of the more prestigious posts in the Consular Service, Casement wrote to Lansdowne's private secretary offering to resign from the Service.

Roger Casement was clearly in a state of considerable emotional turmoil in the months following the publication of his report. His career shows him to have been, in many respects, a man of action with little tolerance of the slow machinations of the political process and an uncertain grasp of its subtleties. This is hardly surprising: the British Consulate at Boma or Loanda was not Whitehall, and imperatives changed. Casement had seen the outcome of the Congo system with his own eyes and was disgusted by it, and although most, if not all, members of the British Government shared his moral outrage in an abstract sense, their desire to do anything about it was diffused by other concerns, not the least of which was the construction of the intricate web of alliances that were to be used in the hope of containing German expansion in Europe. The Belgian role in this was at least as important to the Foreign Secretary and his high officials as the urge to condemn Leopold for his rapacious ill-treatment of his Congolese subjects, but this was something that Casement could not, or would not, understand.

Instead, with the opportunity now to spend more time in the land of his birth, he threw himself wholeheartedly into the Irish cultural revival. The catastrophe of the potato famine of 1848 had led inexorably to a recognition in England that something needed to be done about Ireland, and although it had been a slow process, a number of issues regarding the right to land and the protection of tenants had gradually and reluctantly been addressed, and in some cases settled. In parallel with this came a renewal of interest in ancient Irish history and the forms and language of specifically Irish culture. Roger Casement, through family and social connections, knew many of the Northern Irish Protestant figures who were associated with the cultural revival: he had grown up with some of them, and had long had a deep and enthusiastic interest in Irish history, and as wrangling over his report continued, he spent as much time as he could in Ireland, helping out with the organization at Cushendall, Country Antrim, of a *Feis* – a cultural festival celebrating Gaelic music, dancing, singing and poetry, as well as arts and crafts, games and even traditional agricultural techniques.

It was during this period that Casement established relationships with most of the people who were to form his social and intellectual circle in the last twelve years of his life. They included Gaelic scholars like Alice Milligan and Margaret Dobbs, separatist sympathizers like Francis Bigger, a Belfast solicitor, and Bulmer Hobson, an Ulster Quaker, and most importantly of all, the historian and writer Alice Stopford Green.

Green and Casement came from similar backgrounds. Alice Stopford was born in Meath in 1849, the daughter of a Church of Ireland clergyman, and raised in a bleak and narrow intellectual environment from which she had escaped through intellectual pursuits. In 1874 her father had died and the family moved to London, where two years later she married the historian J. R. Green. Green suffered from tuberculosis and died six years after their marriage, leaving Alice to finish his final work and then to emerge, over the next few years, 'as an historian in her own right [whose] London house became one of the "salons" which influenced some of the more radical thinkers and talkers of the day'.[1] Green and Casement shared an enthusiasm for early Irish history and a concern over colonialism in Africa – Alice had founded, in 1901, a society aimed at stimulating public interest in and knowledge of what was taking place in Africa and had thus become acquainted with Edmund Morel – and Casement had met her after he had written soliciting her support for Morel's Congo Reform Association. It is difficult not to assume that Casement came to see Alice Green as a mother figure in some respects: they corresponded continually and Casement's letters to her often had a confessional quality as he sought her approval for his activities and her forgiveness for his failings. Green, it has been argued, did not make Casement into an Irish separatist, but she did act as the catalyst for his conversion.

It should not be assumed that the relationship between Casement and his Irish friends was entirely one-sided, however. His Congo report had made him into something of a celebrity throughout Britain, Europe and, to some extent, the United States, and he must have become a considerable social prize. One must conclude that there was equal dazzlement on both sides: Casement found a circle of friends totally in tune, intellectually and emotionally, with his romantic Nationalism; his new Irish circle learned that this heroic figure was desperate to be a part of their cause.

After the *Feis* in June 1904, the realities of normal life once more began to intrude. The Consul's post in Lisbon had now become vacant and Casement was due to take over, despite ill health and a profound lack of enthusiasm. In fact he was to last in the appointment for just two months. Although Lisbon represented a promotion, the work was a step down from what he had been doing. In the Congo or Portuguese West Africa, Casement had been the *de facto* ambassador, Britain's senior representative in the territory, but in Lisbon there was a separate diplomatic legation and his work consisted of the normal drudgery of the Consular Service: relieving distressed Britons abroad, springing drunken sailors from jail and booking ships into and out of port. Casement was undoubtedly well organized, though pedantic, pernickety and long-winded, and he could perform the routine tasks of the Consul perfectly well, but as his recent service had amply demonstrated, he had a lot more to offer. On a plea of ill health, he returned to Ireland. His half-formed intention was to resign from the Service but he did not; instead he applied for 'secondment', equivalent to becoming a kind of unpaid Consular reservist.

For the next eighteen months Casement combined work on behalf of the Congo Reform Association with his increasing immersion in the affairs and politics of Ireland. The Congo situation staggered on, with little evidence for Casement that his work had achieved any significant impact. But in reality, he had succeeded in planting a delayed-action bomb under Leopold's colonial regime. For all the personal smears that Leopold launched against Casement, there was no getting away from the fact that he was an official of the British Government and that his report had been published as an official document. Leopold had been forced, in 1904, to institute his own Commission of Enquiry, and whilst it consisted of his own nominees, they were finding that Casement's report was disturbingly accurate. This was not, however, apparent to Casement in Ireland.

After his return from Lisbon he had entered a nursing home for treatment for a fistula, a painful opening in the wall of the anus, normally caused by an infection or abscess, and in his case most likely the result of his sexual preferences. And it seems that at some point in the next months he underwent a form of nervous breakdown or collapse while staying with friends at Richhill Castle in Antrim. It was during this time that his devotion to Ireland and his own Irishness began to be marked by an increasing dislike of England, at least in so far as the English involvement in Ireland was concerned.

The intellectual underpinning of Casement's Irish separatism rested on the question of land ownership. Alice Green argued that the waves of immigration into Ireland from the first millennium onwards – Norsemen, Anglo-Normans and so on – had not actually led to progress in Ireland but had in fact amounted to no more than the imposition of an alien culture on a nation which had a flourishing and advanced civilization of its own. Casement whole-heartedly agreed with this: he saw a parallel between Leopold's imposition of the concept of land ownership in the Congo and the perennial land question in Ireland. In both cultures, land had been held communally by the tribe, and the idea that any one person or family could own it was meaningless. By imposing ownership, Leopold in the Congo and the English in Ireland had automatically excluded those who did not own land from a stake in the community. The Celtic Catholic Irish and the African tribesmen had been reduced to the status of virtual slaves in their own country. This was an attractive analysis, if highly simplistic and somewhat naïve, and in combination with Casement's sheer anger and disgust at what he saw as the pusillanimity of the Foreign Office, it led to a festering resentment.

In the King's Birthday Honours List of 1905, Casement discovered, to his evident disquiet, that he had been made a Companion of the Order of St Michael and St George, the order of chivalry reserved for distinguished service with the Foreign Office. In some respects this pleased him because it was an obvious vote of confidence in his achievement in the Congo, but in reality he was more perturbed by it. His political views were such by now that he felt genuine qualms about accepting British honours and he launched into an immediate round of discussions with his friends in Ireland over whether he should accept. The general view was that he should, and he did indeed do so, but made a small gesture of defiance by refusing to receive the award in person on the grounds of his health; instead, the insignia was posted to him and, according to Casement legend, remained unopened in its package of issue.

While this minor soap opera was taking place, word was filtering back that the Belgian enquiry into conditions in the Congo was likely to agree in substance with Casement's report. Three months after he had received his CMG, on 7 November 1905, the report of the Belgian Commission of Enquiry was finally published in the Congo's official gazette. The findings of Leopold's nominees were broadly that the African natives of the colony had been cheated out of their land and trade, had been abused by the system of forced labour, and had suffered from illegal military actions by the Congo Free State's forces at the behest of the commercial concessions within the colony. Essentially it was a *prima facie* case that Leopold had breached his obligations under the Treaty of Berlin.

Casement was initially delighted by the results of the enquiry, but closer inspection revealed that Leopold had managed to tone down substantially many of the fiercer criticisms and was still refusing to accept that his system was the cause of the abuses, if indeed he even cared. This realization led to further despondency on Casement's part, fuelled by his lack of money (on 'secondment' he remained unpaid), and at the beginning of 1906 he began to look around for a new career. His first thoughts turned to journalism but his friends were unconvinced: they believed that there would be far too much competition for Casement to make a success of it. Edmund Morel was concerned that if his friend left public service he would lose any pension rights he had accumulated, and this seems to have weighed with Casement as well. Instead, Morel began to use his influence, backed up by political changes in Britain, in order to expedite Casement's return to the Consular Service.

The Foreign Office had undoubtedly been annoyed by

Casement's abandonment of his post in Lisbon after only two months, particularly as it had been intended as a reward for him, and there was a disinclination to continue to employ him, especially as he had not entered the Service through the usual route but had somehow managed to penetrate it as an outsider. Nevertheless, his work in the Congo meant that he could not be ignored, particularly as changes were afoot.

In fact, the widespread protests against Leopold's personal rule in the Congo had led to moves among Belgium's opposition politicians to force the issue by seeking to annex the Congo to Belgian governmental control. With an election due in Belgium in May 1906, Leopold had privately agreed that he would not oppose annexation, thus ensuring that the Congo did not feature as a serious issue during campaigning. But with the election concluded, the king had gone back on his word: by issuing a series of reform decrees, he hoped to keep control of the colony and damp down international agitation. To oppose this, and to deal with the protests that it caused in the British parliament, it was crucial for the Foreign Office to keep Casement on its side. Using his parliamentary contacts, Morel was able to force the pace on behalf of his friend: he had a question 'planted' asking why Casement had been given no realistic offer of employment, apart from Lisbon, since the publication of his report two years before. The Foreign Secretary, backed into a corner, gave the questioner assurances that this had been on health grounds alone, and that because Casement was now better these no longer applied. On 25 July, Casement received the formal offer of the Consulship at Bilbao in Spain. As he was contemplating this, a letter from the Foreign Secretary followed offering him the alternative of Santos in Brazil.

This was another key turning point in Casement's career. He had by now spent fourteen years as an official of the British Government, a period which had culminated in his investigation in the Congo with all its consequences. This was an achievement of which he could be rightly proud both as a service to the Government and – without exaggeration – to humanity as a whole. But he had reached a point where, intellectually and emotionally, he had exhausted his loyalty to his employer. He was embittered and emotionally scarred by the experience of compiling and publishing his report and by the lack of support he had received. Instead, he had turned for support to a network of friends whose interests, cultural and political, lay in an entirely different direction, and had allowed himself to be swept up by them. No opprobrium can attach itself to Roger Casement for his change of heart, and even the most small-minded and jingoistic 'Little Englander' can hardly doubt the legitimacy of Irish independence as an aspiration. But there is a central conundrum to be answered: why did Casement choose to continue in the Consular Service at this time?

The most likely answer is also the simplest. He could not foresee getting another job which would be so suited to his tastes and talents. He had toyed for a while with an offer to manage a cotton-growing enterprise in Mozambique but had been put off by the idea of being in 'trade' (he had also disliked Lourenço Marques during his earlier appointment there). He had also considered going back to the Congo as a representative of the Congo Reform Association but this would probably have been futile and perhaps even dangerous: at least one European critic of the regime, an Austrian named Gustave-Marie Rabinek, had apparently been assassinated after his arrest and conviction for illegal rubber trading; and an Italian human rights investigator had allegedly been poisoned while staying at a Free State outpost, although he had survived. Almost certainly the reality is that Casement assumed his loyalty would never be put to the test. By now his position had shifted, and from being a moderate 'Home Ruler', in favour of the devolution of most government powers to an Irish authority, he had become a full-blooded Sinn Fein separatist. Certainly there was a strand within Sinn Fein which conceived a future for Ireland as an independent state sharing a monarch with Great Britain, but there were many more who favoured complete separation.

Casement arrived in Santos in October 1906 to take over a Consulate which had been allowed to run down by his predecessor.

Consuls were paid relatively little but could choose to supplement their earnings by retaining all or part of their office expenses allowance, and clearly Casement's predecessor, Francis Mark, had done that: he had eventually been forced to install a screen in his office to stop disgruntled sailors from throwing things at him. By nature something of a pedant, Casement took a firm grip on the Consulate, revamped the archives and got things running smoothly again, while settling in as a member of the small British expatriate community. One slight oddity was that he had special writing paper printed for the Consulate, headed 'His Majesty's Consul for Great Britain and Ireland', reflecting what was then the official Sinn Fein position, though hardly that of the Foreign Office. His superiors do not appear to have noticed, however.

Casement spent less than a year at Santos before returning to England in July 1907 on urgent private affairs, staying briefly with a former landlady in Earl's Court before leaving for Ireland. There he was offered the appointment of HM Consul-General in Haiti and San Domingo and after consulting with an acquaintance who had previously held the post, agreed to accept it. Haiti was considered one of the better postings in the Consular Service, and an added attraction for Casement was that he 'would save £500 clear out of [his] pay', as he wrote to his cousin.[2] This was important, for a perennial problem faced by Casement was having to bail his brothers and sisters out of financial scrapes. In this case his brother Tom appears to have been in need.

The Haiti posting did not come off, however. To the evident embarrassment of the appointers in the Foreign Office, the Foreign Secretary decided to offer the post to an Old Etonian ex-army officer, and Casement had to be asked to stand down. Instead, he was offered the choice between Santos and Pará, also in Brazil and described to Casement by a friend who had served there as a 'hideous nightmare'. None the less, unable to bear the idea of returning to Santos and reluctant to face the financial squeeze of leaving the Service, Casement opted for Pará.

His stay in Pará, like his tenure at Santos, was short and truncated still further by his ill health. He arrived at his post in February 1908 to find the Consulate in worse disarray than at Santos – his predecessor had been a hopeless alcoholic. Casement was in the process of getting to grips with this when he was stricken by gastro-enteritis during the summer and ordered by his doctor to go to Barbados to recuperate. In fact his illness left him so weak that he was unable to work, and in November he applied for and was given permission to return to Europe. On arrival home he was told that the Consul-Generalship at Rio de Janeiro had become vacant and it was his if he wanted it: he accepted immediately.

The Consul-Generalship of a large country like Brazil was a considerable promotion for a man who was still only forty-four years old, and represented a significant step up from his previous posts. The conditions under which Casement worked were better as well; he now had British assistants and clerical staff, and the Consulate had been well run for the previous fifteen years or so, thus freeing him from the huge effort of reorganization that he had been forced to undertake at Santos and Pará.

As Consul-General, Casement was very much part of the diplomatic circuit which was concentrated around the mountain suburb of Petropolis, but whilst he had been a popular member of the small English community of Santos, this was much less the case in Rio. One reason for this stemmed from Casement's increasingly hostile views on England and the English. His assistant, Ernest Hambloch, reported that Casement had formed a close friendship with the German Consul-General, Baron von Nordenflycht, and was in the habit of attacking England's malign involvement in Ireland to him, so much so that von Nordenflycht mentioned it in conversation with Hambloch. He also reports incidents when Casement would make anti-English speeches at social gatherings, behaviour hardly likely to endear him to a community of largely patriotic English exiles. The second reason to account for Casement's unpopularity came from the whispers that began to circulate about his sexuality. 1910 was the second year for which a 'Black Diary' was found, and if it is to be taken as genuine, the sexual exploits he describes are every bit as lurid as before. For example, one of the earlier entries, on 28 February, reads:

Deep Screw & to hilt. *X* 'poquino'

Mario *in Rio* − *8½* + *6"* *40$.000. hospedaria. Rua do Hospicio, 3$ only fine room. Shut window. Lovely, young* − *18* & *glorious. Biggest since Lisbon July 1904* & *as big. Perfectly huge.* '*Nunca veio maior*'!

Nunca.

The evidence from Casement's diaries is that he liked to be vigorously buggered by young native men with large penises and that he had no qualms about paying for their services. Although Rio was a large town even at the turn of the century, it is likely that some hint of Casement's activities would get back to the expatriate and diplomatic communities, and the evidence from Hambloch, though scanty, is that it did.

After his first year in his post, Casement applied for and was granted leave. At the beginning of March he departed from Rio, heading for Santos where, after a sexual adventure in Sao Paulo, he spent several days visiting friends before continuing his journey to Buenos Aires on 11 March. Here he evidently had a liaison set up with a young man named Ramon, apparently the proud possessor of a ten-inch penis.

Casement stayed in and around Buenos Aires, alternating between visiting friends and meeting Ramon, until 4 April when he took ship for home via Montevideo, Bahia (where he conducted a brief onboard romance with a stevedore) and the Canary Islands, reaching Liverpool on 1 May. For six weeks he travelled happily between London and Ireland, meeting friends, both English and Irish, going to the theatre, involving himself in plans for a testimonial for Edmund Morel and taking whatever opportunities he could to engage in brief sexual entanglements. Then he was summoned back to the Foreign Office for a meeting with the Foreign Secretary, Sir Edward Grey: the subject was a series of disquieting reports of serious human rights abuses in a region of the upper Amazon basin, based on the Putumayo river, that was disputed between Colombia and Peru.

The situation on the Putumayo offered obvious parallels with what had taken place in the Congo. The problem that had arisen was the result of efforts to collect the wild rubber which was to be found in abundance in the area and the fact that commercial control of the rubber-collecting enterprise was largely under the control of one man, Julio Cesar Arana.

Arana was a native of Peru, having been born – in the same year as Roger Casement – into a Spanish family in the Andean town of Rioja. He had begun his career as a trader on the Amazon in 1881 and over the years had established various partnerships as the volume of trade slowly increased. Around the turn of the century, trading stations began to spring up on the major rivers where individuals and small concerns set up shop in the hope of buying rubber from the forest Indians, and Arana and his company were well placed to act as their principal source of supplies and loans and also as a purchaser of the raw rubber. The business had increased by degrees until 1907 when a limited company, known as the Peruvian Amazon Rubber Company and capitalized at £1,000,000, was set up by Arana in London, with himself as managing director.

Arana's great advantage as a trader was the relationship he enjoyed with the Peruvian Government. Most of the traders on the Putumayo were Colombians, but the Peruvian Government was prepared to support Arana's operation with force if necessary. The region was disputed, although under a series of agreements between Peru and Colombia it had been partially demilitarized. But the Peruvian Government understood that having Arana's company in effective control meant that the region was *de facto* under Peruvian rule, and that suited them well.

Not surprisingly, the obvious similarities in circumstances between the Putumayo and the Congo quickly led to markedly similar abuses. As in the Congo, the agents of the Peruvian Amazon Rubber Company found themselves wielding the power of life and death over their native employees, a group of people whom, because of their ethnic differences and supposed backwardness, they regarded as barely human. Reports by travellers and shocked employees of the Company began to be published in Iquitos in July 1907, and whilst many were inclined to ignore or dismiss the reports, there was something particularly compelling about them, as Casement's biographer Roger Sawyer has described.

Content was probably without precedent in terms of horrifying descriptions of torture. The enslaving of Indians might not have shocked a large section of South American opinion, nor the excessively hard working of peons; what might have jolted the public conscience, had it been believed, was the perverted nature of mutilations of men, women and children. The initial motive for torture – to ensure increased rubber yield – had, according to the accounts, long since given way to an orgy of sadism. What was convincing in the testimonies was that men trapped in the middle of the rubber-gathering hierarchy were, in their efforts to destroy the system, willing to incriminate themselves.[3]

Reports from locals were backed up, in late 1907 and early 1908, by the account of two Americans, Walter Hardenburg and W. B. Perkins, who after travelling across the Putumayo and experiencing various adventures along the way, had put together a dossier of eye-witness material about the atrocities. Finding that his own government was not particularly interested in what he had to say, Hardenburg had gone to London and, after trying to interest publishers in his material, had passed it on to the Anti-Slavery Society. In an effort to promote the maximum publicity for the Putumayo atrocities, the Revd John Harris of the Anti-Slavery Society advised Hardenburg to approach the magazine *Truth* with his story, thus initiating a public clamour in London as well as a series of parliamentary questions which prompted Foreign Secretary Edward Grey into action.

Grey instigated enquiries through Casement's successor at Pará, George Pogson, and approached the Peruvian Amazon Company (which had by now dropped 'Rubber' from its title) to ascertain how it responded to the allegations. In the face of the outcry which had resulted, the Company had little option but to volunteer to send out a commission of enquiry.

Casement subsequently explained that he had read the allegations in *Truth* but otherwise knew no more of the situation than any other member of the public. This was not entirely accurate: he was in close contact with many of the key figures in the Anti-Slavery Society, and they formed part of his social round when he was back in Britain and Ireland. He had been in correspondence with the Society about the allegations and as early as 17 June 1910, while he was on leave in Ireland, had received a letter regarding the Putumayo and the Company. A week later he was in London, visiting the Anti-Slavery Society and the House of Commons where he met several sympathetic MPs who may well have told him of the pressure to send him to the Putumayo. This kind of talk obviously persisted for the next two weeks because on 11 July Casement asked his superior, Tyrrell, whether the rumours were true and told him that he was ready. On 13 July his diary records:

. . . To F.O. at 12 & then at lunch Mrs G. & then at 3. Sir E. Grey & others at F.O. Putumayo. To F.O. and saw Tyrrell who told me Sir E. Grey was decided to send me to Putumayo & wished to see me at 3 today. Lunched Mrs G & then back to F.O. Saw Sir E. Grey & long talk with him.

Things moved quickly after this. Casement spent two days reading himself into the Putumayo papers at the Foreign Office, briefly visited Dublin, and left for Pará on the *Edinburgh Castle* on 23 July, in company with, but not formally a member of, the Company's commission.

With 12,000 square miles of territory to cover, the commission clearly was not going to be able to visit every part of the Putumayo and instead resolved to concentrate on two main centres: La Chorrera and El Encanto. Casement joined the first expedition, to La

Chorrera, and the party set out by river steamer, provided by Arana, from Manaos on 17 August, arriving in Chorrera more than a month later on 22 September.

The system in Putumayo bore eerie similarities to the Congo, as Casement immediately discovered. At the top of the hierarchy were the Company owners and senior managers who avoided getting their hands dirty by involvement in atrocities or wrong-doing; below them was a hierarchy of semi-autonomous section chiefs, of European origin, who in turn employed a number of Barbadian blacks as overseers. Below the Barbadians in the hier-archy were literate Indians and half-breeds, and they controlled the *muchachos*★ who 'disciplined' the forest Indians sent out to collect the rubber. Underpinning the atrocities was the fact that the section chiefs relied for their income on commission on the amount of rubber they collected: as in the Congo, this was a certain way of ensuring the mistreatment of the Indians collecting the rubber. Casement recognized this immediately, taking the view that the system in place was sufficient to guarantee that the allegations were broadly correct: to his frustration, he discovered that the commission members were inclined to want to see the evidence first. In fact this was not long in coming. There is a second diary for 1910 – the so-called 'White Diary' – which is an expanded narrative of what Casement and the commission did during the three months they were together. The entry for 24 September describes a meeting with one of the Barbadians, Jasper Dyall, who was working for Armando Normand, one of the more notorious of the section chiefs:

Dyall came at 8 or 8.30 am, and I had Barnes in to hear his statement – one of the most revolting character. The man is a brute but has been employed by greater brutes.

As his statements are so grave, he owning up to five murders of Indians by his own hands, two he shot, two he beat to death by 'smashing their

★ 'Boys'.

testicles' with a stick under Normand's orders and with Normand helping, and one he flogged to death . . .

In many ways, this set the tone for the next three months. On 31 October Casement was back at Chorrera:

Fox and I went out to the store and watched the rubber coming in. Huge loads of it, men, women and children. Dear little bright-eyed boys – tiny girls – mothers with infants – two quite old women and two old men even – almost the very first old people I have seen. Three of the Indian men, too, had beards – stray hairs, it is true, but still beards – one 2″ long. These are the first men with hair on the face I have seen. We weighed several loads – one was just 50 kilogs – on a thin spare enough man too. Then I went one better and collared two small boys with their loads and got these weighed first and then the boys themselves.

One mite had a load of 22 kilogs of rubber on his tiny back and then when put on the balance himself he came to just 25 kos. The next, a little boy whose name he gave as Kaimeni, weighed 29½ himself and was actually carrying 30½ kilogs of rubber! One kilo. more than his own weight. This has been for many miles. The station of Sur itself is only two hours away, but this rubber we were told came from Kaimenes on the way to Encanto, a much greater distance.

Casement left Iquitos on 6 December, to return to Europe to write up his report, and after Christmas at sea and a long weekend in Paris, reported back to the Foreign Office on 5 January 1911. He spent the next four months writing and revising the report and preparing it for the printer. Although this time Casement ensured that no holds were barred in the naming of names, once again the report did not achieve quite the impact that he had anticipated. The Peruvian Government was ready to admit that terrible things had occurred which it had a duty to investigate, but to some extent it was in its interest to do so: by taking responsibility for the Putumayo, it was reinforcing its claim to own it. In fact Grey and the Foreign Office withheld the report at first, attempting to use the threat of publication to persuade the Peruvian Government to take more vigorous action than it had done hitherto. But this was only partially successful: a Peruvian investigation led by a Dr Paredes visited all the sections of the Company's land and eventually produced a 1,300-page report that was considerably more detailed and comprehensive than Casement's, but the problem was that the delay in taking action meant that many of the guilty men named in Casement's report had had time to move on and set themselves up in similar style elsewhere.

As a reward for his work in the Putumayo, Casement was knighted on 20 June 1911. He suffered the same slight qualms that had overtaken him on being awarded his CMG but as Sawyer has said, 'He pretended to hate it but was obviously flattered.'[4]

The day before the award was gazetted, he wrote to thank the Foreign Secretary:

> I find it very hard to choose the words in which to make acknowledgement of the honour done me by the King.
>
> I am much moved at the proof of confidence and appreciation of my services on the Putumayo conveyed to me by your letter, wherein you tell me that the King had been graciously pleased upon your recommendation to confer upon me the honour of a knighthood.
>
> I am indeed grateful to you for this signal assurance of your personal esteem and support, and very deeply sensible of the honour done me by His Majesty.
>
> I would beg that my humble duty might be presented to His Majesty, when you may do me the honour to convey to him my deep appreciation of the honour he has been so graciously pleased to confer upon me.

Although this letter was subsequently presented at his trial as a sign of his hypocrisy, Casement was careful to use neutral and polite language. His life was by now divided into three main compartments: the Consular official, the Irish separatist and the secret homosexual; and he was always wary when these intersected. His anti-English outbursts were usually confined to when he was in company with his Irish nationalist friends, whilst his sexual escapades normally centred on partners of completely different race and class. The knighthood impinged on his career and his politics, pulling him in totally different directions, but at that stage it was more important to him to keep his career going than to make a political point.

Casement returned to Iquitos in October 1911 in order to ascertain how far the Peruvian authorities had got with prosecuting the prime suspects of the Putumayo atrocities. The answer was, not very far: only one, a section chief named Aurelio Rodrigues, was awaiting trial and there had been predictable foot-dragging and obstruction, despite the fact that Paredes had collected an enormous dossier of evidence detailing ghastly atrocities that even Casement had not uncovered. In a state of disillusion, Casement left South America for the last time on 7 December with instructions to go via Barbados to the United States where he was to brief the US Government, including President Taft, on his findings.

Casement's report on the Putumayo was finally published as a Foreign Office 'Blue Book' on 13 July 1912. Publication of the report, which was not substantially factually challenged, was followed by an investigation by a House of Commons Select Committee to ascertain how much responsibility was borne by the London-based directors of the Peruvian Amazon Company and whether the situation required any changes in the law in response.

One curiosity of this investigation, which dragged on for over a year, was that it had emerged that the first reports received by the Foreign Office had come from their Honorary Consul in Iquitos, David Cazes, as early as 1905, whilst Casement had certainly been aware of the situation from 1908 and perhaps before. Casement had glibly explained that the situation in the Putumayo was well outside his territorial remit but this did not fully explain why he had made no move to alert either his superiors in London or the Anti-Slavery Society with which he was in frequent correspondence.

5. England's Difficulty is Ireland's Opportunity

Roger Casement retired from the Consular Service on 1 August 1913 with a pension that would enable him to live his life and pursue his interests in reasonable comfort. Of course, his principal interest, separatist Irish Nationalism, was not what one would normally expect of a retired Foreign Office official with a CMG and a knighthood, but as he left the employment of the Crown, the long-running political crisis over Home Rule was finally coming to a head. The reason for this was simple: the electoral arithmetic of the second general election of 1910 left the Unionists with 272 seats, the Liberals with 272, Labour with 42 and the Irish Nationalists with 82. In short, in order to stay in government, the Liberals were bound to promise Home Rule for Ireland.

The problem, of course, was Ulster. The leaders of the Ulster Unionists, James Craig and Sir Edward Carson, and the British Conservative leader, Andrew Bonar Law, genuinely and sincerely believed that Home Rule would be disastrous for Ireland and for Ulster, this despite the fact that the leaders of the Constitutional Irish Nationalists, John Redmond, John Dillon and William O'Brien, had publicly and unequivocally accepted that the measures on offer would be a full and final settlement of their claim. In fact Home Rule was to be a fairly limp form of self-government, giving an Irish parliament and an Irish executive control over all internal domestic matters, whilst control over anything affecting the position of the Crown – war and peace, the army, the navy, foreign relations and most forms of taxation – was reserved to the Westminster parliament. Nevertheless, the bill in which Home Rule was presented was received with acclamation by Nationalists in Ireland and throughout the Irish diaspora.

The response of the Ulster Unionists was to move an amendment in the House of Commons to exclude Ulster from any Home Rule measures and to organize resistance, by force if necessary. In January 1913 the Ulster Unionist Council voted to set up the Ulster Volunteer Force (UVF) and by the time Casement left the Foreign Office, there were more than 50,000 Ulstermen in training, commanded by a retired English general of the Indian Army, and plans were already being aired for a coup d'état to seize control of the Province before the British army could act.

The Nationalist response to the UVF was the Irish National Volunteers, a similar part-time body composed largely of enthusiastic Home Rulers drilling under the orders of ex-British army NCOs, but lacking the armaments and the degree of organization that the UVF was in the process of acquiring. At this point, it is worth looking at the broad composition of the Irish Nationalist groupings ranged in opposition to the Ulster proposals for the partition of Ireland between a Home-Ruled and a Westminster-ruled state. The largest group were the Constitutional Irish Nationalists led by John Redmond: they enjoyed overwhelming support amongst the Irish Catholic people and controlled the great majority of Irish seats in the Westminster parliament (the remainder being held by Unionists). Considerably smaller was Arthur Griffiths' Sinn Fein, a tiny ultra-Nationalist party which argued for complete political independence for Ireland under the Crown. Smallest of all was the Irish Republican Brotherhood (IRB), inheritor of the traditions of the Irish secret societies and advocate of a complete break with Britain, to be achieved by force if necessary. Although small, the IRB had acquired a new younger membership as a result of the Irish cultural renaissance, and under the leadership of men like Casement's close friend, Bulmer Hobson, and Tom Clarke, was enjoying a rejuvenation. Casement's position at this time was probably closest to that of the IRB: his hatred for England and the English – though not for individual Englishmen – had become almost pathological – it was certainly irrational – but he was not a member of the IRB and was never invited to become one. The reason for this is that even in extremist circles Casement was seen as rather strange, obsessively ranting on about Irish virtue and English villainy, boring even his best friends. He was also self-important to a marked degree (his defence counsel at his treason trial believed him to be a megalomaniac) and saw himself as a pivotal figure in the struggle between England and Ireland, even though he had no home of his own in Ireland and had not lived there for any extended period since adolescence.

Even so, Casement was of value to the Nationalist cause simply because of who he was – an Ulsterman, a Protestant and a man knighted for his services to Britain and to humanity. He undoubtedly carried a good deal of prestige, and he was enthusiastically preparing to lay this at the feet of the movement that had consumed his attention.

The first public expression of this was a meeting at Ballymoney, County Antrim, in October 1913, intended to rally Protestant Nationalists to the cause against Ulster Unionism. This showpiece event was conducted with decorum and restraint: the main speakers, including Casement, made their points with care and consideration for Unionist feelings, and the meeting was held by them to be a great success.

But Casement's increasing extremism was not to be shackled by any real consideration for the feelings of the Ulster Unionists. As far as he was concerned, they were simply wrong, and should be coerced into seeing the error of their ways. From the first he had been involved in the organizing committee of the Irish Volunteers, and by March 1914 he was taking part in Volunteer parades.

In May, when he was in London and supposed to be negotiating with Redmond over the control of the Volunteers, he was plotting with Alice Green and Erskine Childers, the Anglo-Irish jingoist novelist, to import arms into Ireland from Germany in order to arm the Volunteers. The plan was for Childers, who had written the first classic spy thriller, *The Riddle of the Sands*, to sail from Hamburg to Lowth in his yacht, the *Asgard*, in order to land a load of Mauser rifles and ammunition which the conspirators had bought in Hamburg with cash raised in London. Meanwhile Casement, now accredited representative of the arms sub-committee of the Irish Volunteers, had sailed for Canada with the intention of procuring more arms through the expatriate Irish community in the United States.

Casement's principal contact in the US was John Devoy, a veteran Fenian, editor of the *Gaelic American* newspaper and chief of the Revolutionary Directorate of the Clan na Gael, the Irish-American equivalent of the IRB. Although Devoy and Casement had never met, they had corresponded occasionally and Casement had been a subscriber to Devoy's newspaper for some time. None the less, their first contacts were strained. Devoy was aware of the negotiations – to which Casement had been party – which allowed Redmond's representatives on to the committee of the Irish Volunteers and he explained to Casement that this effectively rendered him *persona non grata* to the Clan. The following day, Casement was able to explain himself properly to Devoy who grudgingly accepted him for his obvious sincerity and enthusiasm.

During the next weeks Devoy was able to introduce Casement to the most important figures among the Irish Americans, including Judge Dan Cohalan in New York and Joe McGarrity of Philadelphia, and to brief them on his efforts to provide rifles and ammunition for the Volunteers. In the meantime, Casement was also being used as a celebrity draw at Irish-American fund-raisers, where his Ulster Protestant background and British knighthood made him a doubly exotic attraction.

Casement's single-minded obsession with Irish affairs had, however, blinded him to what was happening in the rest of Europe. His loathing of England had long led him to the conclusion that the malign influence of English foreign policy had formed part of a conspiracy of the corrupt European Imperial powers to deprive Germany of its true role. In an article, 'Irish Freedom', published in Dublin in February 1914 he had argued that 'The true alliance to aim at for all who love peace is the friendly union of Germany, America and Ireland. These are the true United States of the world. Ireland, the link between Europe and America, must be freed by both.'

This was something of a juvenile fantasy and Casement was naïvely puzzled and piqued when the outbreak of war in Europe in August 1914 knocked his speeches to Irish-American groups off the front pages of the newspapers. But having paused to recover his poise, he recalled the old saw that 'England's difficulty is Ireland's opportunity' and, with Devoy and the leaders of the Clan, set about taking advantage of that opportunity.

In fact there had already been tentative contacts between the Clan and the German Embassy in Washington before the outbreak of war, but on 24 August 1914 the first full-scale meeting took place between a delegation led by Devoy on one side and the German Ambassador, Count von Bernstorff, and his senior aides on the other. The Irishmen made it clear what they wanted from the start: arms and training, and a cadre of officers to take control of the Volunteers and forge them into a fighting force, thus enabling them to overthrow British rule in Ireland and, from the German point of view, tie down significant numbers of British troops in Ireland.

Bernstorff gave Devoy a cagey and pragmatic response: he agreed to forward the Clan's request to Berlin, but made it clear that the German response was likely to depend on how the war panned out: if Germany and Britain could reach a swift understanding, it was unlikely that any help would be forthcoming, but if things turned into a war of survival he would recommend agreement to Irish wishes.

Casement, with his enthusiasm for links with Germany, was by now carrying the leadership of the Clan along on his coat-tails, possibly against its better judgement. On 25 August he persuaded Devoy and the Clan to agree to sign a petition to the Kaiser which, among other bizarre claims, suggested that: 'We feel that the German people are in truth fighting for European civilization at its best . . . that Germany did not seek this war, but that it was forced upon her . . .' and, most extraordinarily, 'The British claim to control the seas of the world rests on an unnamed factor. That factor is Ireland . . .'

This kind of rubbish caused some senior Irish-American figures to begin to temper their enthusiasm for Casement. John Quinn, a well-to-do New York lawyer, attempted to restrain him, recognizing that most Americans, including most Irish Americans, saw Germany as the aggressor in the war, but Casement was not having any of this. On 17 September he wrote an open letter to the Irish people from New York:

Speaking as one of those who helped to found the Irish Volunteers . . . I say, in their name that no Irishman fit to bear arms in the cause of his country's freedom can join the allied millions now attacking Germany in a war that, at the best, concerns Ireland not at all and that can only add fresh burdens and establish a new drain, in the interests of another community, upon a people that has already been bled to the verge of death.

This drew a strong protest from the Foreign Office and resulted in the suspension of Casement's pension which he had continued to draw until this point. It also brought him to the attention of the British security authorities, as an unsigned, undated minute in the file MI5 now opened on him makes clear:

Sir Roger Casement: formerly in the Consular Service and employed to investigate atrocities in the Congo and Putumayo.

He identified himself strongly with the Irish National Volunteer movement from its inception and worked energetically with Col. Moore and Captain White in organizing the force.

I am informed that he has been away from Ireland for some time and 'is supposed to have been in America'.

I am awaiting further information on this and also as to his habits (natural and un-natural!).

It is very likely that Francis Joseph Bigger would act as his agent in Belfast.

I have never met Sir R. Casement but was invited to do so by a mutual acquaintance last June, who then described him as a 'sincere Nationalist'

– I declined the invitation and said I was a 'sincere Imperialist' and heard no more.

The jibe about Casement's sexuality is interesting, suggesting that the circle of awareness of his homosexuality was wider than previously supposed.

It would appear that by mid-September 1914 Casement was attempting to persuade Devoy and the Clan leadership to send him as their representative to Germany in the hope of organizing armed support. He seems to have been successful in this, despite the warnings of Quinn, and on 5 October he met Devoy, McGarrity and Judge Cohalan in New York where it was agreed that they would provide him with $3,000 to act as their representative in Berlin. A further meeting took place on 10 October, after which the Irishmen visited the German Club for final negotiations with Bernstorff and his military attaché, Franz von Papen (later to be German Chancellor and – briefly – Deputy Chancellor under Hitler). On 13 October Bernstorff wrote a letter to the German Chancellor, Bethmann Hollweg, introducing Casement and recommending his ideas to him, and on 15 October, with his beard shaved off and travelling on the passport of an American named John E. Landy, Casement boarded the steamer *Oskar II* to take passage for Christiania (now Oslo) in neutral Norway.

The Clan leaders he left behind had mixed feelings, not necessarily about enlisting the support of Germany, although some undoubtedly did have such misgivings, but about the wisdom of sending Roger Casement on this mission. Devoy was impressed by Casement's frugality and apparent asceticism, but his career as an Irish Nationalist activist had been so meteoric and his temperament so odd – W. B. Yeats's father, who met him in New York, heard Casement muttering 'Poor Kaiser, poor Kaiser' with tears in his eyes – that he sought reassurance from McGarrity that they were doing the right thing. McGarrity, who knew Casement no better than Devoy did, assured him they were, and so he was allowed to go to Berlin as their representative.

1. HM Consul Roger Casement.

2. Magherintemple House, County Antrim, where Casement spent much of his childhood.

3. African forced labourers in the Belgian Congo.

4. King Leopold II of the Belgians, proprietor of the Congo Free State.

5. 'Leopold crushes the Belgian Congo', *Punch*, 1906.

6. Putumayo Indians. The rifles suggest these are low-level supervisors rather than rubber collectors.

7. Casement (*left*) with a member of the Peruvian Amazon Company's investigatory commission, 1910.

8. John Devoy (*third from right*) with Eamon de Valera and other Irish-American leaders, New York, July 1919.

9. Casement recruiting for the Irish Brigade, an artist's impression from the *Graphic*, 1916.

10. NCOs of the Irish Brigade at Zossen, 1915, wearing their amalgamation of German and 'British' uniform.

11. Casement (*right*) with Daniel Bailey (*left*) and an officer of the *U19*, April 1916.

12. Casement poses with officers and ratings of the *U19* prior to his departure for Ireland.

13. Captain Robert Monteith, the former British soldier sent by the Clan na Gael to assist Casement in Germany.

14. Members of the Irish Volunteers stretch out their hands to receive arms being landed at Howth, in Dublin Bay, as part of the shipment organized by Casement, Erskine Childers and Alice Green in 1914.

15. Irish rebels arrested in the aftermath of the Easter Rising, 1916, and subsequently executed. It was to prevent this bloody outcome that Casement returned to his homeland from Germany.

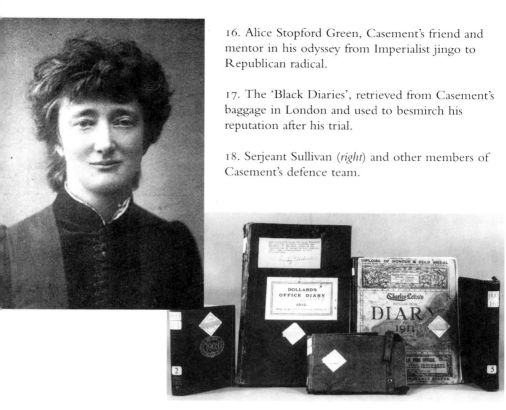

16. Alice Stopford Green, Casement's friend and mentor in his odyssey from Imperialist jingo to Republican radical.

17. The 'Black Diaries', retrieved from Casement's baggage in London and used to besmirch his reputation after his trial.

18. Serjeant Sullivan (*right*) and other members of Casement's defence team.

19. F. E. Smith (later Lord Birkenhead), Attorney-General and prosecutor at Casement's trial.

20. Roger Casement on trial for high treason, 1916.

21. Casement is led away from court after his conviction for high treason.

Even so, both his Irish and German contacts were puzzled by his choice of travelling companion, Eivind Adler Christensen, a Norwegian-American sailor who had accosted Casement on his first night in New York, and with whom he had struck up a friendly relationship. Casement seems to have been one of the few people not immediately repelled by Christensen's manner (presumably effeminate) and decided to take him with him, to Norway and then Germany, as his 'manservant', on the basis that he spoke English and Norwegian fluently and claimed also to be able to speak German. What was not immediately apparent was that Christensen and Casement were having a sexual relationship, and indeed recent evidence has emerged, in the form of a letter from Casement to Christensen, which places their first meeting in South America several years before, that this was the resumption of a relationship.

Casement's voyage on the *Oskar II*, though supposedly secret, could hardly have been calculated to attract more attention from his fellow passengers. Announced as the American Landy, Casement quite obviously had a British accent, and accompanied as he was by the strapping Christensen, most of the passengers and crew assumed him to be a British spy. This impression was reinforced when the ship arrived in British waters and was stopped and ordered into Stornoway harbour in the Isle of Lewis, Outer Hebrides, by a Royal Navy cruiser (ironically the HMS *Hibernia*). Six German officers who had been making their way home to rejoin their units were taken off and interned, but 'Landy' was left unmolested.

Casement and Christensen reached Christiania on 29 October and booked into the Grand Hotel. Casement then departed for the German Embassy to present his letter of accreditation from Bernstorff and set in motion the arrangements to get him to Berlin. Christensen, meanwhile, decided to attempt to earn a little extra cash by betraying his employer and lover. He made his way to the British Embassy where he told a surprised official that he had travelled from the United States with an English nobleman who was being sent to Europe in order to stir up trouble in Ireland. The official, Francis Lindley, reported that the visitor would not give his own name, nor that of the 'Englishman', but that he sounded serious and did not ask for money. It struck Lindley that his story was true. Christensen also gave Lindley the strong impression that he was involved in a homosexual relationship with the Englishman. He was told to come back the following day if possible.

Christensen hurried back to the Grand Hotel to tell Casement an extraordinary story. He had, he claimed, been accosted in the lobby of the hotel by an Englishman who had taken him by car to a large building at 79 Drammensveien – the address of the British legation – where he had been asked questions about his employer: Christensen had loyally refused to give Casement away.

In some respects, this news delighted Casement: it appealed to his self-importance and fed his paranoia, but it was also a worry. If he had been identified by the British, they could presumably make trouble for him in Norway and might even be able to assassinate or kidnap him. The following day he returned to the German Embassy and asked them to change his travel arrangements: could he leave that day? The German Minister, Oberndorff, agreed that this was a good idea.

Meanwhile, Christensen was back at the British legation and having an interview with the British Minister, Mansfeldt de Cardonnel Findley, during which he eventually revealed, for the sum of 25 kroner, precisely who his 'master' was. On a promise of receiving more money for better information, Christensen returned that afternoon with copies of some of Casement's correspondence and a German cipher he had been given. He asked Findley for $100 and received 100 kroner, then hurried back to meet the train he and Casement were taking for Copenhagen and then Berlin. There he told Casement that he had agreed with the British diplomats to lure him to a place where he could be kidnapped for the considerable sum of $5,000.

In fact Christensen's was not the only betrayal that took place during Casement's short stay in the Norwegian capital. Subsequent enquiries by officials of the British legation led them to evidence of a hasty liaison between Casement and another sodomite, 'the

German teacher of languages named Bauermeister'[1] from Bergen.

Convinced that they were being tailed by the British Secret Service, Casement, Christensen and Richard Meyer, a German Foreign Office official deputed to escort them, changed trains during the night and eventually crossed into Germany on 31 October 1914.

In Berlin, Casement had four main priorities as the representative of the Clan na Gael: the first of these was to extract a public declaration of support for Irish independence; he also needed to secure German agreement to provide military help and German public support for Irish aims; and finally to organize an Irish military unit to take part in the fight for freedom. First, however, he needed to persuade the Germans that the Irish cause was worth supporting and to this end he was to meet the Under-Secretary of State, Arthur Zimmermann, at the Foreign Office in Wilhelmstrasse.

Casement had prepared an *aide-mémoire* as the basis for his discussions with Zimmermann and to read it makes obvious the basic reasons why Casement's mission failed in the way that it did. Part of the problem lay in Casement's lack of understanding of the Irish condition. His own experience of Ireland was, as we have seen, limited by his long years abroad, whilst his views were extreme even amongst Irish Nationalists. In consequence a statement like:

Irish Catholics in the ranks of the Army are almost entirely Nationalists and at heart are not proud to be fighting England's battles. They do it from necessity in the first case . . . and in the second case the Irish young men are prone to martial service and like fighting for its own sake . . .

is in truth simply wishful thinking based on supposition and cliché. Casement went on to suggest that although Irish soldiers had an innate sense of 'honour and loyalty' they had entered the British service: 'with all [their] instincts of nationality against them, and solely as a soldier of fortune who preferred the devil-may-care role of a soldier to misery and idleness in the slums of Dublin or

Cork . . .'[2] From a man who had spent twenty years in British
Imperial service and accepted a knighthood and the CMG, and
whose views had only recently turned sufficiently against England
to cause him to resign from the Foreign Office, this is a statement
of shocking hypocrisy. The rest of his memorandum consists of
attacks on Allied propaganda which, no doubt, helped to convince
Zimmermann that Casement was sincere and, in conjunction with
their discussions, led him to decide that Germany had little to lose
and possibly much to gain by giving Casement a measure of support.

Zimmermann reported to the Secretary of State, Gottlieb von
Jagow, on 4 November and on the 7th was given permission to
proceed in a limited way. Jagow told Zimmermann that instructions
had been issued by the Chief of the General Staff to concentrate all
Irish POWs together in one camp but nevertheless expressed great
reservations: 'The military results would be small, possibly even
negative, and it would be said that we had violated international
law. However, it would suffice to have it known that the Irish
prisoners were quite ready to fight against England on our side.'
He also instructed Zimmermann to issue a 'memorandum of a
meeting' (an 'interview') in which German support for Irish
Nationalist aims would be expressed. This was issued and published
in Europe on 20 November 1914:

. . . the acting Secretary of State at the Foreign Office, by order of the
Imperial Chancellor, has made the following official declaration:

The German Government repudiates the evil intentions attributed to it
in the statements referred to by Sir Roger Casement and takes this
opportunity to give a categoric assurance that the German Government
desires only the welfare of the Irish people, their country and their
institutions.

The Imperial Government formally declares that under no circumstances would Germany invade Ireland with a view to its conquest or the
overthrow of any native institutions of that country.

Should the fortune of this great war, that was not of Germany's seeking, ever bring in its course German troops to the shores of Ireland they would land there not as an army of invaders to pillage and destroy, but as the forces of a Government that is inspired by good will towards a Country and a people for whom Germany desires only national prosperity and national freedom.

In theory, this was something of a diplomatic triumph for Casement – Devoy and the Clan were certainly pleased – but as we have seen, the Germans only agreed to it out of propagandist self-interest: they had no great confidence in the ability of the Irish Nationalists to debilitate the British war effort, nor did they particularly like Casement. He undoubtedly had admirers among the German officials he dealt with, but many of the traditionalist Prussians at the top of the hierarchy were deeply suspicious of him for the simple reason that they considered him a traitor to his country.

The next concrete move was to begin recruiting for the Irish Brigade. As well as recruiting among POWs himself, Casement decided that he needed help with his efforts and determined to get it by employing Irish Catholic priests who, he patronizingly assumed, would be able to sway the Irish prisoners from their primary loyalty. The German Minister at the Vatican made the necessary approaches and on 20 November Father Canice O'Gorman and Father Thomas Crotty received permission from their orders in Rome to travel to Germany. The following day, the German General Headquarters issued instructions that all Irish Catholic POWs were to be segregated in a separate camp. Private Michael O'Toole, of the 1st Battalion Irish Guards, describes what happened next:

Towards the end of Nov 1914 all the Irish Roman Catholics were sorted out and transferred to a separate camp in SENNE. Their food was much improved. The Irish were then transferred to Limburg an der Lahn POW Camp. There were already about 4,000 Irish POWs there. The cutting down of food was proceeded with systematically, the rations becoming smaller daily. Propaganda in the sense of an Irish Brigade was made by both agents and by literature . . .

The first setback encountered in this effort came after an address by a German bishop, following which the Irish senior NCOs refused any concessions 'unless they were being received by all prisoners'; because, they informed the camp commandant, 'in addition to being Irish Catholics, we have the honour to be British soldiers'.

Casement arrived at Limburg on 4 December and began his attempts at persuasion. O'Toole takes up the story: 'Sir Roger Casement, who was living in the Alt Post Hotel, Limburg, used to frequently visit the camp and entered into conversation with any-body who wished to talk with him. Bigger meetings were never held . . .'[3]

In fact on many occasions when Casement made his recruiting visits, he was jeered and abused, to his evident fury. Casement's outlook was that he was dealing with men who simply had not awakened to the joys of the Irish world-view and he was deeply angered to discover that he was completely wrong. He was unable to accept that it was possible to be an ordinary Irish Catholic – as opposed to a 'stooge' like John Redmond – and not agree with his views, at least when they had been properly explained. After two days visiting the prisoners, he retired to his bed at his hotel with a sore throat. By now he had attracted just three potential recruits: Sergeant Michael Patrick Keogh of the Royal Irish Rifles, Corporal Tom Quinlisk of the RIR and Corporal P. J. Dowling of the Connaught Rangers. Keogh was immediately made the Sergeant-Major of the Brigade, and Quinlisk its Company Quartermaster Sergeant. Dowling, who was probably only a private soldier anyway (a Ranger), was given his claimed rank of Corporal.

Not entirely undeterred, Casement analysed what had gone amiss and came up with the wrong answer: the men had been concerned by what the consequences of joining up would be. In the somewhat circumspect diary he kept in Germany he remarked: 'I will not accept the responsibility for putting a couple of thousand Irish soldiers into the high treason pot unless I get very precise and secure promises both in their regard, and for the political future of Ireland.'[4]

Instead, in his one and only meeting with Bethmann Hollweg, on 18 December, Casement proposed to conclude a treaty between himself as the representative of Nationalist Ireland – which he was not in any real or implied sense – and the German Imperial Government. On 23 December he submitted the text of a 'treaty' to Zimmermann, setting out in ten articles the principles, purpose and role of the proposed Irish Brigade. Article Two, for example, defined its aim: 'The object of the Irish Brigade shall be to fight solely in the cause of Ireland, and under no circumstances shall it be employed or directed to any German end.'[5]

Control of the Irish Brigade would initially be under German officers appointed 'with the approval of Sir Roger Casement', but these would be superseded as soon as possible by suitable Irish candidates, from either the United States or Ireland. Clothing and equipment would be provided by the Germans as a gift, but the Germans would not pay the Volunteers or provide them with financial remuneration of any kind. In the event of a German naval victory – a prospect that the Germans knew to be entirely unlikely bearing in mind the disparity in British and German naval strength – Germany undertook to land the Brigade in Ireland with sufficient equipment and weaponry to arm any elements of the Irish Volunteers in Ireland who were prepared to join them.

This much was reasonable within Casement's brief from the Clan, but Articles Seven and Eight, which dealt with the prospect of Germany failing to achieve a decisive naval victory over England, are strange almost beyond belief, and reveal Casement's extraordinary self-importance:

Should the German Navy not succeed in this effort the Irish Brigade shall be employed in Germany, or elsewhere, solely in such a way as Sir Roger Casement may approve . . .

In this event it might be possible to employ the Irish Brigade to assist the Egyptian People to recover their freedom by driving the British out of Egypt . . . Short of directly fighting to free Ireland from British rule a blow struck directly at the British invaders of Egypt . . . is a blow struck for a kindred cause to that of Ireland.[6]

The logic of this was, presumably, that any enemy of England was a friend of Ireland, but it was hardly consistent with Casement's refusal to allow the Irish Brigade to take part in operations on the Western Front (and it is inconceivable that any members would have wanted to anyway). During the Christmas and New Year period 1914–15, while British and German soldiers on the Western Front were temporarily putting aside their differences to socialize and play football in no man's land, Casement returned to Limburg and his recruiting tasks: he made virtually no impression and indeed was jostled, spat at and abused; his message of hatred and resentment of the POWs' fellow British army soldiers was not getting through. On 9 January 1915, in despair, Casement wrote to Count Georg von Wedel, a friend and contact within the German Foreign Ministry:

> The favourable impression conveyed to me early in December by the small number of men I then met in the camp and the apparent willingness they then displayed to fall in with my views have not been realized in the much larger number brought together. I daresay a sham corps of sorts could be formed by tempting the men with promises of money; but an appeal to their patriotism is an appeal to something non-existent.
>
> The newcomers, or such of them as I could speak with, seemed very ill disposed . . .
>
> All thought of enrolling the men, I fear, must be abandoned – they are mercenaries pure and simple: and even had I the means to bribe them I should not attempt to do so . . .

So much for 'soldiers of fortune' who 'preferred the devil-may-care role of a soldier to misery and idleness in the slums of Dublin or Cork'.[7]

By this time Casement was becoming more and more involved in what he imagined to be a British conspiracy to attempt to kidnap him. He was still using Eivind Adler Christensen as his manservant and emissary, convinced of his bona fides, and Christensen was continuing to maintain contact, during his occasional visits to Norway, with the British Embassy, to whom he was now routinely giving copies of Casement's correspondence. Christensen was still hoping to extract a large sum from the British, and after some consultation, based on an assessment of the damage that Casement's activities could cause to the British war effort, it was agreed that he might be paid £5,000 for information leading to Casement's capture. Unfortunately this was given to him in writing and, when he crossed back into Germany after the meeting with Findlay, the German authorities, who regarded him with great suspicion, arrested him, searched him and confiscated the letter.

As far as the German Foreign Office was concerned, the British offer simply confirmed its view that Christensen was not to be trusted, but Casement, who was convinced of the Norwegian's absolute loyalty, could not accept this. The £5,000 bribe was evidence of the sheer depravity of the British Government and he must respond by exposing them to the attention and scorn of the world. He decided that he would go back to Norway and confront Findlay in his lair. The Germans strongly advised him against this, but Casement would not be persuaded: he would cross the border into Denmark on 31 January and take a ferry to Norway.

Casement actually set out to do this, with Christensen (no doubt hoping for an opportunity to deliver Casement up and collect the money) in tow but he was thwarted by an out-of-date railway timetable, which meant he missed the ferry he was hoping to catch, and also by his own second thoughts. He returned to Berlin, obsessed with writing a letter to Sir Edward Grey in which he could explain himself and condemn the largely imaginary attempts that the British were making on his life and person.

He duly wrote the letter, dated 1 February 1915, attempting to renounce his loyalty to the Crown and to return any decorations that he had received. This done, he retired to his bed, in effect the victim of a nervous breakdown.

From the beginning of 1915 until shortly before he left for Ireland at Easter 1916, Casement was in the grip of a severe depression that he was unable to shake off. It is clear that for a while – from the time that he had become involved in founding and arming the Irish Volunteers – he had begun to delude himself that he was one of the principal leaders, if not *the* leader, of Irish Nationalism. But his inability to attract recruits for the Irish Brigade, and his obviously skewed judgement in the 'Findlay Affair', as it became known, seem to have catastrophically dented his confidence.

Around this time Devoy, who was unimpressed by Casement's recruiting efforts and believed the Findlay Affair a pointless waste of effort, was horrified to read the 'Egyptian' clause of the Irish Brigade 'treaty'. He could not understand what it had to do with Irish independence: any confidence he had in Casement as his representative in Ireland now evaporated and Casement was, in effect, excluded from the councils of the Clan na Gael, and thus the IRB, until shortly before the Easter Rising.

Meanwhile, efforts to recruit for the Irish Brigade continued on a different basis, as Guardsman O'Toole's interrogator makes clear:

After their [Keogh, Quinlisk and Dowling's] departure a more intensive propaganda campaign was carried on through the medium of pamphlets and the *Continental Times*. This paper was edited by Mrs White, wife of an Englishman named Stewart. She was an Austrian Jewess and considered very influential at the German Foreign Office. She used to entertain very largely the diplomatic personages in Berlin. About the end of April 1915, Casement, Keogh, Dowling and Quinlisk, and a certain Captain Boehm, attached to the German Secret Service, appeared in the camp. The most likely men to become recruits had already been spotted by their agents. These men were called up in groups, and on giving their assent to join the Irish Brigade were removed to another section of the camp. The food and treatment question played a great part on the decision of most . . .

The recruits for the Irish Brigade were after a short time moved to

Zossen barracks. The accommodation and food were good, but they were not allowed to go about freely, but were conducted about in parties by an interpreter. Thence they were transferred to Wunsdorff Mohammedan camp. This would be about May 1915. This turned out to be a regular prison camp. The treatment received there caused the men to make complaints and to rebel; they were then transferred back to Zossen. Here Lt Hagen of the German Army put them through a course of machine gun training. This lasted until about April 1916. When Casement left for Ireland the men refused to carry on with the drilling. General Schneider who was in charge at Zossen was of the opinion that the Irish Brigade caused him more trouble than the 17,000 German troops he had under him.[8]

With Casement only sporadically useful, Devoy was obliged to send another man to assist him. This was Robert Monteith, a former Warrant Officer in the Royal Horse Artillery who had moved to New York after refusing to rejoin the British army on the outbreak of war. Monteith acted as Casement's military liaison officer with the German General Staff but was fatally handicapped by his lack of officer credentials, even though Casement had 'commissioned' him as 'Captain' in the Irish Brigade. Just as the Waffen-SS were to discover nearly thirty years later with the British Free Corps, outside the broad structures which had bounded their lives as soldiers, the Irish renegades were worse than useless.

With Casement no longer able to make a positive contribution, Devoy sent another emissary, Joseph Plunkett, to Germany to ask for arms for the rising that was now being planned for Easter 1916. In March 1916 this was communicated to Monteith and he went to brief Casement in the Bavarian sanatorium where he was staying. By now Casement could not bring himself to trust the Germans: he could not see why they had chosen to inform Monteith and not him. In a state of resignation he partly accepted what was to come, but balked at the idea that the Irish Brigade should be sent into action in a rebellion which he felt was bound to fail without assistance beyond arms and ammunition from the Germans (they had refused to send troops or officers). Instead he insisted that he should accompany the arms.

As the day of departure drew closer, however, Casement realized that if he went with the weapons themselves, he could not give his warning, for what it was worth. Instead, as a final gesture, the General Staff agreed to send Casement, Monteith and Daniel Bailey, a sergeant from the Brigade, ahead by U-boat.

With his two companions, Roger Casement departed in the U-boat *U19* on 14 April 1916.

With Casement's departure from Germany, the Irish Brigade now began inexorably to fall apart. Once he and Monteith had left, the men refused to continue with their training and, in July 1916, were moved from Zossen to a military camp at Danzig-Troyl, where they were restricted to the camp and a local pub. When they made representations to be allowed more freedom, they were informed by the camp commandant that they would only be allowed this if they agreed to work.

The initial terms under which the Irish Brigade members would be allowed their liberty was if they agreed to do agricultural work on the same basis as Russian POWs, for the miserable sum of 30 pfennigs per day. Faced with refusal *en masse*, Hauptmann Nicolai, the camp commandant, capitulated and agreed that they could go out and find work on equal terms with German labourers in the area around Danzig, West Prussia and Pomerania, with the result that by late 1916, the majority of the Irishmen were scattered on farms and in factories across north-eastern Germany. Those who had refused to go out to work, because they were receiving parcels from home and were thus reasonably well off, found themselves doing unpaid labouring within Danzig garrison under the guard of a sentry.

This state of affairs prevailed until the German collapse in November 1918, when the German interpreter to the Brigade, Zerhusen, appeared with a set of passes issued by the 'Workers and Soldiers Council', giving the Irishmen permission to travel freely throughout Germany, at which time they completely scattered: some joining the revolutionaries, some the 'Freikorps' and some making their way home. No serious attempt was made by the British military authorities to capture them and, indeed, when Guardsman O'Toole fell into British military custody in 1920, he was simply released after questioning.

An interesting footnote to the story of the Irish Brigade concerns the unit's Quartermaster Sergeant, Tom Anthony Quinlisk of the Royal Irish Regiment, one of the original three volunteers and a man held in high regard by Casement (although he thought he looked a rogue). By 1920, Quinlisk was back in Ireland attempting to infiltrate the IRA for money on behalf of the British authorities. Quinlisk was detected and killed on the orders of Michael Collins, the IRA leader, thus ending a career in which he had betrayed two masters.

PART II

John Amery

6. 'I'm a Lucky Boy'

John Amery's father, Leopold Charles Moritz Stennet Amery, was born in Gorakhpur, India, in 1873, the eldest son of Charles Frederick Amery and his Hungarian wife Elisabeth. Charles Amery, who was forty years old at the time of his son's birth, was a forestry official, and a member of an old West Country family;[1] Elisabeth had a somewhat more complex background. In his political memoirs, Leopold Amery refers to his mother as being one of a 'stream of Hungarian exiles' who emigrated after the upheavals of 1848 (in which, of course, Roger Casement's father had played his small but distinguished role). In fact, although Elisabeth undoubtedly did come from Hungary, she was a member of a Jewish family and had little or no Hungarian Magyar blood at all. Both her father (who was named Saphir) and her stepfather, Dr Johann Moritz Leitner, had converted to Protestantism, and Elisabeth was a practising Anglican; nevertheless, both ethnically and according to 'Orthodox Jewish law and tradition', she was Jewish, and so were her children.

Leo Amery lived in India until he was three, when his father deserted the family to live in America, leaving them penniless. His mother eventually divorced Charles on the grounds of his adultery and was thus left with the task of bringing up her three children alone, which she managed with some success.

In September 1887, Leo Amery started at Harrow School. He soon established himself as the cleverest boy there, 'effortlessly winning prize after prize and three scholarships'.[2] Not only was he academically brilliant, he was also a ferociously competitive sportsman, excelling at gymnastics, cross-country running, boxing and swimming, despite his small stature (he was 5 feet 4 inches). In fact his distinctive height was to lead him to his first meeting with one of his contemporaries at 'Ducker', the Harrow swimming pool:

One day when I had been no more than a month in the school, I saw a boy standing in a meditative posture wrapped in a towel on the very brink. He was no bigger than I was, so I thought him fair game. Coming stealthily behind, I pushed him in, holding on to his towel out of humanity, so that it should not get wet. I was startled to see a furious face emerging from the foam, and a being evidently of enormous strength making its way by swift strokes to the shore. I fled; but in vain. Swift as the wind my pursuer overtook me, seized me in a ferocious grip and hurled me into the deepest part of the pool. I soon scrambled out on the other side, and found myself surrounded by an agitated crowd of younger boys. 'You're in for it,' they said. 'Do you know what you have done? It's Amery; he's in the Sixth Form. He is head of his House; he is champion at Gym; he has got his football colours.' They continued to recount his many titles to fame and reverence, and to dilate upon the awful retribution that would fall upon me. I was convulsed not only with terror, but with the guilt of sacrilege. How could I tell his rank when he was in a bath towel and so small? I determined to apologize immediately. I approached the potentate in lively trepidation. 'I am very sorry,' I said. 'I mistook you for a Fourth Form boy. You are so small.' He did not seem at all placated by this; so I added in a most brilliant recovery, 'My father, who is a great man, is also small.' At this he laughed, and after some general remarks about my 'cheek' and how I had better be careful in the future, signified that the incident was closed.[3]

Which is how Winston Churchill subsequently recalled the beginning of a lifelong friendship.

From Harrow Amery went up to Balliol College, Oxford, in 1892, where once again he excelled. His field of study was wide-ranging, taking in languages, both ancient and modern, economics, history and other cornerstone subjects of what was to be an intensely political life. In 1897 he was elected a Fellow of All Souls College when that august institution was beginning to enter a golden age – 'in the early twentieth century [it] captured the public imagination as an intellectual elite with real influence in national and international affairs'[4] – and it was through the influence of the Warden of All Souls that Leo Amery obtained employment as a journalist for *The Times*.

He worked for the newspaper from 1899 until 1909, first as a war correspondent in South Africa, later as a leader writer and editor and author of *The Times History of the South African War*. At the same time, he studied for and was called to the Bar and met, courted and, in 1910, married Florence Greenwood, sister of Hamar Greenwood, a Canadian who was a Liberal MP and served as Chief Secretary in Ireland at the height of the Irish rebellion.

Politics nevertheless remained Leo Amery's chief fascination. He was profoundly patriotic and a passionate believer in the British Empire as a force for good. He was an intellectual disciple of Lord Milner, the great Imperial statesman who had masterminded the eventual British victory in South Africa and had subsequently engineered the settlement with the Boers; and a political follower of Joseph Chamberlain, who rejected the prevalent *laissez-faire* economic doctrines of the time in favour of advocating a system of Imperial preference in which the British Empire would maintain itself as a self-sustaining common market, protected from outside forces by high tariff barriers. His political commitment came to fruition in 1911 when, with the help of the Chamberlain family who ran Birmingham almost as a personal political fiefdom, he was elected to the House of Commons as Conservative Member of Parliament for South Birmingham.*

Not long after the beginning of Leo Amery's parliamentary career he and Florence (who was always known as Bryddie or 'B') began their family with the birth on 14 March 1912 of their first son, John.

'Mad; bad; and dangerous to know': Lady Caroline Lamb's opinion of Lord Byron might just as well have applied to John Amery. He attacked life like a fox in a chicken coop; an indelibly corrosive influence on those who came into contact with him. Even so, his spirit and charm enchanted his family enough to forgive

* Later Sparkbrook.

him almost all of his appalling crimes and misdemeanours, and his execution in December 1945 crushed them all. At the root of the bizarre, almost fantastic, behaviour which led John Amery to the gallows at Wandsworth was a severe pathological personality disorder which had held him in its grip from an early age.

At the time of John's birth, Leo Amery was one of the coming men in British politics. Firmly on the right of the Conservative Party, an opponent of reform of the House of Lords and of Home Rule for Ireland, he was nevertheless recognized as a bright new star in the Tory political firmament. The family were living in some style at 112 Eaton Square, an imposing house in the heart of Belgravia, and although Leo Amery was never rich, in addition to his political income his writing and journalism, not to mention the City directorships which came his way as a serious and respectable politician, ensured that they were comfortably provided for. It seems also that Leo and Bryddie were loving parents, more involved with their children than many members of their social class and background might have been at that time, possibly as a result of Leo's unusual 'single-parent' upbringing. Perhaps because of this closeness to their children, Leo and Bryddie noticed that there was something strange about John from an early age.

The first unusual sign to manifest came in the form of frequent panic attacks. John would waken at night, screaming uncontrollably, until he was reassured and settled down by his nanny. He was also very prone to extreme temper tantrums during the day and, it soon became evident, was curiously indifferent to any breakage or destruction he caused. Even before the age of two, his nanny, 'an experienced woman',[5] reported to Bryddie: 'This is a very *hard* child: I don't know quite how to deal with him'.[6] Night terrors were followed, between the ages of three and four, by a 'prolonged attack of bedwetting'[7] and by extreme panic attacks. Leo Amery subsequently recollected:

My wife recalls an occasion of panic terror at the thought of going in a rowing boat at the age of four. I remember myself an occasion in a rowing boat at Exmouth when a little spray blew over the gunwale, and he got into an incontrollable hysterical state and the only thing to do with him was to make him lie down on the floor of the boat. The same thing happened again in a sailing boat a little later.[8]

His father also noticed that there was something peculiar about the way John reacted to instruction:

Rot!!!

I cannot recall John as having been in any way exceptionally ill behaved as a child. But there were several features which at an early date puzzled and presently disquieted me. One of these was a curious unteachability, especially noticeable with regard to any physical action. I would tell him not to do something and he instantly did it again and again, not out of disobedience, but apparently because the message seemed not to have got through. Similarly I found it no use whatever trying to teach him the motions of swimming or ski-ing. The instructions just did not register. But he had no difficulty in teaching himself and became quickly proficient at both.[9]

John's infancy coincided, of course, with the First World War. For the first two years of the war Leo served as an Intelligence officer in 'Flanders, the Balkans, Gallipoli and Salonika',[10] having been rebuffed in his attempts to find himself a political role to play. This changed however, when Lloyd George came to power in December 1916. Lloyd George immediately appointed Lord Milner to the War Cabinet; and Milner insisted upon the appointment of Amery as a member of its political secretariat and special advisor on European affairs, which meant that Leo played a central role in the formulation of policy. Not surprisingly, these events failed to impinge much on the youngest member of the Amery family. In fact, in 1917 when Leo was engaged in work which involved, among other things, helping to draft the Balfour Declaration (whereby the British Government committed itself to work to establish in Palestine 'a National Home for the Jewish race'[11]) and the foundation of the Jewish Legion, the forerunner of the modern

Israeli Defence Force, John was about to go to kindergarten at Miss Ironside's private school in Elvaston Place, South Kensington, a mile or so from the family home. Here again, his unusual character was immediately apparent.

Miss Irene Ironside remembered:

Even at his admission I got the impression that he was an extremely abnormal boy. He always wanted to do the exact opposite of what he was asked to do. This differed from the ordinary forms of rebellious spirit shown by healthy children. It was constant and persistent and gave the impression of being a fixed attitude of an abnormal type. Everything he did had to be startling. He would come to school with an enormous necklace of brightly coloured wooden beads stretched almost to his knees. He was always trying to shock the conventions. If not allowed to ornament his letters, which he called 'putting in fantasy', he would merely write the word 'oxo' and continue to do so. If checked for this he would surreptitiously chalk the word oxo under the tables. He was extremely self-willed and determined. He was violent and destructive, would bully other children, twisting their arms and when quarrelling with other children would threaten to fight but never do it. I had the feeling that if he were disciplined it would send him crazy. It was 'touch and go' with his sanity. He was really unteachable and only learned to read after great pain and effort of all concerned. He showed no interest and had a tendency to shut himself and live inside himself.[12]

Another trait of his son's personality came to Leo Amery's attention at this time:

Another feature that struck me . . . was what I at first thought a curious secretiveness about his doings at kindergarten school and elsewhere when away from home. But I am not sure how far it may not have been a complete lack of interest in anything done once it was done, coupled with a correspondingly intense living in the present. In any case he remained most uncommunicative all through.[13]

A further peculiarity which manifested at this comparatively early age was sexual in nature: after a short-lived phase of masturbation when he was five, he began to draw obscene pictures of naked women, to which he would add a penis. He would then leave the pictures lying around, apparently deliberately, to be found by his young French governess to whom he was apparently otherwise devoted.[14] According to psychiatric theory at the time: 'This behaviour in children is an early sign that the individual is abnormally bi-sexual and prone to develop homosexual perversions.'[15]

The arrival of his brother Julian in 1919 does not seem to have stirred any great resentment in him. An incident was recorded in which John threw a lighted match into Julian's perambulator with the intention of setting it on fire,[16] but such an act, whilst at the extreme end of the scale, is by no means uncommon in children who are in all other respects perfectly normal.

In April 1920, at the age of nine, John was sent as a boarder to the prestigious West Downs preparatory school near Winchester. According to Leo, 'he was on the whole happy there, and did not do too badly. Other boys, I think, found him amusing . . .'[17] Nevertheless, his curious behaviour continued, to the puzzlement of his headmaster, K. L. S. Tindall:

From the first it was obvious that he was a boy of very unusual character and throughout his time at the school his actions caused me considerable anxiety as they did not appear to be prompted by motives which would actuate a normal, healthy-minded boy. Ideas of right and wrong, which are accepted without question by normal boys brought up in the atmosphere of a healthy home and school, seemed to mean nothing to him. Though he clearly felt affection for his parents and for other people, this affection did not prevent him from pursuing a course of action which would be bound to cause anxiety and distress to those for whom he cared.[18]

He was also still prone to hysterical panic attacks. During a family holiday in Switzerland, while walking with his father, he was reduced to a state of abject physical terror by a herd of peaceful Swiss cows. Even after Leo had demonstrated their harmlessness by stroking one of them, his son could not be mollified. Tindall also noted this lack of physical courage:

I recollect one occasion when his conduct had so enraged other boys that one boy of his own age and size asked me if he might fight him. I gave permission on the understanding that the fight was to take place under proper boxing conditions and that I was myself present. Other boys were there as spectators. When the two boys entered the ring, Amery lay on the ground and refused to fight, though he cannot have failed to realize the contempt that such an action would arouse in the minds of the other boys.[19]

This incident so concerned Tindall that he contacted Leo Amery: 'I well remember Mr Tindall telling me how gravely disquieted he was by his complete indifference to the moral standards of others, and quoting the particular instance referred to [above].'[20] Tindall eventually concluded that:

His 'naughtiness' could hardly ever be attributed to motives which actuate other boys – e.g. a love of adventure or the desire to shine in the eyes of his fellows. Amery's 'naughtiness' always seemed purposeless and this was what made me anxious about his future development.
    It would not, I think, be true to say that he had his own ethical code; as far as I could judge, he had no code of morals at all, but would follow the whim of the moment without any thought of where it was going to lead to or what trouble it was likely to cause to himself or others.[21]

By now, Leo Amery was on what appeared to be a political fast-track. At the end of the war he had gained the first rung of the ministerial ladder with his appointment as Parliamentary Under Secretary at the Colonial Office, working for his old mentor Lord Milner, and this had been followed by a junior ministerial job at the Admiralty in 1921. But in 1922 he reached the Cabinet when he was appointed First Lord of the Admiralty, and it was under his auspices that construction began on the huge British naval base in Singapore.

Leo Amery was out of office during the brief period of the first Labour Government, but in 1924 he returned in Stanley Baldwin's first Government as Colonial Secretary; with the British Empire at its zenith, this was certainly one of the most important Cabinet appointments of the time. His increasingly troublesome son must have been a source of considerable additional anxiety to him.

In September 1925 John followed his father to Harrow School where he joined the Headmaster's House, and it was here that his behaviour seriously began to break down and become more and more uncontrolled. Leo Amery felt that 'From the first he seems to have seriously resented the tighter discipline of public school and above all fagging and the authority of senior boys generally. He disliked both work and games and scoffed at house patriotism and all the current schoolboy conventions.'[22] His housemaster, A. P. Boissier, who later went on to be headmaster, recalled:

In the whole of my experience as a schoolmaster, I found him, without doubt, the most difficult boy I have ever tried to manage. He was certainly 'abnormal' in that he seemed unable in those days to distinguish right from wrong. He seemed to think he could be a law unto himself and that every rule and regulation that bound others did not apply to him. I tried every method that I knew to convince him that he must, up to a certain point, fall into line with what the majority do, but I am afraid my efforts were of no avail.[23]

Interestingly, in his first term at Harrow John was reasonably successful academically: he was clearly bright (one of his contemporaries, John Colville, later Churchill's wartime private secretary, found him charming and intelligent): he was bilingual in English and French, which he had learned from his French governess, and his family background was one which greatly esteemed intellectual achievement. He was also reasonably physically fit, a proficient skier and swimmer, and would accompany his father on climbing and walking expeditions (Leo Amery was later elected President of the Alpine Club which, he claimed, ranked with becoming Prime Minister as the twin summit of his ambition). But neither physical nor intellectual achievement interested or motivated John. Instead, according to Boissier:

In a peculiar way he sought notoriety and limelight, and since he was unable to obtain it by the customary means, such as games, he sought it by holding 'ultra' views on many subjects, and expressing them openly on every occasion. He seemed to revel in the fact that so many of his companions thought him mad. Rules and regulations, so far as he was concerned, did not exist, and as a consequence he was continually falling foul of masters and boys. This, I am afraid, gave him a still further 'jaundiced' outlook on life and added considerably to his abnormality.[24]

There was also a sudden deterioration in his behaviour towards others at this time; according to his father he began shop-lifting from local shops and pilfering from his schoolmates. He was never able to make male friends of his own age: this can hardly have helped. He rented a room in Harrow where he and a few other boys would sneak out to smoke and drink in the evenings, and he took to climbing out of his house at night to visit Mrs Meyrick's, a West End night club, encouraging others to do the same. Having had an early puberty, he also now began to manifest a strong interest in sex: during a holiday in Switzerland in 1926 he met and succeeded in seducing a young Dutch girl, losing his virginity when still only fourteen and boasting about it afterwards to his family and schoolmates.

In January 1927, at the end of the Christmas holiday, John decided that he didn't want to go back to the tiresome routine and discipline of Harrow life, and having taken Leo's service revolver, as well as the contents of his wallet, he climbed out of a skylight at the family home with the intention of going to France. Having just learned to drive while on holiday in Britanny, he had formed the intention of becoming a garage hand. Somehow intercepted at the behest of his father, he was taken back to Harrow, but his behaviour was now so peculiar that his parents were forced to consider making unpalatable decisions about him.

At this stage, John was interviewed by Dr (later Sir) Cyril Norwood, the headmaster of Harrow:

[He] could not understand me when I pointed out that he was letting his parents down badly and sacrificing all the splendid future that might have been his: he told me that in the position of a garage hand he would be his own master, would not be driven, and need not do more than he liked. His parents and his prospects counted for nothing: he did not seem to feel that any consideration was due to his father or to his mother.[25]

The conclusion reached by Norwood and the Amerys was that John might benefit from a period in the care of a private tutor, and he was withdrawn from Harrow on the understanding that he would return after a term or two. He was also psychiatrically examined by a Dr Maurice Wright.*

The tutor engaged to look after John was one Leander Jameson; almost immediately he found that he had his hands full:

On the second day of my engagement I was with him on a London bus when he began to smoke. I told him with all the tact possible that this was against his father's wishes and mine, and asked him to put his cigarette out. When he did not comply, I took it from his mouth and threw it through the window. He then left the bus, which was on the move, and, in considerable danger of being knocked down by the traffic, made for the nearest policeman. When I followed, he threatened to give me in charge for indecent assault. On reaching the policeman he asked him the time.

His general attitude at this time was moody and introspective. He had no friends of his own age and his appearance was distinctly dirty and slovenly, and he was a most unimpressive pupil.[26]

* The record of this examination does not survive.

Subverted every schoolboy convention [handwritten marginalia]

Jameson's solution to the problem of John's unprepossessing bearing was to organize riding lessons for him. These didn't work. After three lessons, John had to be removed from the riding school because he refused to be taught and used 'filthy and obscene' language to the instructor in the presence of the other children attending the course.

Jameson surmised that John's behaviour was the result of his utter lack of confidence in himself and his own ability to ride. Further discussions ensued with the Amerys and shortly after the riding-school débâcle, Jameson took John to stay with his aunt and uncle, Mr and Mrs Rodney, in the Hertfordshire countryside at Bury Green.

Being away from home allowed John to calm down a little, although his mood was subject to wild swings. He made progress academically and resumed riding lessons, but Jameson noticed, as others had, an unusual lack of physical courage in his pupil. Certainly John never really enjoyed any of the field sports which Jameson encouraged him to take part in. When he did attempt any physical activity he would normally make a mess of things and attempt to cover his ineptitude with childish and extreme temper tantrums which could become violent.

Jameson liked to break the morning's lessons with some form of exercise but John was never enthusiastic about this, least of all in winter when it might cause him some discomfort. On one occasion when John refused to leave the house, Jameson forced him outside and physically propelled him around the garden. Half an hour after their return, smouldering with rage, John produced a knife and attacked Jameson.[27] After swiftly disarming him, Jameson then gave John a caning, 'and his conduct regarding his morning exercise was ever afterwards exemplary'.[28]

Oddly, outside their episodes of conflict, John's attitude towards Jameson was entirely friendly, even though his behaviour was so unreliable that Jameson felt forced to supervise him almost constantly. One problem that began to arise was that 'If sent on the simplest errand, his main preoccupation would be to get in touch with a girl, usually of the least desirable type'[29] and as a result he was rarely left on his own. To Jameson's surprise, this did not seem to cause John any great irritation: he seems to have accepted that the rest of the world did not approve of many of his tastes and drawn the conclusion that it was best to conceal them.

One point of friction between tutor and pupil was John's invariable habit of sleeping with his bedroom hermetically sealed, which appears to have conflicted strongly with Jameson's outdoor, fresh-air approach to life. Combined with his practice of sharing his bed with a large Irish Setter dog, this led to John's room smelling much like a kennel and Jameson was apparently unable to do anything about it.

Travel in Jameson's company also featured prominently in John's life. In the summer of 1927 they motored together to Scotland, with John driving his own Morgan two-seater, which gave his tutor the opportunity to observe his appalling road manners – if obstructed he became impatient and violently abusive. 'For a boy of 15 he was fantastically arrogant and rude to strangers.'[30]

In the autumn they were on Dartmoor. There they went out on one occasion with the local hunt, but as the day was not particularly interesting, John managed to slip away to the local pub where Jameson found him later the same afternoon, drunk and extremely aggressive. The exasperated tutor managed to persuade his pupil to remount, only for John to take off at a fast gallop along the crown of the tarmac road. Inevitably the horse bolted, eventually ending up floundering in a bog but without causing any injury to its rider. John was so entirely beside himself with rage at this that Jameson considered he had lost control of his actions; nevertheless, two hours later his mood was gay and cheerful.

Their last expedition together was to Norway in the spring of 1928. This trip was marred by an incident in which John stole an overcoat belonging to a fellow guest at their hotel and sold it on to a third party, using the small amount of money he raised to buy a present for the hotel telephonist. When the theft was discovered and the culprit detected, he treated the whole episode as a joke: 'at no time did John have any sense of guilt over the incident'.[31]

Despite his lapses, John's behaviour during his year with Jameson had shown sufficient improvement for his father to want him to make another attempt at Harrow, and in April 1928 he went back, joining a small house with only three or four other boys in residence. He did not last long: in early June he was charged with the grave offence of, in his father's words, 'deliberately slacking at cricket' and reported to the schoolboy Captain of Cricket to be beaten.

At this point John's terror of physical discomfort and pain overcame him and he ran away from school. This appears to have been a spontaneous decision: he simply hid his school boater under a hedge and took off. After he arrived home at Eaton Square, it was the task of His Majesty's Secretary of State for the Colonies and the Dominions to negotiate his son's return to school. This proved impossible. Even though the headmaster had agreed that, on his return, any caning administered to John would be 'purely formal', Leo recognized that: 'his state of mind at the idea of going back was such that he could only have been taken by force and we abandoned the idea'.[32]

In place of formal schooling, therefore, another tutor had to be found in order to prepare John for what his father hoped would be his eventual entry to Oxford. This unfortunate individual was Kingsley Walton:

When I was asked to tutor John Amery for his Oxford Responsions examinations I felt that I could not have been asked to do this on account of my qualifications at Greek or Latin (which were nil), but perhaps because it was thought my previous experiences in life had qualified me to handle 'difficult' cases.

Our first hour disclosed to John that I was his master at mathematics, but I was charmed at John's quick offer to succeed at ancient languages without my help in return for mathematical assistance. I was congratulating myself that I could not have found a more charming, gentlemanly or accommodating boy. Then the first evening out walking together he suddenly turned into a West End hotel, and I was after him, and he had ordered drinks in the lounge. I insisted on him coming out without the

drinks, and he did so without any abashment or resentment or ill feeling
... Whilst we were on the very best of terms, and whilst he quite
definitely felt I was of assistance to him, yet, against his own interests he
would frequently and unaccountably attempt to 'upset the apple cart' by
some sudden lapse. I could only checkmate him by threatening to leave
him, and this he would not allow.[33]

Walton's method for taming John was to remove him entirely
from his usual environment and together they developed a plan to
go to Iceland where they would live in a tent and catch fish for
their food, presumably on the basis that fresh air and the wholesome
life might cure John of the decidedly metropolitan concerns which
appeared to have fixated him.

Their journey to Iceland would be by boat, and this required
them to make an overnight stay in Edinburgh. Walton arranged for
John to stay with a friend of his while he lodged in a hotel. Walton's
friend was a barrister called Francis Steuart, who evidently took a
great liking to John during the evening they spent together before
leaving for Iceland:

Amongst our camping kit was a portable gramophone and a case of twelve
records. These records were superfluous except for three ('Old Man
River', 'Tea for Two' and 'I'm a Lucky Boy'). These three were John's
favourites, and he guarded and *carried* these three records *himself*, and
would not allow them to be put amongst our kit for fear of breakage by
careless handling. It was simply unthinkable to John that we should not
have these three records in our Icelandic tent.

On our way to the boat Francis Steuart, John and I were in a taxi, full
of excitement at our immediate prospects – and poor Francis, I think,
near to tears that he was not young enough or fit enough to come with
us. John was carrying these three records (as usual) as a guarantee of their
absolute safety. Then suddenly, a propos of absolutely nothing, John got
up and put the three records on the seat and jumped up and down and
smashed them.

Luckily there was time for the taxi to call at a music shop in Leith

Walk where we replaced these records. John however, without one word or one flicker of an eyelash about his actions in deliberately breaking these records, I say John insisted on carrying the three new records to make certain they were not broken by careless handling of our baggage by the porters.[34]

There was a further lapse after their arrival in Iceland:

Our tent was small, but John enjoyed the camping life and the fishing so much that he refused my offer of going into more comfortable quarters in an Icelandic farmhouse. He insisted that that would spoil his camping record which he wanted to achieve and so return to London and start life afresh without further lapses. He was counting on a good report from me to Mr and Mrs Amery after his holiday and was determined to earn this. Then, just as if he had a blackout or a sudden lapse, he disappeared from the camp, although he loved the fun of it so much, just as if he were deliberately acting against his own interests. I easily discovered he had gone to Reykjavik, and I sent word through to a reliable man . . . to look after him.

After a week's absence John returned from Reykjavik with all his usual charm, just as if nothing whatsoever had happened. It was just as if there was no connection in his mind with acceptable standards of conduct from a boy towards his camping companion, especially as he had tried to upset our camping endeavour (which he wanted to preserve) by taking our medical stores with him when he disappeared to Reykjavik.[35]

Walton stayed with John until Christmas 1928 but by then Leo Amery had been told of a school for English boys in Château d'Oex in Switzerland, run by a Mr King. Having tried a policy of close supervision with mixed results, Leo now attempted 'out of sight, out of mind'. The Swiss school was well spoken of and there John would be able to indulge his taste for winter sports at which he had become very proficient. He lasted until Easter when King asked the Amerys to take him away. According to Leo, 'there was no particular single offence, but . . . his bar loafing and his approaches to women were calculated to give the school a bad name'.[36] Leo went out to collect John and took him to Zermatt, leaving him in the care of an Alpine guide, Adolf Pollinger, before returning to London to attempt to recruit a new tutor.

On this occasion the black spot was drawn by G. C. Nock, a young schoolmaster, who immediately set out for Switzerland to take control of the situation. Nock took John to Thonon on Lake Geneva where he began the thankless task of educating and controlling his wayward charge.

It would seem that Nock was not up to the job. John felt sufficiently relaxed and in control in his presence to expound what amounted to his philosophy of life; Nock appears to have been utterly overawed by John's baleful egoism:

I had long talks with him in which he spoke of society as consisting of sheep; he fancied himself the lone wolf. He openly wanted to reach great heights by dishonest means. He knew what society expected but had no sense of obligation to do it. He had no obligation to anyone or anything, not even a gangster's code . . . He had all sorts of cunning schemes for raising money and often proposed to rob slot machines. He wanted to get his own back on society in his own way. His behaviour was something to do with forcing his parents' attention. He thought his father was a fool not to have been dishonest and taken advantage of his position. He thought it absurd that his father was comparatively poor. At an early birthday party for his brother he bought and gave him a roulette board, teaching him how to 'rook' his friends . . .[37]

The first instance of Nock's complete inability to control John's behaviour manifested in a strange episode when they climbed the Jungfrau together, during which John insisted on wearing bedroom slippers. More importantly, however, Nock's inadequacies as a guide, philosopher and friend were highlighted by the fact that John contracted syphilis while in his care.

From whom he caught the disease is unclear: he was obsessed with prostitutes and bought sex, but there is another possibility.

According to Nock, John had told him that he had been 'playing the passive role in a homosexual relationship and said it was a good way to make money'.[38] There is no suggestion of when or with whom he did this – it may even have been a fantasy – but the general pattern of his behaviour must lead the observer to conclude that he was probably telling Nock the truth.

It is difficult to imagine the emotions that Leo and Bryddie Amery must have felt on learning that their seventeen-year-old son had managed to acquire this repulsive and, at that time, tenacious disease; their reactions were almost certainly magnified by his indifference and, indeed, hostility, to the medical treatment he received. John was sent to see a Dr Osmond, a specialist in venereal diseases, who treated him with mercury compounds, the only remedy then available, and continued the treatments until 1938. Osmond's conclusion, based on John's attitude towards his treatment, was that he was 'sub-normal'.[39]

Despite this, however, John did succeed in gaining a place at Oxford University. This must have pleased his father almost as much as he was dismayed when John refused to take it up, having conceived an obsession with the film business. Instead, Leo found him a place with British Instructional Films in Welwyn, north of London, where he was to receive training in aspects of film production. Although there were reports of perverse and bizarre behaviour, John was apparently not dismissed from this appointment but left of his own accord to join a small travelling film company which had tempted him with the meaningless role of Assistant Film Director. According to Leo, this soon petered out.

The details of John's life over the next two years are fragmentary. Leo left office in 1929 with the election of the second Labour Government (he did not return to government until Winston Churchill became Prime Minister in 1940) but John, who was still only seventeen, was now slipping beyond the control of his parents. Leo recalled:

I am afraid I have very little record of the next two and half years. He started off with the ambition of being the youngest living film director and somehow persuaded people to find enough money for him to start the production in Africa of a £100,000 film, *Jungle Skies*, in which he directed aeroplane crashes, war dances of native tribes etc. – a remarkable enterprise in many ways for a boy of 18–19. The film was never completed. There were various smaller companies with dubious associates which came to nothing. For one absurd scheme for a company to smuggle in silk stockings by aeroplane, he secured large sums from a school friend. I remember compromising over terms for, I think, £1,000. I also had continuously to find sums running to many hundreds of pounds for worthless cheques issued to moneylenders and other creditors. His doings were an endless source of anxiety, but my chief recollection is of endlessly recurring crises of which the details have happily faded from my memory. The one feature common to all his actions was the complete inability to envisage the inevitable consequences, so long as he could stave off trouble at the moment, and the equally complete lack of regret when found out.[40]

The Amerys were by no means badly off, but it is worth bearing in mind that at this time a backbench Member of Parliament's annual salary was £360 and, although Leo could earn money from writing, journalism and the law, and had an income as director of various companies, John's financial exploits must have been an enormous drain on his resources.

Nor were John's problems simple debts; he had been driving since he was fifteen years old, but his inability to think of anything or anyone other than himself rendered him a menace on the roads. On 7 July 1932 he appeared at Bow Street Magistrates Court on a charge of causing an obstruction with his motorcar in Long Acre the previous month. In fact, on 6 June, John had simply stopped his car, got out and left it for three hours and twenty minutes while he went to a bar. When he was traced and asked to move it by a policeman, he left it for a further thirty minutes. In fining him £5, the magistrate revealed that at this time he had seventy-three previous convictions, of which thirty-one were for obstruction.

It was at about this time that one of John's most celebrated pre-war exploits occurred. On 22 August 1932 Leo, who was in Canada, received a telegram from John informing him that he was getting married that day, but giving no name or any other information. In fact the woman in question was a twenty-two-year-old actress, Una Eveline Wing, who was apparently as surprised by her impending wedding as her future in-laws. She had been under the impression that John Amery was twenty-eight years old and had no family, his parents having died when he was young, and her first inkling of their forthcoming wedding seems to have been when she read about it in the papers, John having issued a press statement at the same time as he informed his father.

John's purpose in getting married was, he later told Una, because of his serious financial difficulties. By getting married he felt that he would give his creditors confidence in him and might also be able to convince them that his wife was rich and might repay some of his debts. If this was indeed the case, his plan was executed with stupefying imbecility.

The major problem that John confronted was that he was still under twenty-one and thus not permitted to marry in England without his parents' consent. Accordingly, when he had applied at Chelsea Registry Office to marry by licence, he had simply lied about his age. However, by issuing a press statement about the forthcoming wedding, he had drawn attention to the fact that he was under age. The result of this was that the Deputy Superintendent Registrar for Chelsea had declined to marry them and had reported John to the police as a perjurer.

By this time John had a fairly close relationship with Chelsea police. On 6 August they had arrested him for dangerous driving, failing to stop when ordered to do so by a police officer, failing to produce a valid certificate of insurance and failing to produce his driving licence. In fact a police officer had spotted John driving along the King's Road in Chelsea with an out-of-date tax disc and had held out his hand to stop him, whereupon John had driven straight at him before swerving away at the last moment, mounting the pavement and then turning into Old Church Street, where he was living at the time. His court appearance on this charge was due on 14 September.

On 23 August a policeman duly called at Eaton Square to interview John and Una and to caution John for having committed perjury by giving false particulars, only to discover that the couple had left for France the night before. On the 23rd, John appeared in Paris to announce to the press that he and Una were to travel to Lithuania where they would marry. By now, John seemed to have forgotten his plan to mollify his creditors and was simply enjoying the limelight. Although his pose was that of a young lover thwarted by his parents' brutal refusal to allow him to marry, the reality was that he could not get formal parental consent because his father was in Canada and not due back until 2 September.

Leo Amery's return home was shortly followed by the arrival back in London of John and Una. In fact Leo did now refuse to give his consent to the marriage, but he agreed to give the couple an allowance so that they could travel together and they departed again on 9 September for France, leaving Leo hoping that they would eventually grow tired of each other.

Five days later, at Bow Street, John was tried in his absence for his latest batch of motoring offences, convicted (his lawyer had entered a guilty plea), fined £50 with £5 costs, and disqualified from driving for five years. The magistrate observed that he 'thought now that the sooner Mr Amery's driving career was checked, the better for everybody'.

The bizarre courtship of John and Una now continued for several more months in France while Leo racked his brains to find some means of straightening out his wayward son. The solution he found was a staff job with Reuter's news agency in Shanghai. His thinking behind this was that John would soon be earning a reasonable income and come of age and so, if he still wished to, he could bring Una out to Shanghai and marry her there. In the meantime, Leo would pay Una an allowance. John immediately agreed and on 24 February Leo travelled to Marseilles with his son to see him off on his ship to China. All appeared to be going smoothly until:

About half an hour before the boat was due to leave he told me that there was a cocktail party of his film friends on board, anxious to have a farewell carouse and that he did not think that I would care to meet them. I foolishly believed this story and left.

No sooner had I gone than he left, having I suppose, resold his ticket, and used the proceeds to sail to Athens with Miss Wing. As the British Consul was not prepared to marry them at once – [John] was still two weeks under age – he announced his conversion to the Greek Orthodox Church and was married on March 31st.[41]

By this time John was twenty-one anyway.

This was not the end of the saga, however. In Athens, John decided to cut something of a figure and the happy couple stayed at the best hotel and ate in the best restaurants, entertaining freely with money that John did not have. On the day of their departure, John extravagantly bought Una some £850 worth of diamond jewellery as a wedding present: he paid by cheque and they left for Paris.

Not surprisingly, by the time they reached Paris, John's cheques were beginning to bounce. Most perturbed was the jeweller who had parted with the diamonds – £850 then was equivalent to about £25,000 now – and his complaints to the police led to the immediate institution of extradition proceedings against John and Una. They were arrested and on 30 May 1933 appeared in the extradition court in Paris on a charge of fraud.

Once again, Leo was forced to bail John out by paying off the Greek jeweller, although Maître Franck, the French lawyer who had been engaged to handle the Paris end of the case, had suggested entering a plea of 'mental deficiency'. For several months after his release from custody, John worked in Paris at the Berger paint factory, of which his uncle, Lord (Hamar) Greenwood, was chairman, before taking off again with Una on travels around Europe, supposedly to look after his film business.

At this point it is worth looking more closely at the relationship between John and Una. They had now been together for about a year, during which time John had revealed himself as a serial liar and fraudster: they lived a marginal existence, trading on John's father's deservedly good name, and they rarely had any more money than the small allowance given to them by Leo. It also became increasingly apparent to Una that John's peculiarities ran much deeper than simple financial dishonesty. Nevertheless, she was curiously passive and uncritical of his behaviour.

From the very beginning of their marriage, John exhibited a range of behaviour that most wives would find puzzling in the extreme, but Una appears to have tolerated it without much thought. Perhaps most worrying was a persecution mania which led John to carry a revolver at all times. During a period when the couple were living in Maidenhead he became so obsessed by the belief that his life was in danger that he would not get out of his car in the evenings unless Una got out and had a look around first, or unless he was actually holding his revolver in his hand. On one occasion when their car was cut up by another driver, John actually jumped out and smashed the offender's windscreen with the butt of his pistol.

Less dangerous but equally strange were fixations he had about his teddy bear and his overcoat. He had had a teddy bear, of which he was very fond, since he was a small child and he used 'Teddy Bear' or 'Baby Bear' as a pet name for Una, but after their marriage he took to carrying the bear about with him at all times: 'he used to take it to cafés and restaurants, sitting it beside him and buying it drinks and comic newspapers'.[42] The overcoat complex was similar: 'For quite a long period he invariably bought an extra seat at the cinema or theatre on which he placed his overcoat and in any restaurant or hotel would insist on taking his overcoat with him into the dining room and would refuse to stay if the staff insisted on placing his overcoat in the cloakroom.'[43]

Other peculiarities that Una noted in John were a strong tendency to react violently against any advice given to him; he was terrified of being without money and would worry uncontrollably about it; he could not sit still or read, and if he wasn't talking or sleeping would walk up and down, sometimes for hours on end, although at one time he channelled this energy into sawing up pieces of wood. In her view, John was happiest when he was 'scheming and laying plans for big financial coups, but never had the patience or self-control to carry them out . . . he had a curious lack of proportion and would spend large sums on schemes whose prospects were always doubtful and whose profit would never have been very great'.[44]

It was in their sexual relationship however, that John was at his most odd. Although they were married, Una subsequently claimed that John continued openly to employ prostitutes and mistresses throughout their time together. Apparently he would pay them to beat him, sometimes severely, or to tie him up. Perhaps even more surprisingly, Una would take part in sex with John with other women present, or would watch John having sex with his prostitutes; this occurred within the first six months of the marriage. No less bizarre was John's preference for sex with a woman immediately after she had had sex with another man: it is not clear if Una obliged him in this taste, but it was certainly she who reported it.[45]

Throughout the marriage John continued to prostitute himself, as he had reported to his tutor Nock, by taking the passive role in homosexual encounters – just as Roger Casement had done, although in a reverse of the financial arrangement. This may not have been too shocking for Una who was no sexual ingénue. Although she was described at the time – and has been ever since – as an actress, before the marriage she had worked as a streetwalker in the West End of London, and had been convicted and fined for soliciting on 13 June 1931.[46] In fact this is probably how John met her: he was obsessed by prostitutes and constantly associated with them. Indeed, throughout their marriage, according to Una, John liked to pretend that she was a prostitute, his mistress or a woman who was keeping him on the basis of immoral earnings. On one occasion, after she let slip in a cocktail bar that she was his wife, he flew into a furious rage and beat her severely.

For two years after John left his job at the Paris paint factory, he and Una travelled about Europe as John apparently attempted to resurrect his film project, *Jungle Skies*. The Metropolitan Police were keeping a weather eye on his activities and associates by now, and had noted that his principal business partner seemed to be John Edward Johnson Noad, alias Count Johnson Noad, who was known to them as a shady solicitor. Police interest in John appears to have been sparked off by a fraud investigation they had mounted against him in 1932, following an incident in which he had sold worthless debentures in one of his many companies to a father and son in Essex for a total of £500. This money had been used by Amery and Noad to return to Africa in connection with the film, but production had never resumed. The police eventually decided that there was insufficient evidence to warrant prosecution.

In 1934, John and Una returned to England to live with the Amery family at their country residence at Maidenhead, and in Chelsea. Leo continued to give John his £10 weekly allowance but despite the fact that this was more than most people were earning at this time, he was always getting into new difficulties as well as being pressed by older creditors. Amongst the schemes that John was operating at this point was a wine merchant's in Marlow, a small town on the Thames near Maidenhead, selling discounted alcohol for 'bottle parties';[47] his other activities remain obscure but we can infer that they were not successful from the fact that at the beginning of 1936 he was finally declared bankrupt, with liabilities of more than £6,000.

Bankruptcy marked a crucial watershed in John Amery's life. When his limited assets had been disposed of, raising little more than £1,000, he left England more or less for good in May 1936, and began the process of being sucked into the vortex of right-wing extremism which was swirling about Europe.

The person who seduced John into the milieu of European Fascism was Jacques Doriot, a fiery rabble-rouser who had, until

1934, been a member of the French Communist Party. Doriot, who had been the elected Mayor of St-Denis, a working-class suburb to the north of Paris, had incurred the wrath of the Comintern by publicly calling for the Communists to instigate a Popular Front against Fascism with their hated socialist rivals. Summoned to Moscow to be disciplined, which in 1934 might well have been a somewhat harsh affair, he refused to go and was expelled from the Party instead – ironically, at much the same time that the Comintern instructed the French Communist Party to organize precisely the kind of popular front that Doriot had been advocating. Nevertheless, in 1935, when he wrote a series of articles explaining how the French Communists were funded and controlled from Moscow, plans were made to assassinate him.

Oddly enough, Doriot's reaction to the election of the Popular Front Government in 1936 was to found his own Parti Populaire Français (PPF), a movement that was explicitly both Fascist and anti-Semitic. Having handed the Communists this propaganda coup, by vindicating their charge that he was a Fascist collaborator, they decided to shelve his murder.[48]

Amery appears to have met Doriot when the latter was in the first flush of enthusiasm at founding his own party. Always a flamboyant figure, Doriot claimed a membership of around 500,000 for the PPF, although the reality was probably no more than one-tenth of that number; nevertheless, he surrounded himself with all the trappings of Fascism: banners, flags, uniforms and uniformed bodyguards. This was clearly attractive to the young Englishman and Doriot was to be his political mentor and hero for the rest of his life.

Many claims have been made about how John spent the period leading up to the outbreak of war in 1939. The accepted version is the one that his family apparently believed:

. . . for the next two years [he] was engaged in working for the Franco cause in Spain, ranking as an officer in the Spanish forces and as such for some three months actually in the field with the Italian division. Most of the time, however, he was engaged, I believe, in sabotage and gun-running work in Germany and France. There were the usual financial scrapes of which I have no details.[49]

In reality, analysis of John's movements does not bear this out. If the evidence of his passport is anything to go by, he did not actually visit Spain until August 1939, and there is good reason to believe that his account of combat service in the Spanish Civil War, as an officer with the Italian and Spanish forces, may have been either a fantasy or a straightforward lie to his family. In the statement he gave when he was captured in 1945, John makes no reference to the Spanish Civil War; instead he sums up this period in his life in a single brief sentence: 'In Spain, in France and particularly with the French politician Jacques Doriot I extensively studied Communism, this led me to Austria, Czechoslovakia and various other countries, including Italy and Germany.'[50]

Of course, this is by no means conclusive, but his passport reveals no period longer than a few weeks, apart from five months at the end of 1936 and the beginning of 1937, when his movements are unaccounted for. In fact his passport shows him to have entered Germany at the end of August 1936, and then Portugal at the beginning of March 1937, aboard the *Highland Princess*, a ship which had sailed from Britain, before travelling on to Genoa a week later on a Dutch boat, the *Titus*. This is a crucial period. During the preparation for John Amery's trial for high treason in the autumn of 1945, his younger brother Julian collected documentary evidence that John had joined the Spanish Foreign Legion on 15 March 1937 and had been granted Spanish citizenship a few days later; unfortunately for John, MI5 was able to prove conclusively that John was either at sea on the Dutch vessel or in Italy on the days when these events were supposed to have taken place.

Was he then involved in some of the other activities that his father suggested: sabotage or gun-running? This is not perhaps so far-fetched: his movements disclose many border crossings between France and Italy and it is certainly possible that he was gun-running, but is it likely? Although a charming and glib talker, capable of mounting a short-term confidence trick, his record hitherto shows no ability to sustain for any period the degree of intense concentration and subterfuge necessary to conduct a long-term smuggling operation, particularly when living in a foreign country with a democratic left-wing government and associating with extreme right-wing politicians of a type that would undoubtedly be under surveillance by the state security apparatus. The reality cannot at this time be proven either way, but it is this author's opinion that if Amery was smuggling anything between Italy and France, it was very likely to have been on his own account.

So what was he doing? In 1940 he told his father that he had secured a contract to make three short films on the French Riviera, and although there is again no evidence to support this claim, it is possible that he was still involved in some way with film production. We do know that his main residence at this time was in Paris at 12 rue de Maistre, in the 18th arrondissement, and that at some point he took up with a Parisian prostitute named Jeanine Barde, and may even have contracted a form of marriage with her despite apparently still being on friendly terms with Una in London. We also know that he was in receipt of an allowance of £10 per week from his father, paid via cash transfers through the Swiss Bank Corporation's London office. Probably the most likely explanation of how he filled his time in this period is that he spent it in the same way that he had done before: in small-scale, marginal business deals on the fringes of fraud whilst at the same time dabbling in, and feeling the thrill of, the extreme right-wing politics which were sweeping across Europe.

7. 'Keep Your Chin Up, Baby Bear'

The launch of the German invasion of France and Belgium on 10 May 1940 came as a total surprise to very few people, and certainly to nobody connected with the making of high policy in Britain and France. But the speed of the German advance, as it drove a wedge between the British and French armies, certainly did. As the *Blitzkrieg* columns made their way towards the Channel ports, fear and confusion spread across France like ripples on a pond.

One of those caught on the hop by the rapid advance of Hitler's panzer divisions was John Amery. When war broke out he was in Spain, having arrived there from France on 22 August 1939 in the course of his nomadic wandering around Europe. He remained in Spain until 13 December when he departed for Estoril in Portugal.[1]

What he was doing in Spain is difficult to surmise. The Civil War had officially ended on 1 April 1939 and the country was returning to the bleak stability of life under General Franco's nationalist regime. The most likely explanation is that Madrid was a congenial place in which John could continue the petty criminality and ducking and diving by which he apparently supplemented the £10 weekly allowance he received from his family. The Spanish economy had been devastated by three years of Civil War, the import of foreign currency was restricted, and there was no suggestion that John was any kind of honoured guest. Nevertheless, the hard currency available to him would have meant that he was comparatively comfortably off.

Similar reasoning may apply to his stay in Portugal. There is a suggestion in his MI5 file that he was involved in illegal currency dealing at this time: he certainly attempted to persuade Una to smuggle a small quantity of jewellery to the United States. In a letter to her written from the Hotel do Parque in Estoril on 25 January 1940, apparently in response to a telegram asking for money, he wrote:

Darling Toto,

Your wire just received, far from being able to send any money to London I am most seriously perturbed as to what is going to happen to me. One thing however is obvious, the value of diamonds has increased by over 25% since the outbreak of war and it is an absolute crime to lose this jewelry [sic] at the moment, especially when it is quite obvious that at the end of the war they will have increased in value by about 100%.

Bearing this in mind it is essential to find someone who will take them out, even if it is to sell them immediatly [sic] in this respect perhaps your bank, or some jeweller, solicitor or anyone else might give the necessary assistance even if you had to sell 2 of them it would give you the third one back. There is also this, Mr Nathan, brother of Mrs Nathan I think, who used to be so often at Eaton Square has an office in London 8 Phillip Lane E. C. and altho he himself might not be able to do anything, he probably or rather certainly has friends in whose line of business that would be.

Under the circumstances the ideal thing would be for someone to take them out and go to America with you and the diamonds, you could wear them in and between you could make at least £1,000 profit selling in New York. This is positive I have this morning made the necessary inquiries.

Please therfor [sic] give your undivided attention to this. In one way or another there is money there for you if you can get busy and use your powers of persuasion on people and don't get discouraged at the first refusal, the family would probably help for introductions etc.

To stall Bravingtons go and tell them I have only just left Spain from where the export of money is forbidden, but am now in Portugal where the money is free and will be delighted to pay there [sic] interest if they will send me the account, this will enable us to gain at least 3 weeks they well know letters take over a week from Lisbon to London.

Lastly if you can do nothing send me the ticket of the ring you put in over Kennet and I will try and compete with that on condition Bravington will either have the ticket in my name or you send me a power of attorney to sell at my discretion, because I cannot hope to get it out but I might be able to sell it here if I had the ticket and sufficient time . . .

I know perfectly well I ought to be there to assist you and arrange everything, however that is impossible and I do beg you baby bear not to sit down and spend your time thinking how bad it is of me not being there because that is f–all good to anybody. React and get busy there is at least even selling in London a very considerable profit for you, but you will have to run around and beard people in their offices; as it is a sensible proposition you should not in the end have any difficulty.

I need hardly say that any profit you make is for you with my love and blessing. I had hoped you might have written to me earlier so that we might have planned your coming here, at the moment my little capital is exhausted, the sands are running out still Sammy★ is well and I still hope to get round the corner to prosperity again. Meanwhile no effort is too great to liquidate this diamond question and I leave it to you knowing that my little girl is going to be really clever and make me so proud. When I am in the money again I will buy you some more ice to make up for what you have know [sic] to sell. Do your best for New York you could leave your income as security. Father would I am sure at least guarantee to continue paying you the £8 a week for another 2 years, and New York and nearly £2,000 in your pocket might be the start to Toto the 'dollar millionairess'.

God bless you, good luck I will do anything I can to help, you know how much I really love you.

Keep your chin up baby bear,
Your John[2]

★ His pet dog.

This pathetic mix of fantasy, exhortation and evasion of responsibilities failed to find its intended recipient. Una had moved from 11 Cheltenham Terrace to 5 Chelsea Embankment without leaving a forwarding address. This did not please John who followed up with a sharp note on 15 February:

> I got back today the letter I wrote you on receipt of your telegram re diamonds.
>
> Of course darling if you are so bloody inefficient you can't get your letters sent from Cheltenham Terrace to Chelsea Embankment what can I do?
>
> Will you *never* have just a little sense? Why did you not tell me the new address in the wire? You get 25 words for 3/6 night letter telegraph.
> Love you
> John
> PS Smack the face of the bloody woman at Cheltenham Terrace at least.[3]

John left Portugal on 4 March 1940 and was given permission to remain in Spain for three days (his visa had initially been issued only for a non-stop journey across the country) after which he apparently entered France on 6 March and 'returned to Paris'.[4]

It was in April 1940 that John was to have his last face-to-face contact with his family before embarking on the path that led ultimately to the Wandsworth gallows: 'In April I had the occasion to meet my father in Paris and I told him that I considered that the French army did not want to fight and would be very rapidly defeated and this gave me cause for the greatest anxiety.'[5] If this claim is true it was a surprisingly prescient view, though one which Amery can have had very little grounds for arriving at: the French army at the time numbered not far short of five million men under arms and possessed almost the same number of modern tanks as the Germans. Not surprisingly, Leo Amery did not share his elder son's pessimism but he did urge him to: 'in one form or another, political, intelligence etc, join up'.[6] It is possible that Una was present at this meeting.

John agreed to his father's suggestion but first he needed to return to the south of France to wind up some business matters – or so he later claimed.[7] In fact at this time he obtained permission from the Préfecture of the Alpes-Maritimes to stay in France until October 1940.[8] This suggests that he had no intention of returning to Britain in the short term, and perhaps not in the long term either. From his point of view, going home can have held few attractions: responsibilities to wife, family and some sort of wartime service were hardly John Amery's *métier*. Better certainly to stick it out in the south of France and hope that something more congenial might turn up.

This was when the hammer blow fell. At dawn on 10 May 1940 Hitler's Wehrmacht invaded Luxembourg, Belgium and the Netherlands, all three of them neutral countries. The aim of this move was to draw forward the British Expeditionary Force and the powerful French forces in north-eastern France so that the main German effort could be launched into France, north of the Maginot line, through the densely forested Ardennes region of Belgium. Which, in broad outline, is precisely what happened.

By 19 May the German panzers of the '*Sichelschnitt*' ('sickle-cut': the main attack via the Ardennes) had reached the Channel near Abbeville, trapping the best of the French armies, together with the British Expeditionary Force, in a vast pocket with their backs to the sea. General Gort, commander of the British force, ignored orders to attempt to break out southwards towards the remains of the French armies and instead retreated to Calais and Dunkirk, where the evacuation followed and was completed by 3 June. Fighting alone, the French attempted to hold out but to little avail. By now their war-machine was in a state of chaos, and collapse swiftly followed. Paris fell on 14 June and by the 22nd, France was forced to accept an armistice to be signed, humiliatingly, in the same railway carriage at Compiègne where Marshal Foch had accepted the German surrender in 1918.

Against the grim backdrop of the disaster of the fall of France
there were a few sparks of good news, not least of which was the
elevation of Winston Churchill to the British Premiership. With
Churchill came a complete change of government: now a coalition,
it included leading Labour and Liberal figures as well as dissident
Conservatives who had supported Churchill's stance on rearmament in the 1930s, together with a few of the leading appeasers from
Neville Chamberlain's tenure, like Lord Halifax and Chamberlain
himself. (In fact at this time Churchill probably had more support
from the Opposition parties than his own.) Leo Amery was among
those who now joined the Cabinet: on 13 May Churchill called
him to Downing Street and offered him the post of Secretary of
State for India. This came as a considerable blow to Amery: he had
hoped and expected to be offered a more senior role, either as
Chancellor of the Exchequer or as Churchill's deputy for Defence.

The reason for Amery's high expectations lay largely with the
position he held as one of the senior opponents of appeasement
within the Conservative Party and also, of course, on the basis
of his almost lifelong friendship with Churchill. Leo Amery had
converted wholeheartedly to Churchill's anti-appeasement cause
in the wake of the *Anschluss* with Austria in March 1938 (which
had so excited John); prior to this he had been in favour of
accommodating Germany's need for an important role in Central
Europe, an outlook that may have been partly brought about by a
meeting he had had with Hitler in August 1935 while on a climbing
holiday with Julian and Bryddie in the Bavarian Alps. Amery liked
Hitler's 'directness and eagerness to let his hearer know all his mind'
and felt that 'intellectually he has a grip on economic essentials and
on many political ones, too, even if it is crude at times',[9] although
events were to change this opinion. Like many others, he began to
recognize that the weakness and inconsistency of Chamberlain's
appeasement policy were simply encouraging German arrogance
and aggression. Although Leo Amery was primarily an intellectual,
'one of the best informed and most intellectually sophisticated men
in British public life',[10] it is also very likely that at the most visceral

level, as a Jew (albeit a 'secret' one) observing the rising tide of anti-Semitic persecution in Germany, he was repelled and disgusted by the behaviour of the Nazis. Having thrown himself into the anti-appeasement cause, he became one of its most articulate advocates, culminating in his famous speech during the debate on the loss of Norway on 7 May 1938 in which he quoted:

. . . certain words of Oliver Cromwell. I will quote certain other words. I do it with great reluctance, because I am speaking of those who are old friends and associates of mine, but they are words which, I think, are applicable to the present situation. This is what Cromwell said to the Long Parliament when he thought it was no longer fit to conduct the affairs of the nation:
    'You have sat here for too long for all the good you have been doing. Depart, I say, and let us have done with you. In the name of God, go!'[11]

Leo Amery's speech caught the mood of the House of Commons precisely. Chamberlain realized that he could not continue to govern without the support of the Opposition parties, and when they declined to give him their support, he resigned three days later. Leo Amery did not bring down the Chamberlain Government – its own inability to manage the war achieved that – but he was certainly one of the catalysts in the events surrounding its fall, and he reasonably expected to be a beneficiary as well.

Despite their long association, Churchill was wary of Amery. He could not ignore him, but he was keen to keep him outside the mainstream business of running the war. Recognizing that democracies are not necessarily ideally suited for the conduct of war, Churchill strongly believed in having as few fingers in the pie as possible: 'All I wanted was compliance with my wishes after reasonable discussion',[12] which he was unlikely to get from Amery. Giving Amery responsibility for India – a subject over which they had quarrelled violently – was a curious solution, and one which Amery considered refusing. And although it brought Leo Amery back into government after an absence of twelve years, it was also the act which gave his elder son the status and 'value', both to the Germans and eventually to the British Government, that was eventually to lead to his death on the gallows.

John Amery's description of the fall of France is short and succinct: 'the French army collapsed, the Armistice was signed and I found myself virtually trapped in the Free zone of France, where by the terms of the Armistice visas outgoing were not granted to British subjects of military age'.[13] In fact this is a somewhat disingenuous version of events: although France fell astonishingly swiftly, it did none the less take some six weeks, long enough for visitors or temporary residents in the south of France in possession of a motorcar (Amery owned a Ballat car, registration number 7397RF3[14]) to make good their escape. Options available, all within an easy day's drive of Cannes, where Amery was staying, included Spain, Switzerland and, until 20 June when the Italians attacked southern France through the Alps, Italy. This is an important point: when P. G. Wodehouse's home in Le Touquet was overrun on 22 May 1940, he and his family had literally a few hours' warning of the imminent arrival of the German army (they had been assured by both the BBC and locally based British officers that any German assault would be 'hurled back'). The Wodehouses had enough time to throw a few clothes into a suitcase and attempt to flee but they were caught because their car broke down.[15] In fact they had been permanent residents at Le Touquet since 1934 and had roots there – good reasons for an unworldly, sedentary couple to stay put – nevertheless they attempted, at least, to get away. In contrast, it is by no means unreasonable to speculate that Amery made no effort to leave France at this time.

The France in which John Amery now found himself trapped, however, was a considerably less congenial place than it had been before the German invasion. On 22 March 1940 President Albert Lebrun had appointed Paul Reynaud as Prime Minister. On the face of it he was an ideal choice to inject some energy into a French Government that had been characterized by weakness and vacillation for many years: he had been an opponent of the Munich

Agreement in 1938 and was a strong supporter of rearmament and an advocate of the modern, manoeuvrist approach to warfighting typified by German *Blitzkrieg* doctrine. (Other adherents included such diverse figures as the Fascist-supporting Major General J. F. C. Fuller in Britain and the then little-known Colonel Charles de Gaulle in France of whom Reynaud was something of a political patron.) Perhaps even more importantly, Reynaud had a combative and quick-witted temperament and was even something of an Anglophile: certainly Winston Churchill – then still First Lord of the Admiralty in Chamberlain's Government – had been delighted by Reynaud's elevation to the French Premiership and wrote to him to tell him so:

> I rejoice that you are at the helm, and that Mandel is with you, and I look forward to the very closest and most active co-operation between our two Governments . . . we have thought so much alike during the last three or four years that I am most hopeful that the closest understanding will prevail, and that I may contribute to it.[16]

The reality, however, of the corrupt 'crony' politics of the Third Republic meant that the majority of Reynaud's apparent virtues were actually flaws: 'he was essentially a loner and, by virtue of his opinions, an outsider'.[17] He had little support among the cliques who, as their country collapsed around them, continued to manoeuvre for petty domestic and personal advantage. Recognizing the miasma of defeatism that had engulfed the French body politic and armed forces, Reynaud attempted to rally the nation around the heroic figure of Marshal Philippe Pétain, the eighty-four-year-old 'victor of Verdun' during the First World War, by appointing him Vice-Premier on 18 May 1940. It turned out that Pétain's heroic days were behind him: senescent (a subsequent nickname he acquired as head of state was 'Philippe le Gaga'[18]), defeatist and Anglophobic, the Marshal recommended capitulation and began to intrigue against Reynaud almost as soon as he had joined the Government. As the military situation worsened, Reynaud's hold on power weakened, and on 16 June, with Paris now in German hands and his Government in still-unoccupied Bordeaux, Reynaud was forced to resign in favour of Pétain.

Acknowledging military defeat, the Governments of Belgium, the Netherlands, Norway, Poland and Czechoslovakia had eventually re-established themselves in exile in London and continued to conduct their limited business beyond the reach of German duress. Uniquely for a defeated major power, however, Pétain's Government continued *in situ*, in the provincial spa town of Vichy.

The terms of the Armistice, which was agreed and duly signed on 22 June, recognized the continued existence of a sovereign French Government and accepted that part of France would not be occupied by the victorious Germans. These concessions are surprising with hindsight but Hitler was undoubtedly concerned that France might continue the war from North Africa or the more distant colonies – the French fleet, as well as the colonial army, remained powerful and largely undamaged. Nor were claims made on French colonial possessions. Nevertheless, the French army was to be reduced to 100,000 men – the same number allowed to the Germans after the Treaty of Versailles in 1919 – and the French Government was to accept German military control in strategically important parts of the country – in effect, Paris, the north and the Atlantic coast – while the massive costs of the German occupation, set at 400 million francs per day, would also be met by France.

The material effect of the Armistice on those who, like John Amery, were nationals of France's erstwhile ally was not at this stage clear, but the situation did not remain as it was for long. On 3 July 1940, the British naval commander in the Mediterranean, Admiral Somerville, was instructed to ensure that the French fleet at Mers-el-Kébir, in Algeria, could not fall into the hands of the Germans or Italians. Somerville was instructed to take his 'Force H' to the French port and then to issue an ultimatum. The French fleet had a number of options: to put to sea and join forces with the Royal Navy; to sail with reduced crews to any British port where the ships would be impounded and the crews repatriated; to sail with reduced crews to any French port in the West Indies where the ships would be immobilized; or to scuttle the ships within six hours. Admiral Gensoul, the French commander and another Anglophobe, transmitted a truncated version of the ultimatum to France: he claimed to have been told that he had been given six hours to scuttle his ships or force would be used; not surprisingly, he was instructed to resist, and equally unsurprisingly, the British attack was more or less a massacre.

The result of the British operation, codenamed CATAPULT, was 1,297 French dead and the severance of diplomatic relations between the British and French Governments. Amery and other British subjects, who until then had been citizens of a state which was at least in formal alliance with France, suddenly found themselves almost enemy aliens. The breakdown of diplomatic relations meant that the United States' Consular Service now took formal responsibility for safeguarding the interests of Britain and British citizens in the unoccupied zone of France.

John Amery was to prove a source of considerable trouble to the officials who dealt with him at the US Consulate in Nice. In order to keep on top of the extra work which responsibility for British nationals entailed, the Consulate employed a number of British subjects who had remained in unoccupied France, among them an insurance assessor named Wilfred Brinkman, who worked for the London firm of Toplis and Harding as one of their representatives on the French Riviera. Brinkman's first contact with Amery came in July 1940 when he was instructed by the American Consul to 'deal with a telegram . . . requesting that Amery be taken to Switzerland, bearing in mind his medical condition'.[19]

John Amery claimed then and subsequently occasionally maintained (though not in the statement he gave to MI5 after his capture) that he was a victim of tuberculosis. In reality, as the post-mortem examination after his execution in 1945 showed, he bore no sign of ever having had the disease: there was 'no sign of tuberculosis either active or healed'.[20] Even so, Brinkman asked Ogilvie, former secretary of the Queen Victoria Memorial Hospital in Nice who was working in the Consulate, to take charge, as it appeared to be a medical case and [he] checked up what Ogilvie was doing. [Brinkman] was able to arrange for an ambulance to take Amery to Switzerland and arranged with the Swiss Consul and the French that a visa be granted. When arrangements were completed, Amery turned them down as he could not take his dog and lady friend★ with him.[21]

It seems likely that Amery's claim of serious illness was a symptom of his personality disorder. The only way in which he appears to have profited from pretending to have tuberculosis was in extracting money from his family to fund his supposed treatment: as we have seen, he could have used it as a pretext for escape to a neutral country; instead, he chose not to do so. Rather, it seems likely that he used his claim to have TB as a way of drawing attention to himself, just as he boasted of his fictional exploits as a combatant officer in Spain. This impression is strengthened by one of the earliest MI6† reports relating to Amery which was passed to MI5 in 1942: 'Amery has a habit of picking up in the streets the stub ends of cigarettes which he smokes and when the BANBAN-ASTEs‡ remonstrated with him, he replied that it did not matter as far as he was concerned as he was in an advanced state of TB.'[22] Amery was a self-confessed heavy smoker and as the result of German demands and subsequent rationing, tobacco was difficult to obtain in unoccupied France: the habit of collecting cigarette ends for subsequent re-use was by no means unusual amongst the general population, though perhaps surprising in the son of a British Cabinet minister.

★

★ Jeanine Barde, his prostitute girlfriend.
† MI6 was the wartime cover-name of the Secret Intelligence Service which collected Intelligence from overseas sources.
‡ MI6's informants.

From a political point of view, Amery maintained a fairly low profile during the first year or so of the Vichy regime, but this is not entirely surprising. Although Marshal Pétain's Government actively sought to collaborate with the Germans in the most craven manner, it was by no means in political sympathy with them. In so far as the Government had power, it was in character a militaristic dictatorship, lacking a coherent ideology but seeking to unite the French by harking back to an imaginary 'golden age' when rulers and peasants worked in harmony to feed and clothe themselves untroubled by the strange alien scourges of socialism, capitalism (and, indeed, Fascism).

The first of the three pillars underpinning the Vichy regime was the personality cult which developed around Pétain himself. As a genuine hero of the First World War, with a reputation for courage and humanity, he had the respect and affection of a large proportion of the population; his regime sought to translate this into an absurd cult of veneration. The basis of this was the decision of the National Assembly, taken by an overwhelming majority on 10 July 1940, to hand over all its powers – including the power to change the constitution by decree – to the Marshal himself. In response, and on the same day, Pétain issued three decrees: the first appointed himself Head of State (rather than President); the second changed the constitution to give himself full power; the third suspended the National Assembly indefinitely.

It was not long before every school classroom and government office in France featured its own colour photograph of the Marshal, blending 'benevolence with sternness'[23] and often accompanied by the slogan: 'Je fais à la France le don de ma personne',★ invoking the supposed courage and patriotism the Marshal had shown in remaining in France rather than fleeing elsewhere. Every morning, children in every school – in the unoccupied zone at least – would sing the regime's appalling anthem:

★ 'I give to France the gift of my person'.

Maréchal, nous voilà!
Devant toi, le sauveur de la France.
Nous jurons, nous, les gars,
De servir et de suivre tes pars.

('Marshal, here we are before you, France's saviour. We, your men,
we swear to serve you and follow in your footsteps'.[24])

Large crowds would be assembled to greet the Marshal during his
walks about the town of Vichy, at his weekly visits to church
(Pétain was by no means pious, but the symbolism of service and
obedience surrounding Catholicism was not lost on him or his
supporters) and during his tours through the unoccupied zone.*

The cult of the Marshal combined with a strange militarization
of French society. One of the first acts of the Vichy regime was to
found a veterans' organization, the Légion Française des Com-
battants, ostensibly as a self-help group for ex-soldiers and a support
organization for the hundreds of thousands of POWs still in German hands, but with an explicitly Pétainiste agenda and adorned
with symbols of the new France – the 'Francisque' and the slogan
'*Travail, Famille, Patrie*', meaning 'Work, Family, Homeland'.† The
Légion, membership of which became essential for preferment
under the Vichy regime, was soon joined by the Chantiers de
Jeunesse, a youth movement founded as a substitute for national
military service which was prohibited under the Armistice. Soon
almost everyone in Vichy France seemed to be regimented and
clad in some kind of uniform.

But unlike what was happening in Nazi Germany and Fascist
Italy, there was nothing particularly new about what Pétain wanted
to achieve in France: his 'National Revolution' was not forward-
looking, even in the grotesque sense that Germany's and Italy's

* Pétain visited the occupied zone only once, in April 1944.
† And which, of course, replaced the old, republican and hard-won '*Liberté,
Egalité, Fraternité*'.

were; he simply required an obedient and compliant population which would not cause friction with the German occupiers. Pétain was not a traitor in the sense that he was consciously acting against France's interests or even against a narrow perception of what they might be: he simply assumed that the war was lost, that Britain would shortly be in the same position as France, and that a better deal could be obtained for France in the long term by cooperating – collaborating – with Germany rather than offering futile resistance. In attempting to unify the population and submerge political differences beneath himself as a figurehead, he assumed that Hitler's Germany might show some gratitude when the war was eventually over. At this early stage in the war, a great many French people agreed with him; keeping their heads down, returning to what Pétain regarded as traditional values and trying not to antagonize their *de facto* rulers seemed like wise counsel. The Vichy Government was undoubtedly Anglophobic, anti-Semitic, anti-Bolshevik and militaristic, but it was reactionary rather than radical, and it was still very unwilling to tolerate the activities of openly pro-Nazi and Fascist groups in the unoccupied zone.

Amery continued with his career as an irritant to the Consular officials in Nice through the winter of 1940 into 1941. As a British subject in distress, he was entitled to a small relief grant of up to £10 every month paid through the Consulate, but for a man of his habits – and, presumably, lack of resources – this was not enough. Wilfred Brinkman later recalled: 'I . . . had considerable trouble with Amery over his relief allowance, as he expected to receive more than I was authorized to grant, the matter being adjusted after telegraphic communication with London.'[25] An MI5 informant subsequently alluded to the resentment that this engendered: 'Asked what he knew about John Amery, Leaver★ said that he had never met him but knew that he was loathed in Nice. For

★ Leaver is identified in the MI5 file only as a man who had been in France and got away to Britain.

some unknown reason he was allowed £20 a month instead of the usual £10.'[26]

This may have been a rare example of Leo Amery using his influence to help his wayward son. There are occasional allusions from British and German contacts of Amery to assistance John received during this period from his godfather, the British Ambassador in Madrid, Sir Samuel Hoare, but there is no concrete evidence as to what this might have consisted of. Although Amery's British passport was renewed by the US Vice-Consul at Nice in June 1941, he did not use it for travel again. Nevertheless there is an intriguing suggestion from Brinkman:

I heard that there was a traffic in Sterling cheques which apparently was being done in the Consulate. I traced this to Ogilvie who was subsequently arrested by the French Police, apparently on denunciation by a third party.

A few days later I happened to be in the French Police Headquarters in connection with the detention of British subjects, when I noticed Amery walking in and out of offices in the building, showing he had a certain authority to do so. A French Inspector who knew me well, confided that Amery had denounced Ogilvie for the purpose of collecting the reward on cheques seized on Ogilvie [sic]. Also that these cheques had been smuggled over the Spanish frontier by Amery himself, who had utilized a British Diplomatic passport he held.[27]

It is difficult to imagine how Amery could have obtained a genuine diplomatic passport or *laissez-passer* of some kind unless through the good offices of his godfather; equally, there is no corroborative evidence to show that this is anything more than a rumour: certainly Amery makes no mention of having left France prior to his decision to throw in his lot with the Third Reich the following year.

The major event of the first year of Amery's sojourn in Vichy France came on 22 June 1941 when Hitler unleashed Operation BARBAROSSA on his erstwhile ally, Josef Stalin, in an attempt to 'crush Soviet Russia in a swift campaign'.[28] One hundred and fifty three divisions, comprising nearly 3,600 tanks, 2,700 aircraft and 3.6 million German and Axis soldiers, crossed into the Soviet Union, intent on defeating the Red Army west of the Dvina–Dnieper rivers. This was marvellous news for John Amery:

It was my considered opinion . . . that Europe was in the greatest peril of a Communist invasion, that this invasion would sweep the whole continent and that nothing could stop it, unless the different countries of Europe pushed through a social revolution which would spike the guns of the Communists in their world-wide revolutionary activities. It was also [my] view that the Jewish race was mixed up and working hand in glove with Moscow.[29]

Fortunately, however, 'The German army attacked first.'[30] Excited by this news, John took himself to Vichy to see how Pétain's regime would respond. He was to be disappointed.

I went . . . to Vichy to see what was going on, determined to do what I could to create a situation whereby a united front of all nations might be organized against Russia. I found there that there was no intention whatsoever of carrying out any kind of Social Revolution. That, in a word, Vichy was an ultra-reactionary government; of priests, the worst type (in my opinion) of French industrialists and militarists.[31]

It may well be that this visit by Amery to Vichy first brought him, as the son of one of Churchill's senior ministers, to the attention of the upper echelons of the Pétain regime: 'If I did not take kindly to these people, they did not like me either . . .'[32] Nor did they care for his French associates: neither Jacques Doriot nor Marcel Déat, a former socialist minister and pacifist, now promoting his own pro-Nazi party in the occupied zone, would enter the unoccupied zone for fear of arrest. Doriot was busy organizing the Légion des Volontaires Françaises Contre le Bolchévisme, a force of French anti-Communist volunteers, to fight on the Eastern Front. Vichy had now identified Amery as an enemy. In November 1941, following the arrest of a Pétain loyalist in Syria, a Vichy territory which had recently fallen under the control of de Gaulle's Free French forces after a British-led military confrontation with Vichy forces, a number of British subjects were arrested in the unoccupied zone. Amery suffered a considerable indignity when the Vichy police 'took me from my bed at 3 o'clock in the morning and threw me into jail at Vals les Bains, where I found myself with Paul Reynaud and Mandel★ of all people'.[33]

Notwithstanding the irony of his situation, John's behaviour remained much the same as ever. While interned in Vals les Bains, he 'frequently drank in a night a whole bottle of gin or *fine* which he took to bed with him'.[34] Fortunately for him, 'the united efforts of my friend Jeanine Amery-Barde and Doriot extracted me from there after 18 days'.[35] Doriot's efforts recruiting on behalf of the German war effort in Russia clearly gave him some influence, even though he still dared not enter the Vichy zone; Jeanine made a less successful impression: 'the Banbanastes describe her as a "morue", i.e. a woman of the streets . . . a Frenchwoman of the worst type . . . who completely dominates him'.[36]

Immediately following his release from Vals les Bains, Amery removed himself to Marseilles. By now, yet another MI6 contact was taking an interest in him:

Amery, the son of the English Minister, has been released from the Concentration Camp at Valses de la Sol [sic] in unoccupied France and is at the moment living at the Hôtel Noailles in Marseilles.

Source regards Amery with considerable suspicion. The Hôtel Noailles is much frequented by members of the German Armistice Commission, and it seems strange that he is able to stay at a hotel of this class on the £10 per month allowed to British subjects in France.[37]

★ Georges Mandel, Reynaud's Minister of the Interior, one of the leading 'hawks' in Reynaud's Government who was subsequently murdered by the Vichy Milice in July 1944 while being transported to Germany.

Amery himself saw things differently. After his brief stay in Marseilles, he was 'only allowed to reside in the Isère. In the country town of Grenoble and later at Paladru I planned what I could do useful [sic].'[38] The problem facing John, or so he later claimed, was the alliance between Britain and the Soviet Union; the idea was such anathema to him that he 'thought that the people responsible in London were acting in a manner that no longer coincided with British Imperial interests'.[39] To his surprise, 'the American authorities representing the British interests seemed to find the Russian alliance normal'.[40] He seems also to have been feeling isolated: 'I was cut off from evryone [sic]. Including England.'[41]

On 3 March 1942 the RAF launched a bombing raid on the Renault industrial complex at Boulogne-Billancourt in the suburbs of Paris, as a result of which 623 French civilians lost their lives. In so far as the plant was being used to produce war *matériel* for Germany, the raid was unremarkable – ultimately France lost more than 60,000 civilians to Allied raids – but it prompted a response from John Amery in his isolation in the French Alps: he wrote a letter to the *Petit Dauphin*, a French newspaper:

Grenoble 6 Mars – M. John Amery, fils de l'ancien ministre britannique des Colonies, sejourment [sic] actuellement à Grenoble nous a fait parvenir la protestation suivante:

Devant le deuil qui frappe si cruellement la nation française, il est évident que la décemi même impose à tout Anglais le silence.

Néanmoins, je désire declarer très haut – et je crois que cette pensée est partagée par nombre de mes compatriots – que des operations telles que le bombardement des quartiers ouvriers de Boulogne-Billancourt nous remplissent de tristesse et de honte, que nos ailes soient salies à pareille enterprise.[42]

Up until the publication of this letter, Amery was little more than a shabby, disreputable and disturbed fantasist who had spent his adult life trading on his father's well-deserved reputation. But by publishing criticism of his own Government in a newspaper controlled – or at least supervised – by the enemy, he had crossed a Rubicon; he was 'giving aid and comfort to the enemies of our lord the King'.

What caused John Amery to take this step? His statement to MI5 gives no clue to his motivation – nor indeed suggests that he gave it much thought at all. It is possible that he was encouraged to write the letter by one of his French collaborationist friends, but equally he may have decided to do so as a means of drawing attention to himself or even as an attempt to ingratiate himself with the Vichy regime. In any event, the impact of the letter was not immediate; MI5 first learned of it towards the end of April 1942 via letters sent home from British residents in the unoccupied zone but it was not until 22 July that a copy of the text arrived in London.

It was at this point that the British Intelligence Services began to take a serious interest in John Amery. D. C. Orr, an MI5 official serving in Room 055, the liaison section at the War Office, submitted the cutting from the *Petit Dauphin* together with the comment that 'these should be sufficient to deter the young gentleman from ever setting foot on British soil, or if he does, he should be assured of a reception at the hands of a firing squad'.[43] A somewhat more considered note was placed on the file the same day by Sydney Albert of B. 4a branch after a conversation with the Director General, Sir David Petrie: 'We spoke about John Amery, son of the Secretary of State for India . . .'[44] Albert went on to note that it had been decided to inform SIS of what was known about John, to place him on the postal censorship black-list, to obtain any correspondence or files about him from the Foreign Office, to investigate the possibility of cutting off his relief allowance in order to force his return and, finally, to warn the ports. No attempt appears to have been made to seek the views of Leo Amery at this time. A subsequent letter from Miss V. Gibson, an MI5 officer, sent to SIS a week later, informed the Intelligence Service that Amery 'was living in the Grand Hotel d'Angleterre in Grenoble but is now back in Nice', and that he had been 'arrested once again for trafficking in stocks and shares'. She concluded by remarking:

'I think he is more a crook than anything else, but I am considering having him put on the censorship suspect list to find out with whom he is in contact over here.'[45]

Unaware of the stir that his activities were causing in London, Amery now began to dig himself deeper into trouble. Apparently feeling desperately isolated, he 'decided at this period to attempt to talk to Dino Grandi, previously Italian Ambassador in London, to see if Italian diplomacy was not capable of organizing an end to this kind of "civil war between the civilized when the barbarians were at the gate"'.[46] Grandi had held the post of Under Secretary and then Minister of Foreign Affairs in the Italian Government between 1925 and 1932, and had then been appointed Ambassador to London, a post he held until 1938 when he was recalled to Rome because Mussolini believed him to be 'too moderate'; it is certainly possible that Amery met Grandi at some point during his time in London.

Now appointed Minister of Justice, Grandi was a senior figure in the Italian Government but experience of Mussolini's wartime leadership had been a cause of severe disillusionment to him, as to many other high officials in Italy. In early 1941, along with other ministers and officials, Grandi had been mobilized by Mussolini and sent to the Albanian front as a stunt to raise public morale, and it was at this time that the first stirrings of the plot which would eventually remove Mussolini from power began.

Amery gave the Italian Consul in Grenoble a letter for Grandi, seeking a meeting 'in the European interest',[47] but he received no reply; possibly Grandi, if he did indeed receive the letter, was in no mood to encourage a foreign admirer of Mussolini. Changing tack, Amery wrote to the Finnish representative in Paris offering his services in Finland's war against the Soviets – he had already donated his 'skis and various other things' during the Winter War of 1939–40 – but was politely rebuffed.

It was at around this time that the German Foreign Office first began to take an interest in Amery. The mechanism by which this came about is unclear. Dr Fritz Hesse, the Foreign Office official with responsibility for British renegades, was under the impression that Amery had been arrested by the German army near the Spanish frontier in 'the early part of the war'[48] and that his views and outlook had been passed on by the military through their chain of command: this is unlikely. It seems much more probable that Amery's general behaviour and relatively high profile brought him to the attention of the German authorities supervising the terms of the Armistice in the unoccupied zone; certainly, in addition to the overt German presence, the Abwehr ran a number of spies and informers throughout the region. It is also possible that contacts of Amery in ultra-collaborationist circles in Paris brought him to the Germans' attention. In any event, in August 1942 he was visited by Graf Ceschi, the German Armistice Commissioner for the Savoy region, whom he had met in Vienna in 1938, together with Werner Plack, a member of the German Foreign Office who had spent several years in the United States, to ask whether he was interested in going to Berlin for 'political discussions'.

Amery did not immediately leap at this offer, even though his vanity must have been enormously tickled. Despite his apparently lifelong delusion that he was an important person in and of his own right, he seems to have recognized that the Germans may have had an ulterior motive in attempting to get him away from the relative security of unoccupied France. Amery told Ceschi that he was willing to go but only if he was given 'a formal guarantee that [he] could leave without let or hindrance should [they] disagree'.[49] Ceschi was not in a position to give this guarantee, but he was able to prevail on the Vichy authorities to allow John to leave the Isère to visit Jeanine's family in Bergerac.

It was there, on 26 September, that Werner Plack returned to tell Amery that Berlin had granted a safe conduct for him and Jeanine: 'he gave me the necessary assurances and we departed almost immediately'.[50]

8. Rather a Sensation

For all his delusions and fantasies, Amery was initially suspicious of the German approach to him, but the German Government hardly dealt with him as wide-eyed innocents. Dr Hesse, chief of the Third Reich's England Committee, explained: 'The Police reported his arrest* to the authorities concerned, including the Foreign Office, being of the opinion that Amery was a British agent sent over to pry out military and political secrets . . .'[1] Clearly this was not the case, but it does indicate the puzzlement which Amery's defection caused among the officials set to deal with his case. Foreign Minister Ribbentrop asked Dr Hesse for advice:

I was of the opinion that it would harm Anglo-German relations if the son of a British Cabinet minister were executed for espionage, without just cause. I suggested that he should be brought to Berlin to see whether we could use him for any political purpose. Ribbentrop accepted my view, and the Propaganda Ministry also agreed, and so he was brought to Berlin.[2]

'I might say that it caused rather a sensation in Berlin when it was known that the son of a British Cabinet minister had volunteered to work for the Germans . . .'[3] recalled Dr Reinhard Haferkorn, who was in charge of the English section of the Foreign Broadcasts Department of the German Foreign Office. And the convoluted

---

* Hesse was confused over the circumstances of Amery's first contact with the Germans: notwithstanding his belief that Amery had been arrested by the German authorities – not a possibility, as Amery was living in unoccupied France – his impression that Amery's presence was initially reported through military rather than political channels is correct.

way in which Amery's intentions became known to the Germans
also ensured that news of his defection – and of the ideas he brought
with him – reached a very high level indeed.

Hitherto the British renegades in Germany had been recruited
and managed mainly by the Foreign Office and in a few special
cases, including Joyce, by Goebbels' Propaganda Ministry. Amery,
however, had come to German attention via the military authorities
in unoccupied France, and it seems likely that it was with them
that he first raised the possibility of forming an anti-Bolshevik
legion of British volunteers to fight on the Eastern Front alongside
his friend Jacques Doriot's Légion des Volontaires Français which
had clearly inspired it. Evidently a report of Amery's ideas, through
military channels, reached the Führer himself; Dr Hesse, as Ribbentrop's special advisor in English matters, thus received something
of a surprise: 'The first I knew about it was when I received,
through Ribbentrop, a direct order from the Führer to organize [a
British unit], as he thought it would have great propaganda value
on the Eastern Front.'[4]

Thus from an early stage, Amery's collaboration with the Third
Reich ran on twin tracks: the German Foreign Office wanted to
use him for political purposes; but there was a secondary, military
strand as well. In fact the more important, although even Amery
did not recognize it as such, was the former, because the political
purpose which Hesse and Ribbentrop had in mind for Amery –
and for which they sought, and received, the Führer's approval –
was the role, hitherto unsuspected by historians, of acting as a
conduit for German peace feelers.

Like many other aspects of government and high politics under
the Third Reich, the control of foreign renegades was a somewhat
haphazard and *ad hoc* affair, but the body that had most responsibility
for their employment and use was Dr Hesse's England Committee.
The original concept behind the Committee was to centralize and
coordinate advice available to the Government on British affairs:
Joachim von Ribbentrop, the wealthy former wine merchant who
had become Hitler's Foreign Minister in February 1938, had access

to a number of people with some expertise in British matters but he often found that their advice varied widely. Consequently, in November 1939 he ordered the establishment of the Committee so that he could get one considered view on any matter of importance.

Initially, membership of the Committee was restricted to employees of the Foreign Office and the Büro Ribbentrop. The original participants in the meetings included Ambassador Gauss (Ribbentrop's legal advisor); Ambassador Woermann (who acted as Chairman); Professor Dr Friedrich Berber; Dr von Kries; Ambassador Dr Paul Schmidt (who was Hitler's interpreter); and Dr Hesse, who had been Press Attaché at the German Embassy in London and a conduit for secret discussions between the British and German Governments right up until the outbreak of war, acting as secretary. Their brief was to 'keep Ribbentrop generally advised on the question of how, when and under what circumstances peace could be brought about again with Britain'.[5] This began to change in January 1940 when Ribbentrop asked the Committee to 'give advice on the general political line of propaganda'.[6]

This change came about as the result of a decision made by Hitler shortly after the war had started. Almost as soon as he had taken over the role of Foreign Minister, Ribbentrop had started to take a close interest in foreign propaganda, hitherto the almost exclusive preserve of Goebbels and his ministry. However, in the late 1930s Goebbels had fallen from Hitler's favour to a considerable extent as the result of his marital problems, caused by his affair with the Czech actress Lida Baarova, and with Germany at war, Ribbentrop was able to launch a bid for control of foreign propaganda. On 8 September 1939, Hitler issued a decree to the effect that the Reich's Foreign Minister would issue 'general guidelines and instructions' on foreign propaganda, and that Ribbentrop would make known his 'wishes and orders'[7] to Goebbels regarding leaflets, radio, film and press. Goebbels protested as far as he dared and was mulishly uncooperative with the Foreign Office. In fact, in practice, the Foreign Office was not equipped to handle the execution of propaganda on the scale required and a further secret clarification of the responsibilities of the departments limited Ribbentrop's department's role simply to giving advice.[8]

The new role for the England Committee advising on propaganda gave it practical responsibilities it had not hitherto enjoyed, and its membership was increased by the appearance of Dr Haferkorn. However, the sudden and largely unexpected defeat of France in June 1940, which left Britain and the Empire as Germany's sole adversary, suddenly made the Committee much more important. Hesse related that:

In the middle of 1940, the character of the Committee was changed, in so far as we were allowed to invite representatives of various other departments to the meetings. This measure was taken because other departments had complained that they did not get any political information about Britain, and other world affairs, from the Foreign Office, and so the departments concerned were invited to send a representative to the sittings of the England Committee, where they were supplied with a review of what had taken place during the past week. The departments invited to these sittings were:

Propaganda Ministry

OKW★ (Wehrmacht Propaganda – W. Pr.)

Navy (Propaganda Dept)

Luftwaffe (Propaganda Dept)

Ministry of the Interior (who later dropped out, as they were not interested)

Press Department (Dr Dietrich's† representative)[9]

The reconstituted England Committee convened every Friday morning from June 1940 until the end of the war at the Wilhelmstrasse offices of the Foreign Ministry, where the representatives of the Armed Forces and Propaganda Ministry were joined by

★ Armed Forces High Command.

† Otto Dietrich (1897–1952), Nazi Party press chief from 1931 to 1945 and State Secretary in the Propaganda Ministry.

members of various Foreign Office sections, including the Political Department; the Economic Department; Radio Department; Press Department; Information Department; Legal Department (for prisoner-of-war affairs); Ambassador Bieckhoff of the Amerika Committee; Ambassador Stulenburg of the Russland Committee; and Counsellor Adam von Trott zu Solz.★ The Chairman or Dr Weber, head of the British sub-department of the Political section, would give a review of what had happened in the world and how it affected Britain and then each department would give an account of its own activities in relation to British affairs; finally, the Chairman would sum up and issue guidance accordingly, and the meeting would break up.

By the end of 1940 Ambassadors Woermann and Gauss had ceased to take an interest in the affairs of the Committee and Dr Hesse assumed the chairmanship instead, combining this with his job of reading and assimilating open-source political and diplomatic intelligence (i.e., newspaper and media reports) from Britain. In his own words, he thus became a 'living dictionary'[10] on events and personalities in the UK, and the leading authority on how Germany might regain peace with Britain.

It is a surprising fact, in view of the ferocity with which Germany prosecuted some aspects of its war with Britain, that Hitler was not necessarily interested in the destruction or occupation of Britain or the Empire; indeed, it is quite evident that the thrust of German foreign policy towards Britain in the period leading up to and actually throughout the war, was to attempt to gain British acquiescence, or at least neutrality, towards German manoeuvrings in the east and particularly against Russia.[11] A negotiated peace with Britain would have removed all military pressure on Germany in Western Europe, the Mediterranean and North Africa, and lifted the crippling British blockade which severely restricted the free inward flow of raw materials. Under those circumstances, it is not

★ Both von Trott and Stulenburg were later executed for their part in the 20 July 1944 assassination attempt against Hitler.

difficult to imagine the superbly organized and led Wehrmacht defeating the Soviet Union in the autumn of 1941 or, indeed, at any point up until the summer of 1943.

There were, however, a number of significant obstacles to any kind of peace settlement. Hesse recalled that:

Ribbentrop looked on me as an authority on the question of how to get peace with Britain again . . . I would say that Ribbentrop had a fair appreciation of the difficulties of this task but he always had great difficulty in getting the Führer to accept his views. According to Ribbentrop, the Führer had a somewhat primitive idea of the English mentality, and rather thought that it was just a question of time before the English got tired of the war, and then the two countries would shake hands over the conference table. He would never accept the view that certain conditions and concessions were necessary in order to make at least negotiations possible.[12]

This is an interesting revelation on the state of Ribbentrop's relationship with Hitler and their differing views on foreign policy. It is widely believed that Hitler held Ribbentrop in excessively high regard as the result of his success in negotiating the Nazi–Soviet Non-Aggression Pact in August 1939; Hitler had been known to describe Ribbentrop as 'a second Bismarck'.[13] This treaty and a range of secret protocols had effectively carved up Eastern Europe between Germany and the Soviet Union while providing each with reassurance about the other's intentions. This had left Stalin free to gobble up Eastern Poland, Bessarabia and the Baltic states while Hitler grabbed Western Poland and turned his attention on Western Europe: a major diplomatic coup from the German point of view, if a deeply cynical one. Apart from Hitler, however, few in the upper echelons of the Third Reich had much regard for Ribbentrop and he was widely perceived to be vain, boastful and incompetent.

In fact, Ribbentrop was perfectly capable of responding to reasoned arguments:

. . . after the defeat of France Ribbentrop asked me under what conditions I thought Britain would be prepared to negotiate for peace. I pointed out that the evacuation of all conquered countries in Western Europe and the restitution of Poland and Czechoslovakia as independent states, would be an essential condition that Britain would require. Ribbentrop accepted this view and put it before the Führer, who considered it but turned it down, and accepted the view that the so-called Greater German Reich required parts of Denmark, Holland etc.[14]

That Ribbentrop was prepared to argue on this basis, and that Hitler was prepared to give it some thought at this stage shed an interesting sidelight on the Führer's war aims. Hesse continues: '[Hitler] was of the opinion that he could not agree to any conditions for negotiations, as the war was, in his eyes, not yet finished. I subsequently realized he had in view the invasion of Russia.'[15]

But by the autumn of 1942, when John Amery was about to embark on his journey to Berlin, several major spanners had been thrown into the works.

'One has only to kick in the door, and the whole rotten structure will come crashing to the ground'; so Adolf Hitler had assured his generals before launching his attack on the Soviet Union on 21 June 1941, and at first his prophecy appeared to be borne out by events, as the Russians' failure to prepare left their armies practically on their knees. By the end of August, however, German casualties had reached 400,000[16] (four times the manpower strength of the current British regular army), lines of communication were being stretched to breaking point, and more and more Soviet divisions continued to appear to face the advancing German formations, despite losses totalling well over two million soldiers and probably as many non-combatants.

Hitler, none the less, was reluctant to concentrate his main strength against Moscow, arguing against his generals' advice that the granaries of the Ukraine and the Baltic ports were more important to German success, even though Moscow was such a major centre of communications and industry as well as having the symbolic value of being the Russian capital. Indeed, it was only in September that he finally agreed to concentrate his forces against Moscow, and by then the advance of winter left the German generals in a race against time.

It was a race that they lost. Although, by 28 November 1941, reconnaissance units of the 4th Panzer Group were in the western suburbs of Moscow, the German formations were now exhausted and beset by the extreme conditions of the Russian winter. Digging in in the hope that they would be able to resume their offensive in the spring, the Germans were surprised by the launch of a Soviet counter-offensive on 5–6 December, using troops and equipment freshly arrived from the Far East. The Soviets broke easily through the weakened German positions and, by the end of December, had pushed the Germans back some 280 kilometres from Moscow. By the end of January 1942, when the front had more or less stabilized, the invasion of Russia had swallowed up nearly 918,000 German soldiers: wounded, captured, missing or dead.[17]

Hitler resumed campaigning in earnest in the summer of 1942, concentrating his forces this time almost entirely in the southern sector with the intention of capturing the Caucasus oilfields and destroying what he assumed were the remnants of the Soviet reserves. On 24 August, soldiers of the 6th Army under General Paulus reached the Volga river, traditionally the boundary between Europe and Central Asia, a few miles to the north of Stalingrad, and on 12 September they entered the city with the intention of capturing it. For the next seven weeks, 6th Army attempted to capture Stalingrad, fighting street by street for control against dogged Soviet resistance.

Simultaneously with the fighting in Stalingrad, the only other significant land campaign involving German forces was reaching its climax. At the battle of El Alamein, between 23 October and 4 November, the British 8th Army, under Lieutenant General Bernard Montgomery, finally managed to punch through the defences of Rommel's Panzer Armee Afrika★ and force it into retreat towards Tunisia. This was followed on 8 November by the TORCH landings of American, British and Free French troops in Casablanca, Oran and Algiers, which meant that although there was still considerable heavy fighting to come, the writing was on the wall for the Axis presence in North Africa.

What this meant in strategic terms was that, for Germany, the war was in the balance and that balance was beginning to tilt inexorably in favour of its enemies. The Third Reich did not have the resources to sustain major operations on two fronts and the choice which they needed to face was between the East and the West: they had to bring an end to the fighting against either the Soviets or the Anglo-Americans before a major second front was opened in Western Europe which would inevitably result in their destruction. The alternatives they had were either victory or a negotiated peace, but evidently, if they did not have the resources to defeat the Soviets at Stalingrad – and the Germans were undoubtedly at the end of their tether there – they were unlikely to be able to come up with the wherewithal to challenge the almost limitless capacity of the United States, which was now being brought to bear on the European theatre of operations almost a year after Hitler's declaration of war against the US. Would it be possible, at this crucial turning point in the war, by making some concessions, to persuade the British and Americans that it was in their interests to make peace with the Third Reich, in order to allow it to complete its mission to destroy Communism? It might be worth a try.

Amery's celebrity as the son of a British Cabinet minister was important for Germany. Up until this point, the star turn of their English-language propaganda broadcasts had been William Joyce, notorious throughout the English-speaking world as Lord Haw-Haw. Joyce was actually a United States citizen by birth: he was born

---

★ It is worth noting that Rommel was actually absent from Africa on sick-leave at the time of the battle, and that, despite its German name, Panzer Armee Afrika contained more Italian than German troops.

in Brooklyn, New York, on 24 April 1906, the eldest son of Michael Joyce, an Irish Catholic immigrant to the US, and his wife Gertrude, who came from a Lancashire family. The Joyces moved to Ireland in 1909, probably because Michael had done well enough as a business-man in New York to return as a wealthy man to his homeland, and quietly forgot about their American nationality. In 1922, when Ireland was partitioned, the family, who were staunch loyalists, moved to England and eventually settled in London, where William continued his education at Battersea Polytechnic and Birkbeck College.

Joyce's value to the Germans rested on three main pillars: he was academically gifted, having achieved a first-class honours degree in English Literature at London University; he was a lucid, witty and able speaker; and he was a fanatical anti-Semite and Fascist. In the 1920s and '30s, Joyce lived out a kind of double life, as student and later teacher by day and extremist gutter politician by night. In 1933, he followed many of his friends into the British Union of Fascists (BUF), Oswald Mosley's attempt to bring Fascist solutions to the many problems that beset Britain and were not being addressed by the 'Old Gang' of politicians who took it in turn to run the country. Joyce thrived in the BUF, soon becoming one of its senior paid officials as Director of Propaganda, but he was less than enamoured by Mosley, whom he deemed insufficiently radical and anti-Semitic. This problem was solved when Mosley fired him from his salaried post as a cost-cutting measure: Joyce left the movement and set up the National Socialist League, a tiny rump of cranky anti-Semites and extreme racists, renting an office doubling as a club-room on the Vauxhall Bridge Road behind Victoria Station in London.

This was a happy time for Joyce: he made his living teaching English to foreigners at his flat in Onslow Square, South Kensington ('No Jews or Coloureds'); and spent his evenings making inflammatory speeches from soap-boxes to minuscule gatherings, or heckling other street-corner orators. But the approach of war in 1939 had thrown him into a dilemma: although in many ways he was fiercely patriotic, he could not face the prospect of his country fighting a war against a political system which held him in such thrall. In the event, and following warnings from a contact within the Security Service that he was likely to be detained and interned as a security risk, Joyce and his wife decamped to Germany just before war broke out.

Joyce had contacts in Berlin, and within a few weeks of arrival there he secured a job as a newsreader on the Reichsrundfunk's English-language 'Germany Calling' service, joining a small group which included Norman Baillie-Stewart, a former British army officer convicted of passing secrets to Germany in 1933, and Mrs Frances Eckersley and her sixteen-year-old son James Clark. Oddly enough, Baillie-Stewart, who affected the drawl of the British upper classes, was the speaker – at that stage anonymous – who was first picked out by the British press as 'Haw-Haw', but as Joyce became the principal British voice on the station, the sobriquet passed to him, even though his accent was the unaffected standard English of a well-educated member of the middle classes, with a somewhat nasal inflection.

Joyce achieved a wide audience in Britain, as much the result of curiosity as anything else, as listeners tuned in, for the first time in a major war, to uncensored news and comment from the enemy, but the problem was that as propaganda, Joyce appeared to be precisely what he was: a mouthpiece for and adherent to the German cause. There was no ambiguity about him – he wanted Germany to win and he wanted to impose a National Socialist system in Britain. Even John Amery recognized this:

As is well known there were numerous other Englishmen in Berlin and notably William Joyce and his friends and Bailey Stewart [sic] and his. These people had come to Germany on or before the declaration of war. Also they had adopted German nationality and considered themselves Germans, in consequence their views and outlook widely differed from mine . . . It was in my view quite insane to carry on as they did calling the British 'the enemy' and so forth as was their custom; if we wished to get together.[18]

★

Together with Jeanine Barde, Amery had spent a few days in Paris, during which time he had possibly met Marcel Déat, before moving on to Berlin, 'travelling under the names of Mr and Mrs Brown'[19] and accompanied by Werner Plack. Now, for the first time, Amery was interviewed by Dr Hesse to establish whether he would be suitable for the task the Germans had in mind for him.

Amery was aware, presumably because Plack had broached the subject with him either in France or on the way to Berlin, that the Germans would want him to make broadcasts to England. This would fit in well with Amery's delusions of political grandeur and also, it should be noted, with Plack's experiences: he had previously been one of the two German officials, both pre-war acquaintances from Hollywood, who had persuaded the naïve P. G. Wodehouse to make his short series of humorous talks to the United States in May 1941. Plack is unlikely to have been aware of the real purpose behind Amery's forthcoming appearances on 'Germany Calling': Amery certainly was not. The key factor in the Germans' calculations which made Amery attractive to them was that he came from a political family: Joyce had become a celebrity because of the novelty of having an apparent Englishman broadcasting Nazi propaganda, but in many ways he was regarded as a figure of fun outside his tiny circle of admirers and, although his talks were monitored by the BBC and digests were circulated in the Government, his broadcasts were not *de rigueur* in political circles; Wodehouse was not even broadcasting propaganda. But if Amery broadcast, Hesse, Ribbentrop and even Hitler presumably calculated, then at least one member of the British Cabinet would be listening to him:

We put a lot of bad language into these talks to distract the ordinary people from understanding the real purpose of them, but the idea behind it was that if anyone of importance should listen to them in Britain he would infer that Germany was prepared to negotiate with Britain. Therefore, according to my memory, no insult to Churchill was contained in these talks.[20]

Amery's first meeting with Hesse was a cagey affair as the latter sounded him out on his political views and what he was prepared to do. For his part, Amery adopted a tone of some hauteur:

I told Dr Hesse perfectly frankly that I was not interested in a German victory as such, that what interested me was a just peace where we could all get together against the real enemies of civilization, and that the British Empire as it was intact must be a part of this and not a dependant of such a regroupment [sic].[21]

Like many who had spent the entire war in continental Europe, Amery was clearly still under the impression that the Germans were likely to win it. In his statement to MI5, Amery claimed to have asked to be allowed to speak 'uncensored and uninterfered with' in a special British hour on the radio, and requested that the German Government give 'precise guarantees' that their policy towards Britain 'remained based on the proposals of the German Chancellor to the British Government of July 1940'.[22] It is probable that, describing the events three years after they took place, Amery had inflated his demands and taken credit for suggestions originally made by Hesse; it is certainly evident that he did not see any ulterior motive in Hesse's demeanour. In a further flurry of self-importance, Amery also told Hesse that he was 'perfectly aware of the enormous losses of the Germans of the preceding winter in Russia as also the folly of their policy in Vichy, in Croatia and elsewhere'.[23]

Hesse, for his part, seemed to be reasonably satisfied with the meeting: 'I approached him on the matter [of the broadcasts] . . . without telling him the full details, i.e. that the Führer was interested.'[24] Finally, Hesse got down to brass tacks: what would Amery want in return for his cooperation in this project? John's response seems to have come as a surprise: 'I told him that far from wanting anything I was not disposed to accept anything other than that he consider me as a guest having no resources of my own available . . .'[25] Hesse was quite taken aback, Amery concluded somewhat self-righteously.

John Amery spent the next two weeks in Berlin staying in
Werner Plack's apartment while Hesse reported back to Ribbentrop
and decisions were sought on how to advance the Amery project.
Unfortunately, Allied bombing in 1943 destroyed the majority of
German documents relating to this process and we must rely on the
testimony of participants, but it seems clear that both sides of the
compact were very keen for it all to continue to fruition. It seems
reasonable to suppose that Amery welcomed it became he felt he
would no longer need to live the kind of life in which he had to resort
to picking up cigarette dog-ends from the streets, while the German
side imagined they were getting a hot-line into the heart of Churchill's Cabinet: they cannot possibly have realized how John's entire
life up to this point had discredited him in the eyes of the one
person they were directly addressing, no matter how much Leo
Amery loved his son. In any event, after two weeks of waiting,
John was summoned back to the Foreign Office to meet Hesse:

When next I saw him he told me the following. That I could consider
myself a guest of the Reich, that I could go where I pleased, that he
suggested I should make on the radio a series of weekly speeches which
would be officially dissociated from the German senders and entirely
uncensored. At the end of this time the problem would be once more
wholly revised, he hoped, to my satisfaction.[26]

More gratifying still for Amery, one suspects, was that the German side swallowed his request for an 'expenses-only' existence.
According to Hesse, 'He did not get a salary, but I was ordered by
Ribbentrop to cover his expenses and be as liberal as possible, as he
thought that the son of a British Cabinet minister should live at a
certain scale. Amery made liberal use of this arrangement.'[27] Dr
Haferkorn confirms this: 'Amery – so far as I know – never received
a regular salary for the work he did for the German authorities, but
it is obvious from the way that he lived that he was allowed fairly
unlimited expenses . . .'[28]

The next step for Hesse and his colleagues was to start the ball rolling for Amery's broadcasts. According to Hesse, 'I suggested certain ideas for talks to him, and asked him to submit me drafts . . .' Amery did so. Haferkorn recalled that 'Amery's main theme was to bring about a better understanding between Britain and Germany, and also to deal with anti-Bolshevik matters.'[29] On such a sensitive and important matter, the German Foreign Office was keen to get things right. Haferkorn supervised the production of Amery's first script:

Amery's first broadcast was written and typed by himself. The manuscript was passed by him to Dr Hesse who in turn passed it to me for editing. I disagreed with certain items and discussed these with Dr Hesse, and later saw Amery in regard to the matter. I went over the manuscript with him and made certain suggestions to him, to which he agreed. A fair copy of the original manuscript, together with a German translation, supplied by a member of my staff, was then submitted to Ribbentrop, who took a personal interest in the matter and reserved his approval.[30]

Hesse concurs with this summary: 'I went through these drafts very carefully with him, with Haferkorn and FitzRandolph,★ and then they were sent before Ribbentrop. Ribbentrop made certain alterations and then ordered them to be broadcast.'[31]

With practical preparations in train, Germany now had to play the propaganda hand. Up to this point, Amery had been 'on ice' in Berlin, kept away from places where he might encounter neutral journalists and diplomats who might leak information about his presence back home, but now the time had arrived to advertise their propaganda star. Haferkorn organized a meeting with Eduard Dietze, the British-born chief of the Reichsrundfunk's English *Redaktion*, to compose some radio advertisements for Amery's talks, while the Propaganda Ministry alerted a correspondent of their 'Transocean' news service to the forthcoming scoop.

★ A member of the German Foreign Office, evidently of British or Irish extraction.

At some point during the week following the Operation TORCH landings in North Africa, and probably after the German occupation of his adopted home in France's unoccupied zone on 11 November 1942, Amery was escorted to the Reichsrundfunk's Charlottenburg headquarters to record his first talk. Haferkorn's deputy, Friedrich Wilhelm Schöberth, a former lecturer at Newcastle, Liverpool and Cardiff Universities, was also present. Haferkorn recalled that 'it was necessary for Amery to record this talk two or three times before a suitable recording was made', and Schöberth agreed: 'He was much too nervous to broadcast directly.'[32]

With advertisements now running on the 'Germany Calling' service, Amery could finally go public; he and Jeanine moved from Plack's apartment to the luxurious Adlon Hotel in central Berlin. On 18 November, *The Times* and other British newspapers, which had picked up on the 'Germany Calling' publicity, ran the news that John Amery was in Berlin. The enterprising *Daily Mirror* door-stepped Leo Amery and asked him directly about his wayward son; his reply reflects the confusion and anxiety that he must have been feeling:

I last heard of him through the Red Cross as an invalid in unoccupied France. It is just conceivable that John asked to go for treatment for lung trouble.

Somehow I cannot quite credit the German message, but I cannot say definitely that he is still in the south of France because communication is still very difficult.[33]

But the doubts and confusion in Leo's mind were dispelled the following day: 'Transocean' splashed the Amery story as a news lead:

When John Amery heard in Berlin of the landing of Americans and British in Algiers and Morocco, he decided to approach the Wilhelmstrasse★ with

---

★ The German Foreign Office.

a request to be permitted to address his compatriots at home over the German wireless . . .

John Amery arrived in Berlin three weeks ago and his presence there had been kept a dead secret. Several months ago he had already written to the German authorities in Paris asking for permission to go to Berlin. At first, he wanted only to have talks and study conditions on the spot. The attack on French North Africa prompted him to come into the foreground. He will broadcast on Thursday. He and his wife are living with friends in the southern Hartz Mountains. But he is at present in Berlin, at the Hotel Adlon.[34]

To MI5's transcript of this message, the desk officer, D. C. Orr, evidently a somewhat smug and bloodthirsty individual, appended the following note: 'I wonder whether the influence of his unfortunate and much to be pitied father will save young Amery from the fate he so richly deserves?'[35]

That same evening, interested Britons including, presumably, members of the Amery family, listened as the anonymous announcer on the 'Germany Calling' programme introduced their latest attraction:

Tonight you will hear an Englishman who is speaking to you at his own request and of his own free will: Mr John Amery, son of the Secretary for India of the British Government, the Right Honourable Leopold Stennet Amery. The German Government bears no responsibility whatever for what Mr Amery is going to say. The German Government has merely sought fit to place its station at the disposal of Mr Amery for what he desires to say, since the world may be interested to hear what an Englishman who looks at his country from the outside has to say. We believe that Mr Amery's observations will be of special interest to you also . . . Mr John Amery . . .[36]

Bearing in mind what we now know about Hitler's intentions in allowing Amery to speak on the German radio, this stupefyingly inapt introduction almost defies belief. It is by no means clear what discussions took place within the British Government over Amery's broadcasts, if indeed any formal notice was taken of them, but few who knew Leo Amery and his family can have had any illusions about John and the way that he behaved. By dissociating the Government from what Amery was about to say, the Germans were inviting Britain to attempt to fathom hidden messages from a man who was known to be somewhat odd at best. Unsurprisingly, this confusion can only have been increased by the content of John's first talk.

Listeners will wonder what an Englishman is doing on the German radio tonight. You can imagine that before taking this step I hoped that someone better qualified than me would come forward. I dared to believe that some ray of common sense, some appreciation of our priceless civilization would guide the counsels of Mr Churchill's Government. Unfortunately this has not been the case!

For two years living in a neutral country I have been able through the haze of propaganda to reach something which my conscience tells me is the truth.

That is why I come forward tonight without any political label, without any bias, but just simply as an Englishman to say to you: a crime is being committed against Civilization![37]

Anyone hoping for reasoned argument after the rhetorical flourishes of his introduction was to be disappointed. Amery's listeners were now treated to a disquisition on how the heritage of the British Empire was being thrown away as a result of Britain's alliances with the Soviet Union and the United States; not surprisingly, the hidden hand behind both Allies are the Jews.

. . . our alliance with the Soviets! What is that really? Is it not an alliance with a people whose leader Stalin dreams of nothing but the destruction of that heritage of our fathers? Morally this is a stain on our honour, practically it can only lead sooner or later to disaster and Communism in Britain . . .[38]

But, we learn, we are pursuing this alliance blinded by Jewish propaganda:

There is not one, not one single great daily paper in London that is not Jewish-controlled, not one news reel; it's so easy to check it at Somerset House. You are being lied to, your patriotism, your love for our England is being exploited by people who for the most part hardly have the right to pretend to be English. Of course in a thing like Dieppe, Emanuel Shinwell and the rest of the Jewish clique, Leslie Hore Belisha for example, don't care very much about the two or three thousand Christians that died there.[39]

Not surprisingly, John did not add the name of Leopold Amery to his list of successful Jews in British politics.

This incoherent drivel continued as Amery railed at 'English priests' who were apparently calling on God to help the Bolshevik armies, even though the Soviets were attempting to crush 'gallant little Finland'. 'We have been betrayed,' he cried, 'we have been sold out to the international interests of New York and Moscow, who will not hesitate to leave us once they have sucked up all our resources, when the last Englishman has died for their criminal war.'[40]

Up until this point, Amery's text had shown no evidence of the influence of Hesse or Haferkorn, or Ribbentrop, for that matter, but the central passage of his tirade does in fact reveal a calmer and more assured propagandist hand, capable of rising above the anti-Semitic cat-calling which characterizes Amery's material:

Ask yourselves just one question only: Is this war really necessary? Who are these men who are urging you to go on and on? Who are those men who persistently undermined any possibility of coming to reasonable terms with Germany? There is more than enough room in the world for Germany and Britain. Your leaders say Germany seeks world domination. Did it ever enter your mind that this is but another trick of that long-planned strategy of Jewish propaganda, expected to thwart Germany's commanding position on the Continent, to which she is after all entitled?

Whereas Germany never – and you know this – denied Britain her Imperial position. It is up to you to say the word, to come slowly, gradually, but irresistibly back to common sense.[41]

This passage is important because it was a principal theme of Nazi propaganda aimed at Britain, as well as restating Germany's – in fact Hitler's – position in relation to Britain. As recently as 3 September, Hitler had held forth on this theme over dinner at his forward headquarters in the Ukraine: 'We must persist in our assertion that we are waging war, not on the British people, but on the small clique who rule them. It is a slogan which promises good results. If we say we are fighting the British Empire to the death, then obviously we shall drive even the last of them to arms against us . . .'[42] Indeed, the section quoted above is clearly the only part of Amery's speech which was inserted by the German Foreign Office. From the propaganda point of view, however, its impact is entirely swamped by the sea of juvenile racism which surrounds it: the very next paragraph is a suggestion that Britons should feel ashamed that the only two candidates in a recent election for Lord Mayor of London were both Jewish.

The conclusion of the first broadcast was almost surreal in its imbecility:

. . . so long as the German Government allows me, I shall be here to help you, to guide you, that we all may see again the sun of peace rise over Europe! Between you and peace stands only the Jew and his tool, namely the Bolshevik and American Governments. I am saying that not as a defeatist but as a patriot whose primary concern is the preservation of the British Empire.[43]

At which point the recording ended and the continuity announcer informed the listeners that:

You have been listening to Mr John Amery, son of the British Secretary of State for India, the Right Honourable Leopold Stennet Amery. We should like to remind you of the fact that Mr John Amery spoke in his own name and that the German Government bears no responsibility for what Mr Amery has said.[44]

The first Amery broadcast caused considerable interest in the British national and regional press, which quickly picked up that he seemed to be enunciating some kind of peace offer. As far as the Amery family were concerned, it is difficult to imagine the anguish that they must have felt listening to John: Leo was well aware of how his elder son's actions would be viewed by the prosecuting authorities in Britain. Bryddie Amery appears to have gone into denial: in a letter to a friend, intercepted and copied by MI5, she claimed that the voice that she had heard was not John's, but that of someone who sounded like him.[45] In a kind-hearted gesture of support, Winston Churchill asked his old friend to travel with him to a commemoration at Harrow School, offering his sympathy for the family's misery.

In the wake of the first broadcast, and as a 'teaser' for the second, Amery gave an interview to another 'Transocean' correspondent which was put out over the wires on 25 November. A classic tabloid article, it reiterated many of the lies and fantasies that underpinned John Amery's public persona:

'Many Englishmen who share my views would now be in Berlin if there was no channel between England and the Continent,' declared John Amery, son of the Secretary for India, the Right Honourable Amery [sic], when I interviewed him at the Hotel Adlon in Unter den Linden on Wednesday. This small, dark-haired man in the early thirties, young Amery might be taken for a native of France, where he lived for many years. The inglorious collapse of the Third Republic made a profound impression on young Amery, who stresses however that he was anti-Communist and anti-Semitic ever since he left Harrow.

John Amery had ample occasion to study the Jews. He saw Zionist leaders at his father's house in England and he was no longer surprised that British press reports on the situation in Palestine completely ignored the Arab viewpoint, when he began to realize that the British press was virtually controlled by Jews. He knew what Communism means from his own experiences during the Civil War in Spain. He saw Madrid immediately after its liberation from the Red yoke and he thus knows what he is talking about.

In view of his anti-Communist and anti-Jewish attitude, young Amery was frequently shabbily attacked by the British press. He admits that there might be some truth in some of the charges brought against him by British papers, but he emphatically denies he was fired from Eton school, as some Swedish paper recently asserted. John Amery has travelled a great deal, and he has studied conditions in many countries. He has been in Abyssinia and speaks with disgust of 'the damned slavery and barbarism under the regime of the Negus'. He knows practically all countries of Europe, paid at least ten visits to Germany.

In the year 1939 he rushed to Prague to witness the entry of German troops into that city. In the preceding year he had just crossed the Swiss-Austrian frontier on the eve of the entry of German troops into Austria. He spent the entire night with German officers in Feldkirch and then accompanied German Panzers to Vienna in his Hispano-Suiza car. John Amery stresses that he has no political ambitions.

'I left England because I could no longer bear to see my country governed against its own interests. Since 1930 I have lived in France as a private man and I hope to live in the same way after the war.' When I asked Amery for the reasons which prompted him to enter politics by addressing the British people over the radio from Berlin, he explained, 'I considered it my duty to tell the British people that they are not fighting for England as they believe. They will be fighting for England only when they are fighting side by side with the Germans on the Eastern front.' Amery frankly expressed his views when he was still living in unoccupied France, by writing a series of articles for *Éclaireur de Nice* early in May this year. Since he was convinced that he could do more effective work from Berlin, he asked the German authorities to allow him to come to Berlin. Permission was granted by the German authorities, and travelling under the name 'John Brown', young Amery arrived in Berlin at the end of October, accompanied by his pet dog Sammy, who during this interview was peacefully slumbering, curled up under his master's chair.

When I asked John Amery what his father might be thinking of his son's present activities he declared after brief reflection, 'My father is doing what he considers to be the right thing, and he knows that I am doing the same.' Through his godfather, British Ambassador in Madrid Sir Samuel Hoare, young Amery had during his stay in occupied France still been in contact and communication with his family in England. Relatively recently he received a cordially worded letter from his father. 'You cannot expect an old man and Right Honourable like my father to find a way out of the old rut, but a large and growing number of young people in England are thinking the same way as myself.'[46]

The pomposity and self-aggrandisement of this interview give a good idea of how Amery's mind was working at this time: it is quite clear that he greatly enjoyed the flattery and attention he received as a result of his new project and that he is retrospectively applying it to aspects of his past which fitted in with his new role: his random wanderings around Europe become 'studies' of 'conditions'; his brief visits to Spain in 1939 and 1940 are transmuted into participation in the Civil War; his single letter to a French newspaper becomes a 'series of articles'. It is a commonplace but entirely false belief that Third Reich propaganda was routinely deliberately untrue: in fact it was Propaganda Ministry policy to stay as close to the known facts as possible. The reason for this is straightforward: the more often a given news source is shown to be false, the less credibility is allowed it by its audience. German propaganda broadcasters often got their facts wrong, but they rarely made them up: 'white' propaganda achieves its impact by the 'spin' it imparts to stories, not by falsification. This strongly suggests that the inventions in this interview are Amery's own rather than the journalist's or the Propaganda Ministry's.

The second talk to be broadcast shows much greater focus than the first effort and was evidently much more closely edited within the Foreign Ministry. If anything, Amery's first talk was characterized by confusion: he was unable to sustain an argument or train of thought for more than one paragraph at a time. The second talk, although a nasty piece of racist propaganda, is actually coherent:

I am going tonight to expose to you two questions of the very greatest interest to us all: firstly whether any interest has been or is being served by our declaration of war against Germany, and secondly whether victory as it is at present seen and understood in London, is really a British victory or even a desirable thing at all.[47]

Amery's argument is that the British declaration of war against Germany in 1939 was unjustified because no British interest or community was threatened by the Germans. In fact, we learn, the group that is most affected by German expansion in Eastern Europe is, of course, the Jews: 'the international Jewish trusts had suffered by the action of the German National Socialist authorities very heavy practical and moral losses. I am not here to discuss whether the steps taken against these trusts were justified or not . . .'[48] Apparently these international trusts were sufficiently forceful to compel Neville Chamberlain to make his declaration of war in September 1939, notwithstanding the efforts of the 'Italian, Spanish and Belgian' Governments to prevent the outbreak of hostilities 'or, at least, to limit them to Poland'.

We discover that

If you wish to look at Germany in good faith you can find abundant proof that Germany does not seek an extension of her power which is not as over-reaching as propaganda would wish you to believe: extension of living space – yes! But World Domination – no! A certain sensational type of yellow journalism attempts to identify the present day fact of a largely German occupied Europe – which is an automatic result of war, after all – as a *lasting* prospect for 'poor haunted Europe'.[49]

This is an extraordinary statement to have emanated from an official German propaganda source – the language is too measured to be

Amery's – and we must assume that it was written by Hesse or Haferkorn, or even Ribbentrop, to represent Germany's negotiating stance at the close of 1942: that Hitler would withdraw from parts of occupied Europe at least, and would make no territorial demands against Britain and the Empire in the event of a negotiated peace. The rest of the talk, however, is obviously Amery's, as he jibes at Jewish bankers and Jewish members of the Bolshevik revolutionary leadership from the 1920s, seeking to link the two.

The desire for a negotiated peace in the West was probably now in the forefront of the minds of the German leadership. On 19 November, the very day that Amery's first talk had been broadcast, General Zhukov, Deputy Supreme Commander of the Red Army, launched operation URANUS, a massive strike against the 3rd and 4th Romanian Armies, which had been assigned to protect the flanks of Paulus's 6th Army as it struggled for control of Stalingrad. Zhukov's plan worked very well: the Romanians collapsed under the first assaults and by 23 November, 6th Army was encircled in a pocket in and to the west of Stalingrad, trapping nearly 250,000 soldiers, together with their equipment. This news was kept secret in Germany until mid-January – Amery would certainly not have known of it – nevertheless, the desperate airlift attempted by the Germans, and the efforts of Army Group Don to re-establish contact with 6th Army threw into sharp relief Hitler's pressing need to resolve the war on at least one front.

The theme of the third broadcast, condemnation of Britain's interference in European affairs, was again clearly dictated by the German Foreign Office. By seeking to maintain a European balance of power, Amery argued, Britain had been exercising an unwarranted influence over Europe which was entirely unnecessary because Britain had at its disposal an Empire which is: 'a self-contained unit capable of giving for hundreds of years all the outlet our people need. Capable of supplying the home country, in abundance and more, with all the things we can possibly need.'[50] By implication, the German position is restated: Germany will not interfere with Britain and the Empire if Britain leaves Germany and the other European states to sort themselves out.

The fourth and fifth broadcasts are aberrations, bearing no obvious traces of input from Amery's paymasters. The fourth takes the form of an attack on the American contribution to the war and, particularly, on American involvement in the TORCH landings in North Africa. In the first instance we are assured that the Americans were only able to land in France as the result of the sacrifice of British lives and shipping in the transport and escort fleets. These losses will mean further food shortages in Britain but the actual end result will be: 'that the Jews of the ghettoes of Algiers, of Oran, stabbing the backs of the French soldiers who have so long defended them, were able to embrace the soldiers in the pay of World Jewry, to found the beginning of American and Jewish domination over Africa. Africa has always been a European hunting ground: what is America doing there?'[51] Of course, what will happen is that American Jewry will take over the British Empire, American soldiers will eat the British people's meagre food rations and rape their wives 'in the name of democratic solidarity'.

The fifth talk is a similar attack upon the Soviet Union and Bolshevism. The essential theme is that whilst the Soviets are Britain's ally, they are none the less plotting against the Empire: Stalin is holding back troops in the Caucasus to invade India; and even if he does not invade *per se*, the Soviets may decide to retreat into India instead. The problem with Bolsheviks is that they are, of course, Jews: 'Bolshevism is the most terrible menace that exists. In every country they have organized an element of trouble from the riff-raff — an element of trouble which menaces England's social fabric and her Empire . . .'[52]

The final two broadcasts in the series are complementary and, again, reflect the persistent themes of German 'friendly' propaganda: the close cultural and racial ties between Britain and Germany, and the benefits to be accrued from a peace settlement:

Let us look closer – we see that the Germanic and Anglo-Saxon races are near cousins, and are in our hemisphere the two dominating and allied Nordic races. Religiously we see in both Empires a Protestant majority, a large Catholic minority and, even to this day – the Jewish question apart – a basic principle common to both nations of religious toleration based on 'render unto God what is God's and unto Caesar what is Caesar's'.[53]

The reason that antagonism has arisen between the British and German peoples is that the Jewish-controlled press has whipped it up: Amery does not regard the war as a factor.

The final broadcast had a wistful, almost regretful, valedictory air to it:

Don't you see how marvellous it will be to see all the lights of Piccadilly Circus again? How much better life will be when one can have a drink amongst Englishmen in an English pub, without the American soldier, the insolent Jew, the professional Communist agitator.

And above all to have your husband back, to look at your child and to know he will never grow up to see the horrors we have seen.[54]

Amery had recorded ten talks but only seven in the series were broadcast before they were discontinued 'as there was no response from Britain and as the Japanese complained about the political tendencies of these talks'.[55] In fact Amery himself was dissatisfied: 'It was absurd for me as an Englishman to talk about us all getting together if five minutes later from the same station another Englishman was to yell out abuse of my countrymen.'[56]

Amery's recollection was that he decided: 'to betake myself to Paris to talk these matters over with my French friends and to consider what next might be done under these circumstances'. Hesse's recollection was that 'I then sent Amery back to Paris, to have a good time and enjoy himself.'[57]

The last talk went out on New Year's Eve, 1942. In the Caucasus, 6th Army's situation was becoming increasingly desperate: an attempt by General Hoth's 4th Panzer Army to reach 6th Army had stalled in the face of another large Soviet operation. In Libya, Panzer Armee Afrika was in full retreat towards Tunisia. At the Rundfunkhaus in Berlin-Charlottenberg, the English Service's celebrity propagandist was appearing by courtesy of a black lacquer recording disc, recorded some weeks beforehand: the bird had flown. On 17 December, accompanied by his prostitute mistress, Walter Plack his German minder, Sammy the Pomeranian and, most importantly of all, his unlimited expense account, John Amery had booked into the Hôtel Bristol in Paris.[58]

9. 'I Personally Have No Great Belief in This Unit'

The secondary, military strand running through John Amery's treason was the creation of a British anti-Bolshevik legion to fight against the Soviets on the Eastern Front; an idea, as we have seen, that was clearly derived from his friend Jacques Doriot's Légion des Volontaires Français (LVF). The LVF had been brought into being after a meeting in Paris in July 1941. Leaders of the collaborationist groups had gathered at the Hôtel Majestic in response to the German invasion of Russia, and had agreed to sponsor a French military force to fight alongside the Germans. The Vichy regime was extremely unenthusiastic but was not in a position to block the move, whilst Hitler personally welcomed it, though stipulating that the force should consist of no more than 15,000 men.

The original plan conceived by Doriot and Marcel Déat, that the LVF would fight in French uniforms, was vetoed by the Wehrmacht who pointed out that this would be contravening international law unless France declared war on the Soviets. Instead, they were to wear German field-grey and fight as a unit of the German army, though equipped with a distinguishing French badge. Consequently, in September 1941, the first drafts of volunteers began to move towards the Heidelager training area at Debica in Poland, where they were to be worked up as a military unit.

Although Hitler had placed a ceiling of 15,000 on the size of the unit, in reality no more than 13,400 men ever volunteered and nearly 8,000 of these proved to be unsuitable, either on medical grounds (mostly as the result of bad teeth!), or because of their criminal records.[1] Nevertheless, one of those who were successful in joining was Doriot himself, who entered the LVF in his old

French army rank of sergeant-major. After an initial baptism of
fire in the fighting before Moscow in the autumn and winter of
1941–2, the LVF spent two years participating in the vicious
anti-partisan warfare that took place in areas bypassed by the Germans during their initial advance into the Soviet Union.

John Amery was at least realistic enough not to imagine that he
could attract as many recruits for his British legion as the LVF had
gained: he thought it would be enough to have a few hundred men
available for propaganda uses rather than forming a proper combat
unit, and he undoubtedly saw himself as playing a significant role
in the British legion. This particular ambition was not, however,
shared by his German sponsors, and certainly not by the Waffen-SS
which eventually assumed responsibility for the unit. In fact, it was
recognized that an intensive psychological campaign would be
necessary to persuade anti-Bolshevik British POWs to change their
allegiance, and it was quite obvious that Amery had neither the
application nor the ability to contribute much, if anything, in this
direction. According to Dr Hesse, 'Amery was kept in ignorance
of what was really being done, as the whole affair of the British
Free Corps was a first-class state secret, but he frequently came back
to the idea of creating such a body. I do not think he ever knew
exactly what was the position.'[2]

Hesse was distinctly unenthusiastic about the British legion: 'I
gave it as my opinion that the whole plan was extremely difficult
and that I thought it practically impossible to get British people to
fight for Germany as long as war between Germany and Britain
existed, even if these people were promised that they would only
be used against the Russians . . .'[3] Hesse believed that the first
essential would be to try to create a better psychological climate
among potential recruits by improving conditions for British
POWs in Germany and accordingly, he pressed for two significant
changes.

The first of these was the establishment of two holiday centres
for British prisoners where they would be allowed better food and
a range of freedoms that were not possible in the highly restrictive

'Stalags'* and working parties in which most prisoners spent their time; the second was the distribution of English-language anti-Bolshevik propaganda among POWs. These ideas were accepted and implemented during the first half of 1943, with Hesse and the England Committee acting as advisors to the POW Department of the Wehrmacht High Command (OKW). As liaison officer between the Foreign Office and the OKW, Hesse appointed a publisher who had previously worked for the Propaganda Ministry and had been an internee in Britain during the First World War, Arnold Hillen-Ziegfeld.

There is a popular myth of life in German POW camps during the Second World War, fuelled by film and television, which is completely at odds with reality. In the mythical version prisoners lived a relatively comfortable life, organizing games, sports and amateur theatricals to pass the time while secretly plotting escapes, fuelled by the contents of Red Cross food parcels and ingenious raids on German food-stores. In reality, prisoners were subjected to a somewhat harsher regime. The first point to make is that although officer prisoners had a lot of time to kill, soldiers were obliged to work and their NCOs were required to supervise them. Under the Geneva Conventions on the treatment of POWs, they could not be made to work in any capacity that would be directly contributory to the German war effort, but there were plenty of grey areas, and many prisoners found themselves doing back-breaking labour in quarries and coal-mines, on building sites and road projects. The food they were given by the Germans, though supposed to be of the same type and quality given to depot troops, was anything but that: rations were meagre and unwholesome and, had they not been supplemented by food parcels from Britain, which were delivered by the International Red Cross, starvation and malnutrition would have been widespread (at the end of the war, when the Red Cross parcel system did finally break down, long-term POWs did indeed begin to die from malnutrition).

---

* *Stammlager*, the main POW camps.

Along with the immense psychological stress of capture, prisoners also had to contend with frequent breakdowns in discipline resulting from the circumstances of their captivity: the strict hierarchies of military units were broken up and often relatively junior, inexperienced officers and NCOs were left in command of large bodies of men who neither knew, respected nor necessarily much liked them. The Germans interacted with the prisoners' leaders or 'confidence men', passing on orders and instructions and leaving the prisoners to organize themselves to the best of their abilities, while keeping an eye on them through specialist security personnel. Known to the prisoners as 'ferrets', these men were normally Sonderführer of the Wehrmacht, English-speaking civilians called-up for non-combatant military service.

The result of the general treatment of British POWs during the first three years of the war was that the two 'holiday camps' that were to be set up were necessary and welcome but also regarded with the most intense suspicion, and this was compounded by the British POWs who were selected to run them.

Among the 100,000 or so British prisoners of war who were then in German hands, it is not entirely surprising that a few had emerged, over and above the small number already working for the Büro Concordia and the Deutsches Rundfunk, who were more or less sympathetic with National Socialism or who were sufficiently corrupt to seek advantage by pretending to be so. The most significant amongst this group is a fascinating character, John Henry Owen 'Busty' Brown, a Battery Quartermaster Sergeant of the Royal Artillery, who was captured on 29 May 1940 as he attempted to get to Dunkirk.

Despite his rank, equivalent to that of a staff sergeant* in the rest of the British army, Brown had very limited military experience, having been a member of the Territorial Army – the part-time reserve – for less than a year at the time of his capture. His real employment was as an office manager for Truman's Brewery in the

---

* In US terms, he ranked as an E-5.

East End of London. In fact Brown was a graduate of Oxford University – unusual for a British army NCO – but even stranger was his political background: 'Busty' Brown, the educated white-collar worker called up to fight against National Socialist expansionism, was also 'Teddy' Brown of the British Union of Fascists and National Socialists, perhaps the most senior and committed member of the BUF to fall into German hands.

BUF colleagues of 'Teddy' Brown remember him as an enthusiastic and long-term partisan of the organization, clever but fond of a rough-house on the streets of Whitechapel and Bethnal Green against the hated Reds and of course their Jewish co-conspirators.[4] The details of Brown's early career as a POW are somewhat obscure, and in the absence of outside evidence and the full version of the statement he gave to MI5 investigators at the end of the war★ one must rely – with caution– on the memoir which Brown wrote after the war and which was published posthumously in 1979.[5] In this, Brown describes being taken to Stalag VIIIb at Lamsdorff in Germany, and from there being posted as foreman of a group of thirty or so British POW labourers at a work camp, Arbeitskommando E/3 at Blechhammer, where nearly 20,000 British and other prisoners were constructing an artificial rubber and oil plant.

Brown describes gaining the confidence of the German POW camp hierarchy on the basis of his welfare work on behalf of his men, his Christianity, his education and his rational demeanour; in reality, it is evident that Brown worked hard to ingratiate himself with the Germans and that he managed to surround himself, from an early stage, with a coterie of BUF members who acted as his assistants. In the straitened circumstances of the POW camp system, Brown soon became a major black-market baron, trading with his

---

★ This has yet to emerge in its entirety, although a number of extracts from it are in MI5 and Home Office files in the PRO. It is possible that the full version contains details of how Brown was able to communicate with MI9 which remain secret.

German captors – and with others as well – in a wide range of goods; some of these were undoubtedly used for the benefit of his fellow prisoners, others were utilized for Brown's own ends.

In February 1942, Brown was transferred from Blechhammer to Stalag IIId at Steglitz, a suburb of Berlin, which was used as a special POW camp to administer prisoners of particular interest to the German military and civilian authorities. Brown describes a brief meeting with William Joyce whom he claimed to 'know by sight' from before the war – in reality, he knew Joyce well from the latter's days as BUF Director of Propaganda[6] – but in other ways is reticent about what he did in Berlin, glossing over the episode in a few pages of his book: in fact he spent seven months in Berlin before returning to Blechhammer in August 1942.

At some point during the autumn of the same year, Captain Julius Green, a Jewish Glaswegian dentist, arrived at Blechhammer to tend to the prisoners there. Green was evidently a difficult customer for the Germans to deal with – according to Brown, 'even the [British] Sergeant-Majors were shocked by his behaviour'[7] and he eventually wound up in the notorious Colditz Castle as a result of his obduracy – but he was in possession of the secret letter-writing codes developed by MI9* for covert communication with Britain, and he passed these on to Brown.

Had Captain Green noticed some special qualities in BQMS Brown that were not evident to the other British senior NCOs and warrant officers at Blechhammer, who universally believed him to be sailing close to the wind of collaboration? Probably not; Green's attitude to security was reckless in the extreme. In March 1944 he gave a tour of the prisoners' quarters of Colditz to Sub-Lieutenant Walter Purdy, a former BUF member and renegade naval officer who had just been confined there after going absent without leave from the Concordia Büro in Berlin, for whom he

---

* The service of the British War Office designed to exploit the intelligence potential of POWs in captivity; to train the armed forces in escape and evasion; and to organize escape and evasion lines in occupied territory.

was a regular broadcaster. In the course of this brief tour, Green managed to show Purdy the entrance to a tunnel that was being dug by British prisoners and to tell him about Brown's activities as an MI9 correspondent – information Purdy promptly used to buy his freedom (although it is worth mentioning that the British prisoner hierarchy had delivered a threat to the German Kommandant that Purdy would be executed if he was not removed). It is likely that Green passed the codes on to Brown simply because he seemed bright enough to use them.

In his memoir, Brown claims that he was initiated into the secret code system before the outbreak of war, but this claim is contradicted in one of the extracts from his statement which appears in Intelligence files; there he claims to have been able to communicate with Britain 'from about the end of 1942'.[8] Thus he had cleverly placed himself in a position whereby he could legitimately cosy up with the Third Reich as a known and trusted British Fascist without compromising his position at home at the end of the war. He was careful never to do too much on behalf of the Germans: he neither broadcast nor joined the British legion, but he did enough to become their trusted intermediary in various matters and to ensure his own material comforts and those of his small group of assistants; it is worth noting that when most British POWs were on a near-starvation diet towards the end of 1944, photographs of Brown show a bulky and clearly well-fed man. So it was that during the early half of 1943 Brown was approached by the Germans to act as the camp leader at the other ranks' holiday camp at Genshagen in the south-western suburbs of Berlin and agreed without hesitation.

Together with Brown, the Germans assembled a small staff of British POWs, many of whom had been with Brown at Blechhammer, to run Genshagen and set the correct moral tone. Bombardier Fred Blewitt, evidently a genial individual despite his former membership of the London BUF, was 'confidence man'. The immediate medical needs of the prisoner-holidaymakers would be met by Sergeant Frank McLardy of the Royal Army Medical Corps

(RAMC) and Lance Corporal Gordon Bowler of the Queen Victoria Rifles: McLardy had been district secretary of the Formby BUF and Bowler an East End activist. In charge of discipline was Corporal Francis Maton of 50 Commando, also, as it happens, a BUF member from the East Midlands. Running the library and canteen was Sergeant Arthur Chapple, a Yorkshireman with a whining voice who had been mobilized as a NAAFI manager but was also, coincidentally, an adherent of the BUF. In fact the only non-BUF sympathizer on the original Genshagen staff appears to have been Sergeant Trinder, a veteran of German POW camps during the First World War, who was in charge of hygiene and cleanliness.

Blewitt, Bowler and Trinder were members of Brown's clique, but Maton, McLardy and Chapple had all made themselves known to the Germans via different routes: both Maton and McLardy had already independently volunteered to serve in the Waffen-SS to help defeat the Soviet Union.

Genshagen opened in June 1943 as a hutted camp of eighteen rooms, with a wash-house and a concert hall, built around a field which would have made a good football pitch had it not been criss-crossed with air-raid trenches. Soon after the British staff had been installed, yet another strange character turned up: this time, a British Waffen-SS NCO, Thomas Cooper.

Cooper was born in London in 1919 and brought up as the pampered only child of his English father, Ashley Cooper, a photographer and commercial artist, and Anna-Maria, his German wife. Educated at the prestigious Latymer Upper School,★ a mile or two from the family home in Brook Green in west London, Cooper was a cranky loner who made no close friends at school. When he left in 1936, having matriculated, he did not go on to

★ A 'direct grant' grammar school in Hammersmith, West London, established in 1624 by the Edward Latymer foundation to provide education for the 'poor lads' of the borough. By the early twentieth century it had become a key route through which the middle classes of west London got their sons to university.

university – the usual route for Old Latymerians – but instead sought to join government service, investigating career possibilities in the Foreign Office, the Royal Air Force, the Navy and the Metropolitan Police. He failed to enter any of these professions, ascribing this to the fact that his mother was German, although she had acquired British nationality on marrying his father in 1910; instead, he joined a firm of essential oil importers in the East End and began to fall increasingly under the spell of the organizer of the Hammersmith branch of the BUF.

As Thomas Cooper slumped into a slough of petulant teenage despond at his failure to make a huge impact in life, his parents began to look for a way to improve things. Having made the necessary enquiries, and filled out the necessary forms, they ascertained that the German Academic Exchange Organization, based in Russell Square, ran a working-visit scheme under the auspices of the Reichs Arbeitsdienst (RAD), a German militarized labour force. This would enable Tom to acquire work experience while improving his German language skills and visiting his mother's family.

In July 1939 Tom and his mother duly took the boat train from London to Chemnitz to stay with her family, before moving on to other relatives in Stuttgart where the RAD camp was also situated. There they found disappointment: the office in London had failed to complete the paperwork correctly and Tom had not been allocated a place on the scheme: he could not enter the camp. He and his mother stayed with their relatives while they attempted to sort out the problem, but after a week with no further progress, his mother left to return to London and Tom resolved to follow a few days later.

Then, out of the blue, the situation changed. The day before Tom was due to set out for home, a letter arrived for him from the RAD, offering him a post teaching English at a school in the Taunus mountains. He jumped at the opportunity and began work there on 20 August 1939, seemingly oblivious to the international situation.

Everything changed with the outbreak of war. On 5 September Tom was summoned by the school principal to be told that as he was an enemy alien he could no longer be employed, and that he must immediately report to the Ordnungs Polizei (Orpo) in Frankfurt am Main to register as an enemy alien. As a bewildered twenty-year-old, he did just this and from there was ordered to report to the headquarters of the Exchange Organization in Berlin. Three days later, while still in Berlin, he was arrested by Orpo who, believing him to be an enemy citizen of military age, intended to have him interned. At this point his mother's assiduous groundwork intervened: among the many forms that had been filled out correctly in anticipation of his stay in Germany was an application for him to be considered an ethnic German (*Volksdeutscher*) and he had duly been issued a certificate to that effect.

As a *Volksdeutscher* in the hyper racially-conscious Third Reich, Cooper was in some ways in a fortunate position: he was not liable for internment because he was recognized as a fellow German, but at the same time he could not be called up for military service because he was a citizen of one of the enemy powers. Nevertheless, the problem that he now faced was to maintain himself on his own, completely cut off from his hitherto very protective family. He managed this for a few months but in January 1940, in a state of near desperation, he decided that he would join the German army.

In fact he could not. The Wehrmacht did not accept recruits from foreign countries, particularly not from the principal enemy power. Instead Cooper was directed to the main recruiting office of the Waffen-SS where, after a medical, an interview and an examination of his racial antecedents, he was accepted as a recruit for the premier élite unit of the Waffen-SS, the Leibstandarte Adolf Hitler.

After basic recruit training, Cooper was posted first to the Leibstandarte's artillery regiment and subsequently, in March 1940, presumably because of the impending military action against British forces in which the Leibstandarte was to be heavily involved, to a different unit of the Waffen-SS, the Totenkopfverbände or Death's Head units.★ The Leibstandarte was by no means an unsullied part of the Waffen-SS, but the SS-Totenkopfverbände had blood all over their hands. Formed from the paramilitary units set up to guard the concentration camps for political and ethnic enemies of the National Socialist regime, it provided personnel – one hesitates to describe them as soldiers – to perform a variety of unsavoury tasks.

Cooper proved a capable soldier. Given temporary NCO status, his first role in the 5th Totenkopf Infantry Regiment based at Oranienburg, north of Berlin, was to train new recruits in the use of indirect fire from machine-guns and he was soon promoted to the substantive rank of Rottenführer (roughly equivalent to a lance-corporal in the British army). Late in 1940, his unit was redeployed as a garrison unit to Plock on the Vistula river in Poland, and in March 1941 he was sent to the Waffen-SS NCO school at Lauenburg in Pomerania.

Cooper's NCO course finished in May 1941 when he was sent to join yet another new unit, a detachment of the Wachbataillon Oranienburg based at the SS training centre of Heidelager, near Debica, nor far from Krakow in Poland, and he was shortly afterwards promoted to Unterscharführer. It is fairly clear that during his service with this unit Cooper was involved in a number of activities that were unambiguous crimes against humanity.

The ostensible task of Cooper's unit was the security of the Heidelager area and '[to] guard the Polish and *other* prisoners at work'[9] – a group made up of Soviet POWs, forced civilian labourers and possibly Jews as well – but the unit was also available for tasks in neighbouring towns, and Cooper spent some time regaling the British Fascists at Genshagen with stories of his military career. Francis Maton later recalled one such account:

★ It is likely that this was because of the forthcoming invasion of Western Europe. The Waffen-SS might well have considered that Cooper would have been placed in an impossible position by having to fight against British troops.

One story which always stands out in my mind, told by Cooper, is one he told me about Warsaw. He said he was at that time in charge of a squad of Ukrainian volunteers and they were conducting a purge through the ghetto. His attention was drawn to a house by reason of loud screams issuing from the back of it. On going inside the house he found in the top flat a bunch of these Ukrainians holding at bay with pistols some twenty Jews. On asking them what the noise was about they told him in broken German that they had found a new way of killing Jews. This was done simply by opening the window wide and two men each grabbing an arm and a leg and flinging the Jew through the open window. The small children and babies followed their parents because they said they would only grow into big Jews.[10]

Cooper's Polish sojourn lasted until the beginning of 1943 when he and his fellow NCOs were transferred into the SS–Polizei Division and sent to the Eastern Front near Leningrad. Within days of arrival, Cooper was severely wounded in the legs by a Soviet artillery barrage and evacuated. He was convalescing at a hospital near Nijmegen in the occupied Netherlands when he was transferred to act as a recruiter at Genshagen.

Another who arrived at this time was Lance Corporal Roy Courlander, a member of 2771 Intelligence Section of 18th Bn, the New Zealand Expeditionary Force (NZEF). Courlander was born in London, but as one of his two stepfathers had owned land in the New Hebrides he had lived in Auckland from an early age, although he had received part of his education at an English boarding school. After joining the NZEF in 1939, he had served in the Western Desert campaign between June 1940 and February 1941 and had then been sent to Greece. From the moment they arrived there, the Commonwealth forces were involved in a rearguard action against the German invaders that culminated in surrender on 29 April 1941 under Brigadier Parrington at Kalamata. After a period acting as interpreter in his POW camp, Courlander volunteered to serve against the Soviets on the Eastern Front, possibly because he saw this as a means of escape, more likely because he simply wanted to widen his options in case Germany did win the war. As soon as Genshagen was set up, Courlander was transferred there, and even before the British legion project had got off the ground, he was spending part of his days reading scripts for 'Radio National'.

The point about people like Brown, Courlander and Cooper is that they were cleverer, better educated, far more organized – and indeed saner – than Amery. They could see the benefits to themselves from their involvement in aspects of the British legion in a way that Amery could not. It is fair to guess that one of the main reasons for John suggesting the formation of the British legion in the first place was simply so that he could emulate his idol Jacques Doriot.

The most significant German figure at Genshagen was the Sonderführer, Oskar Lange. Although actually an infantry lance-corporal, Lange had worked for several years as a longshoreman on the wharves of New York and spoke fluent English with a strong American accent. Known widely among prisoners at Stalag VIIIb at Lamsdorff, where he had originally worked, as 'Canadian Joe', he had allegedly shot and killed two British prisoners there in the early days of the war. Like many of the Germans associated with the British legion, Lange saw in it an opportunity for considerable personal advancement. Through his connections with other Sonderführer, Lange had an idea that might beef the British legion up into a proper unit. Friends of his at the nearby Luckenwalde POW camp ran a special compound where newly captured British prisoners were interrogated by a small team of renegade British and Canadian soldiers. Lange argued that this facility might be used to recruit for the British legion and accordingly a programme was put in place to use techniques of intimidation and conditioning against newly captured prisoners.

In one sense, intimidation was to prove a very effective means of gaining recruits for the British legion. In September and October 1943, sixteen recruits were netted by this method but, of course, they were hardly well motivated or enthusiastic, and when they were taken from Luckenwalde to their new billet in a disused café in Berlin, they soon discovered that they had been duped. The reason for this was that whilst they had been given the 'stick' of threats of violence and continuing bad treatment, they had been offered the 'carrot' of joining a powerful brigade of 1,500 soldiers, commanded by a British brigadier. When Hillen-Ziegfeld discovered what had happened, he offered the Britons the opportunity to go to a 'normal' POW camp, and the majority of them took it.

By now it had been decided that the British legion would be incorporated into the Waffen-SS and, at about the same time that the Luckenwalde experiment was taking place, recruiting was taken away from the direct control of the OKW and placed in the hands of the chief of the SS-Hauptamt, SS-Obergruppenführer Gottlob Berger, who was responsible to Heinrich Himmler, the Reichsführer-SS, for recruiting manpower for the rapidly expanding Waffen-SS. Berger was not overly enthusiastic – 'I personally have no great belief in this unit'[11] – but he was happy enough to start the ball rolling. Cooper and five of the earliest volunteers accordingly attended several meetings at the SS-Hauptamt where aims and priorities for the unit were thrashed out.

The first thing they fixed was a name: the British Free Corps (BFC) seemed suitably dramatic and was similar to the Freikorps Danmark, a Danish volunteer legion in the Waffen-SS (which would shortly be disbanded). John Amery had envisaged 'his' British legion as something of a prop to accompany his propaganda activities; he wanted to travel to European capitals to make his speeches with a small phalanx of soldiers available to pose for photographers, but the actual volunteers were completely against this. Several of them were undoubtedly sincere in their intention to fight against Bolshevism; some of them had come forward to escape the hard life of the POW camps; but they were united in their view that they were not going to traipse around Europe as the plaything of a drunken, dilettante playboy. With this in mind, Courlander told the SS of Amery's partly Jewish background (how he knew about this is a mystery) which ruled out the possibility of even honorary membership of the unit. Instead, until a suitable British candidate came forward, the BFC would have a German commander and was thus placed under the control of SS-Hauptsturmführer Hans Werner Roepke, an English-speaking lawyer who had been serving as an artillery officer with a Waffen-SS division on the Eastern Front.

The basic plan developed by the SS-Hauptamt was to attempt to create a British unit of platoon size or larger, which could then be incorporated into the elite Wiking division and used in action against the Soviets, accompanied by a furious blast of propaganda. With the right personnel, this might have proved possible, but with John Brown, a British Intelligence agent, acting as the kingpin of recruiting and propaganda efforts, it was doomed to failure. Having attracted no more than a handful of recruits from Genshagen, efforts were switched to direct recruiting tours by members of the BFC in and around POW camps and working parties.

The results of the BFC's own recruiting efforts were sufficiently ambiguous to persuade the Germans that they were worth persisting with. A steady trickle of volunteers came forward, but most had been recruited on the basis that they were getting out of their POW camps to have a good time at the Germans' expense, rather than to fight against the Soviets, and this caused a schism in the unit between the true believers and the opportunists. This meant that the numbers of men in the unit constantly fluctuated as individuals left, either disillusioned or deemed unsuitable, while others appeared to fill the gaps. Although a total of fifty-eight men joined the unit during the nearly two years of its existence, the strength never exceeded twenty-nine at any one time, and was usually around half that number.

The BFC formally came into being as a unit of the Waffen-SS in January 1944 and in the same month was stationed at Hildesheim near Hanover in western Germany, based at a Germanic studies centre in a former monastery. In October 1944, the then thirteen members of the BFC were sent to the SS-Pioneer School at Dresden to be trained as combat engineers, and in February 1945, in the wake of the massive British and American raids on the city,

they were moved back to Berlin and finally prepared for action
against the Soviets. Between 15 March 1945 and the final surrender,
about ten members of the BFC were attached to the 3rd Germanic
SS Panzer Corps to the north-east of Berlin. For a period they were
members of the armoured reconnaissance battalion of the 11th
SS Panzer Grenadier Division, but the senior German officers
responsible for them were sufficiently realistic about the outcome
of the war to realize that they might get themselves into serious
trouble by using the BFC men as combat soldiers: instead they
were reassigned as truck drivers, which is how they spent the rest
of the war. Following Hitler's suicide and the final German collapse,
they found themselves under the command of Tom Cooper in the
town of Schwerin where the majority were arrested by British
army officers – an inglorious end for the British Legion against
Bolshevism.

10. England Faces Europe

Back in Paris after the first series of broadcasts, things must have seemed considerably rosier to John: perhaps as good as they had ever been. With his German expense account in place on the orders of Ribbentrop himself, the fear of being without money had been lifted from his shoulders, and as a protégé of the German Government in occupied Paris, he was now a man of genuine consequence. On 17 December 1942, he and Jeanine booked into the Hôtel Bristol in Paris, under the disapproving eye of M. Vidal, the manager. Vidal, who had known the Amery family for some time, had had the opportunity to compare father and son: '[John] was too delicate and drank too much',[1] was his verdict; nor was he particularly impressed by the alias John had adopted, presumably for security reasons: he recognized 'Mr and Mrs John Brown' at once.

With the loose ends of his existence now firmly tied up, John could assume the pose of political man of affairs, which he swiftly did, moving back into the circle surrounding Jacques Doriot and the other significant ultra-collaborationist leader, Marcel Déat. In discussions with them he deplored German policies in occupied Europe:

The news from Russia was getting pretty bad and that in France worse.★ (All German occupied Europe in fact).

We were very disturbed. The problem, which amounted to a vicious circle, was this. We were partisans of a social revolution and of a getting

---

★ It is difficult to see how minor problems in the application of occupation policy in Amery's country of residence can be compared with the loss of an army of 250,000 men. His sense of proportion was always somewhat suspect.

together of all European nations in a customs union etcetera. The Germans however were controlling Europe and instead of, Norway excepted, carrying out any social revolution at all they were getting together with the reactionaries and what was worse the kind of people who were uniquely interested in getting rich quick at anybody's expense. Moreover they seemed to possess no one who understood the other nations of Europe, their people and mentality, and more especially the Latins; this was the rule amongst the Embassies and Army chiefs. Amongst the SS and Political Police (not to be confused with the Sipo or Gestapo) things were individually much better but carried little political weight, strange as it may seem. On the other hand the only people who were fighting the soviets seriously were the Germans . . . from that there was no getting away. Doriot's view was that it was better to go to the front in Russia and make things abundantly clear, 'and when I come back with the Iron Cross I will send this bloody Embassy to hell'. He thought, and I equally, that Vichy must be overthrown, peace made between Germany and France and an end of occupants and occupied, the creation of Europe. Déat's view leaned more to peaceful continual pressure on Abetz★ until he finally grasped it: 'he means well, he is badly surrounded, with time . . .'

And there we were. We had been right when we said sanctions would throw Italy into Germany's arms, we had been right when we said Franco would win, when we said France would collapse, when we said Russia was faking her fighting strength in the first Finnish war. Here on the eve of Stalingrad we were saying Russia will destroy us, and all Europe with us, the chances were we were right again and nobody had listened to us or ever seemed likely to do so . . . and we were not so many . . . but we must try somehow?[2]

Ignoring Amery's execrable prose style, one must still wonder at both his lack of grip on reality and his delusions of grandeur. His association with Jacques Doriot and, latterly, Marcel Déat as well,

---

★ Otto Abetz (1903–58), a Francophile Nazi and German Ambassador to France after the Armistice. As representative of the German Government, he was one of the *de facto* rulers of the country.

seems to have given him the false idea that he was a political thinker of some consequence: in reality his views were an odd mixture of Doriot's Fascist-Socialism and Leo Amery's Imperialism, leavened with the casual racism of the time and his own special brand of ugly anti-Semitism. Fired up with determination as the result of his meetings with his French friends, Amery headed back to Berlin to 'confront' Dr Hesse:

I returned to Berlin bearing numerous documents of my own, of Déat's and other people, confirming all that we had always said concerning the mad foreign policy that was being carried on.

I tackled Hesse again. He was a man who had never got over the criminal folly of the bombardment of England in '40–41 and he listened patiently to me. I told him that in my view we must create a British anti-Bolshevik Legion however small and that perhaps on the things going on in the other countries in Europe it would be possible for me to attempt to help some sort of improvement of the situation based on the following principle. If England saw that Europe was uniting against Bolshevism, she would come in as well, the problem would be shifted away from 'Germany the mad dog of Europe' to 'All collaborating to the common good'. I also told him that without delay I would write a short book.[3]

Amery did not know, because Hesse did not tell him, that plans were already well in hand for a British anti-Bolshevik legion but that it had been decided to keep John away from it. The book idea was one that Hesse was happy with: it fitted into his general framework for propaganda and might prove a useful propaganda tool, and with Hesse's blessing, Amery and Jeanine settled into their suite at the Kaiserhof Hotel and John began to write.

Surprisingly, perhaps, in a sustained effort of concentration, fortified by evenings at Berlin's better restaurants and cafés, and late-night drinking sessions at the Foreign Press Circle, a Propaganda Ministry-funded bar with telegraph and telephone facilities in the Fasanenstrasse, John managed to produce, by the end of

March, a 45,000-word manuscript describing what he believed to be the state of the British Empire in 1943 and portentously entitled *England Faces Europe*.

A detailed analysis of the text of *England Faces Europe*, published in Berlin in July 1943, is unnecessary: it is an unedifying read, consisting of crude anti-Semitic insults dressed up in the high-flown phrases of a semi-educated waster attempting to sound like a serious political commentator. It is, none the less, a useful guide to the basic prejudices, hatreds and misconceptions that motivated Amery and perhaps help to account in some ways for the course his life followed. It should go without saying, of course, that the great majority of opinions, 'facts' and allegations stated by Amery, which are described below, are ridiculous, idiotic and without foundation.

In Chapter One, 'The Underlying Reasons and Causes', Amery describes what he believes to be the general historical background to Britain's entry into the war, our relationship with Europe and our relationship with the Empire:

Once we had evolved beyond the concepts of an absolute monarchy, that is, from the end of the reign of James II, the real power in England became the 'City' as it is now called.

The parliament existed, but its members were from those early days only the agents and instruments of the great merchants.[4]

Experienced readers of anti-Semitic tracts will undoubtedly be able to predict how this argument will develop. In fact, Amery tells us, when this situation first arose, in the days of 'Merry England', the British standard of living was far superior to that available elsewhere but:

The one terrible fragility of this edifice was precisely this: 'He who controls the City controlled everything'. And our friends, the Jews, were beginning to come back to England again . . .

We can safely date the day on which the poison first permeated our body politic; the night after the Battle of Waterloo, when the House of Rothschild scored a greater victory than Wellington.[5]

The Rothschilds, Amery alleges, were more interested in trade with Europe than the Empire and although originally only a tiny minority in the 'City', 'The body politic was infected, even though the City remained British; day by day it carried with it more extra-national considerations which have ended in becoming anti-national.'

In the period prior to Queen Victoria, the expansion of trade with Europe had obstructed the development of the Empire, but not sufficiently, Amery contends, to prevent the Empire from developing by itself. Then came the era of Disraeli:

where the first dreams of world Jewry begin to become apparent, that is, to control first the City, to engage it in a policy of a balance of power in Europe, and, having thus eliminated possible enemies, to develop in a haphazard way the British Empire, but not in a commercial sense so much as in the sense of obtaining throughout the world vantage points, or pirates' nests, from which world domination might be achieved.

This attempt at world domination, however, could only work while we kept the rest of Europe at each other's throats. When the Jewish imposed system of the balance of power broke down, we had the First World War, which was followed by the arrival of Bolshevism in Europe. Europe then divided between two 'currents': 'that of the men who were decided to have their countries to themselves, and to expand and develop regardless of the City and international finance, and the Judao-plutocratic conception of a European conquest, not by the force of arms but by the force of gold'. Thus, he tells us, the Jews bought up the small countries of Europe one by one, and established control over the 'press . . . the cinema, the broadcasting, the key administrative positions and so forth'.

What follows is an extreme distortion of views which Leo Amery might once have recognized as his own: that the Empire was failing to live up to its full potential through lack of investment and through the inability of successive British Governments to recognize where the true 'national' interest lay. Naturally, this is the result of Jewish control over the levers of power. Oddly enough, John cites his own philo-Semitic, pro-Zionist (and, indeed, ethnically Jewish) father as a victim of the Jewish hold over the press:

Here was a politician with a brilliant record, and who had, moreover, sufficiently flirted with Jewry and international finance not to be accused of Fascism.

At the time of the Italo-Abyssinian war, realizing the folly of the Government's policy, he went up and down the country, and in a series of speeches, and by direct attacks on the Government in the House of Commons, he upheld the justice of Italy's claims and showed up the barbarity of the Negus★ and his nigger dictatorship. Not only did the great Jewish newspapers not once publish any of his utterances, when but a short time before his smallest declarations had been front-page news, but mysteriously none of his numerous directorships were renewed.

Thus the British Empire has become a 'jumping off point' for international Jewry to achieve world domination.

Chapter Two, 'Official Views and Conceptions', purports to describe how participation in the war has damaged the British Empire. It is a simple survey of events, described from John Amery's bleak and ignorant standpoint, and need not detain us long. His argument is that Britain has always sought to fight wars using Allies as proxies, but that German and Japanese successes had dried up this supply, and instead, Britain and the Empire had now become the proxy of American-based Jewish international financiers:

★ 'Ruler of Ethiopia' (Amharic), adopted as a term of abuse by Fascists in the 1930s.

Thus, but two and a half years since the City and Winston Churchill had embarked the British Empire in a war, to be conducted contrary to the most elementary, proved and sacrosanct principles of Imperial strategy, our Empire was trapped; trapped in a cul-de-sac that had no possible issue; where victory and defeat were equal, and complete ends to the heritage our fathers left in our keeping.

The answer to the problems facing the British Empire is, of course, obvious, as Amery points out in Chapter Three, 'A Solution': an alliance with Germany. Regrettably, there are a few matters which will need to be straightened out along the way. The British would have to renounce their interest in Hong Kong and Singapore, already lost to the Japanese anyway; Cyprus and Malta might need to be ceded, presumably to Italy; and they would, of course, have to leave Gibraltar, perhaps, in exchange 'against one of the Canary Islands'.

This was a small price to pay against domination by 'Judao-Plutocracy' from Washington and 'Judao-Mongolism' from Moscow, and, as we soon learn, 'Jewry' is a religion which advocates the overthrow of all other nations 'not from religious motives but from racial ones':

Here are a few extracts from the Talmud, which is the book whose thought and conceptions are taught in the synagogues the whole world over, and which is the supreme directive and code of the Jewish people:

'All the peoples of the world will be chained to the throne of Israel, at the end of an atrocious and bloody war, in which three-quarters of the population will be decimated.'

'We order that every Jew should curse three times a day the Christian peoples, and pray on God to exterminate them utterly with their Kings and their Princes.'

'It is a commandment, that every Jew should exert all his efforts to annihilate everything that touches the Christian Church and those that serve it. Christ is the son of a prostitute.'

'The Jew who rapes or corrupts a non-Jewish woman, or even kills her, must not be found guilty before the Court of Justice, because he has only harmed a mare.'

'The best of the Christians must be strangled, for he who offers the blood of these men, makes a sacrifice agreeable to God.'

'The Jews are the very essence of God, but the non-Jews are but the spunk of animals.'

'God gave all power to the Jews over the wealth and the blood of all peoples.'

'The non-Jews have only been created to serve Jewry night and day.'

'No oath and no promise has any validity for a Jew, in so far as Christian people are concerned.'

'The Jews are men, the other nations are but a variety of animals.'

This farrago of pornographic forgery is merely the introduction to a further barrage of anti-Semitic drivel, seeking to link Judaism with Communism, and thus all the ills of the world, until we finally reach the meat of Amery's proposals in the final chapter, 'Outlines of a Programme'.

It is important once again to re-emphasize that Amery's ideas contain no profound political thought or insight: they are simply an admixture of his father's progressive Imperialism, Jacques Doriot's Fascism and his own anti-Semitism. Thus, in outline, we find that a future Britain should have no Jews in public office of any kind (and, oddly, that 'By giving the Jews a national status of their own, by sending them to their own country, we will not need to make statutes of exception because [they] . . . will no longer be there';[6] a mixture of Leo's Zionism and John's anti-Semitism); that capital, business, etc. are to be commandeered in the national interest; surplus goods are to be distributed free; all member nations of the Empire are to be equal, and the King will live in each in turn. And finally, of course, Britain will be in military alliance with Germany: 'Courage, fellow countrymen! Our banners will soon fly high in the noonday sun by the banners of civilization, that Judah and Bolshevism may perish, that Europe and England may survive.'

John handed over his manuscript at the end of March 1943 and, well satisfied with his work, commenced a round of carousing which was brought to a sudden halt just a week later: 'On April the 7th to 8th my beloved friend and brave political revolutionary Jeanine Barde died.'[7]

This terse statement covers an event which has been the subject of speculation, rumour and innuendo ever since. Helen Wies, an Australian-born employee of the Reichsrundfunk, recounts the version prevalent in Berlin shortly after the event.

I first met Amery at the Café Roma and saw him there frequently over a period of two or three months between May and August 1943. . . . He was regarded as a person who was not nice to know, even by the Germans who knew him. The Germans also considered him a traitor. . . . Amery told me he had to leave England following a dispute when he was riding on his estate. He was married to an Englishwoman I learned from discussions with other people, and from two or three different sources that he was later married to a very eccentric Frenchwoman. She had a daughter, who in 1943 was seven years old and living in the south of France with the mother's parents. This wife died, according to stories I heard, in rather odd circumstances. After a party in Berlin, a political discussion ended in a quarrel and Amery's wife is reported to have said that she would rather die than live with him, whereupon he is supposed to have put some powder in her drink saying 'Good luck to you', and the next morning she was dead.[8]

Ribbentrop's secretary, Reinhard Spitzy, who met Amery several times during 1943, recounts an equally macabre rumour. He was told that Amery had accidentally killed Jeanine by giving her a suicide pill instead of a headache tablet and had thus become an inconsolable alcoholic. Although, like all rumours, both stories contain a kernel of truth, the reality was in fact somewhat different. Notwithstanding his celebrity status as a well-connected renegade, it is unlikely that the German Foreign Office would have tolerated a murderer on their payroll, and a discreet investigation was launched by the Prosecutor-General of the Tribunal of the 1st

Instance for Berlin. A summary of its findings, written by Hesse on 21 April 1943, was subsequently discovered during a search of the German Embassy building in Paris after the Liberation:

According to the statement of Amery he was present, in the company of Jeanine Barde, his mistress, in the Foreign Press Circle, Fasanenstrasse 83, Berlin-Charlottenburg, during the evening of 7 April 1943. The pair were having a discussion. Complaining of a headache, Jeanine Barde took from her handbag a powder contained in a small box carrying the inscription 'Asciatine' and Amery gave her a glass of water in which she then poured the powder. Before tasting the contents of the glass, Jeanine Barde said that she was going to poison herself. Amery thought the powder inoffensive, and didn't take his mistress's statement seriously. Both had already been drinking heavily.

When, at about one in the morning on 8 April, the couple left the Circle, wanting to catch a tram to go to the Hotel Kaiserhof at the Zoological Gardens★ where the two shared a room, Jeanine Barde fell unconscious at the tram stop. Amery, who attributed her state to drunkenness, then got a taxi to take his mistress to the Hotel Kaiserhof. As they arrived, Jeanine Barde regained consciousness and was able to get to their room unaided. Arriving there, she collapsed again and he put her on the sofa where she was seized with a fit of vomiting. After that, he undressed her and put her in her bed. She had regained her calm and was breathing deeply, in a way he now attributed to her drunkenness. Then, having taken a sleeping-tablet, he lay on the other bed and went to sleep. When, at around 11 o'clock on 8 April 1943, he awoke, he realized that Jeanine Barde was dead and that, after he had gone to sleep, she had vomited again in the bed where he had lain her. He immediately called the hotel management.

To discover the causes of the death of Jeanine Barde, Professor Doktor Müller-Hess, Director of the Institute of Criminal and Legal Medicine at the University of Berlin, and Doktor Neugebauer, chief doctor, were ordered to proceed with a forensic autopsy of the cadaver; at the same

★ A railway station and neighbourhood of Central Berlin close to the actual zoo.

time, a chemical examination of the blood-alcohol level, the remains of the Asciatine found after the discovery of the body and the viscera removed at the autopsy (stomach and contents, intestines, liver, kidneys, urine), was effected by Doktor Brüning.

The results of the autopsy permitted the conclusion that death was due to the inhalation of stomach contents which had been vomited by the victim. The chemical examination revealed a blood-alcohol level of 1,50 o/oo. The concentration of alcohol in the blood was not therefore enough to conclude that she had a fatal level of ethyl alcohol intoxication. Subsequent chemical analysis revealed only traces of Asciatine, which is to say a mixture of pyramidon and butychlorhydrate. In fact, all the organs examined revealed no other poison (mineral or vegetable). In any case, none of the researches indicated any finding which would permit the attribution of death to the effect of poisons, venomous plants, hard drugs, and particularly sleeping-tablets, together with the Asciatine.

Conforming with these findings, the expert report of Professor Doktor Müller-Hess concludes that Jeanine Barde, under the influence of alcohol, during the course of her sleep and as a result of her drunkenness, was seized by a fit of vomiting and inhaled the material that she had vomited.

As a general conclusion of the enquiry it is clear that the hypothesis of death by asphyxiation agrees with the statement of Amery concerning the state of drunkenness of Jeanine Barde, her collapses, her repeated vomiting, to conclude that his statement appears to be in good faith. If, as a result of the statement made by Jeanine Barde and reported by Amery, in which she declared she would poison herself, there were grounds to look at a hypothesis of suicide, this hypothesis is contradicted by the results of this enquiry. Finally, there is no evidence to support a criminal action.[9]

Shocked, Amery accompanied Jeanine's body back to her native Bergerac where she was buried soon after her death. Subsequently, he was able to dismiss events that took place in the latter part of April by claiming that he was 'too distraught to pay any great attention at the time'[10] but this is probably not true, because by 14 April, when he returned to suite number 505/6 at the Hôtel Bristol in Paris, following Jeanine's funeral, he was already in the company of a new 'fiancée', Mlle Michelle Thomas,[11] another Parisian prostitute, whom he had met on the train from Bordeaux to Paris.

It was during this stay in Paris that John Amery committed what were subsequently deemed in Britain to have been his worst acts of treason. As we have seen, although Hitler liked Amery's idea of founding a British anti-Bolshevik legion, John's German sponsors did not envisage him having any active role in it and the England Committee, together with the OKW, set the operation in train without his assistance or knowledge. Nevertheless, it was an idea, according to Dr Hesse, that Amery frequently came back to, and while he was in Paris, escorted by Werner Plack, he conceived the idea of entering the internment camp at St-Denis and canvassing for recruits. Hesse later recalled:

He once blundered badly in Paris where – according to information I got later – he and Plack went together to a camp for British internees . . . There, on his own initiative, he tried to get volunteers for his British Free Corps, but he had no success whatever, and there was a brawl at the camp, and numerous complaints about his and Plack's behaviour, because he was going against all orders. In addition, they got posters printed in Paris, calling for volunteers for a British Legion of St George. The title was entirely an idea of Amery's. The posters were never used. All these activities of Plack and Amery were quite unauthorized and on their own initiative. My impression is that they were both almost continually under the influence of alcohol.[12]

The visit to the camp took place on 20 April 1943 and its *ad hoc* nature means that we can only piece together the sequence of events from the statements of participants: there are no surviving German records. It would seem that the German camp Kommandantur had sufficient notice of the visit to draw up a list of thirty to forty prisoners who were thought to be suitable candidates for proselytizing by Amery. The Camp Secretary, a British internee called G. D. Pugh, thought that a majority of them had been chosen because they spoke German or had business or family connections with Germany[13] but there was certainly no deeper meaning than that, and it is possible that the camp authorities did not know the real reason for Amery's visit until he actually arrived there.

Amery's audience were rounded up by the camp runner who told them to report to the visiting hut where a visitor was waiting for them. When the group had assembled, there was much speculation as to why they had been brought together – it wasn't a visiting day – but this ended ten minutes later with the arrival of Amery and Plack, together with the camp commandant and a few others. Amery stood on a small podium, used for giving lectures, to speak to the assembled prisoners. The gist of what he said was described by one of the inmates, Royston Wood:

You mustn't think that everybody in England is in favour of continuing this war. Three days ago a British plane flew over from the RAF and joined the Legion of St George. In the British prison camps in Germany we have already got several hundred (I forget the exact figure) to join the British Legion of St George. Should you wish to join you will leave the camp immediately and you will never come into it again. You will have to wear German uniform and you will have German officers, but you will have non-commissioned officers who are English or British. You will never be called upon to fight in any sector where British troops are.[14]

This bizarre statement seems to have stunned the majority of the audience; Wood reports that 'the general attitude of the people present was a passive one'. Purcell Purcell-Jones, another internee, reported that

we, the internees present, were most annoyed to be subjected to a talk by this traitor. Amery is a small, slight individual, and we gave him a very bad time by cross-examining him. He said he was anxious to recruit people to fight against Bolshevism. He was asked for news of the fighting on the Russian front and he said the Russians were on their last legs. He was then asked why the Germans wanted to recruit people to fight them.

Someone asked Amery if we could have a radio set in the camp, but he declined to assist in this way, though he made extravagant promises to any who would step forward and volunteer to join his Legion.[15]

One internee who was not in the least passive was Wilfred Brinkman, whom we last met dispensing relief aid to Amery from the British Interests section of the US Consulate in Nice. He had been interned in St-Denis in March 1943, following the German takeover of the unoccupied zone.

I was advised by my friend James Henderson, agent in Paris for Klein-wort's, that Amery was actually in the visiting hut. . . . I hurriedly dressed and ascertained that the men in the hut had been called upon individually and told they were wanted in the visiting hut. They were given a chit with their name and number to enable them to enter. Most were under the impression it was a personal visit. I wrote my name and number on a piece of paper and forced my way past the German sentry. I found Amery supported by about half a dozen obvious Gestapo men in civilian clothes, together with the camp commandant Möbius, and several German officers in uniform. About thirty-five men were listening to Amery. The interruption of my entry caused Amery to turn round and I asked him whether he recognized me. He said he did. I then asked if he remembered his friend Ogilvie* – which put him out of his countenance. I then asked him what he was doing there. He replied that he was explaining the advantages of joining in the fight against Bolshevism by joining what he called St George's Legion. I asked on what authority he was acting. He replied he was representing a committee existing in England, the names of which he could not divulge, which was fighting for the freedom of England. I asked what the St George's Legion was. He replied: a body of about 1,500 men recruited in prison camps, to join which three four-engined bombers had flown over to England complete with crews. I then asked where they would fight. He replied, on the Russian Front.

* It will be remembered that Amery had denounced Ogilvie to the Vichy police for illegal currency dealing.

I asked what would happen if they were confronted by British troops. He replied that they would be moved to another sector. I asked what would happen if they were taken prisoner. No reply was given. I then asked what would happen to them after we had won the war. No reply. I then asked, did these men realize that they would be traitors to their country, as he was. No reply.[16]

It is an interesting thought that it is quite likely that Amery had not, at this point, considered in any real sense that Britain might win the war. In his delusional world, it probably seemed such an unlikely outcome as to be not worth considering, notwithstanding his well-documented inability to foresee the consequences of his actions.

Brinkman's appearance had clearly greatly discomfited Amery because

[He] then turned round to the men and said he had nothing further to add, thanked them, and said he would send in literature explaining his statement – upon which the men filed out. I was about to leave with them, when Amery asked me to wait. I did. When the last man had gone, the Gestapo men crowded around us, but the German officers began walking away.

Amery said to me that I seemed to misunderstand his position. I said I was fully aware of his past, particularly his activities in Nice. He continued that his work had been solely on behalf of the Vichy authorities for the common good. To which I replied that I doubted it. He then begged me not to mention in the camp anything that would appear derogatory to him. I replied that that was precisely what I intended to do. He repeated his request, and offered me his hand to shake. I replied that I was not in the habit of shaking hands with traitors. He said nothing, and I walked away.[17]

The other internees were equally unimpressed: the Canadian-born George Edward Beckman: 'had never heard anything more ridiculous, for after all I am a veteran of the Boer War and the [First

World] War, now being aged sixty-six years'.[18] In fact the only individual to be swayed at the first meeting appears to have been an elderly academic named George Logio, who, after hearing the talk was 'prompted by the apparent sincerity of Amery to make the approach [to work for Germany] through him with a view to achieving his object'[19] which was, rather strangely, to go to the University of Sofia where he had friends. Logio was certainly released from the camp and apparently allowed to proceed as requested.

Amery's exit from the camp was somewhat fraught. By the time his talk had finished a crowd had gathered outside the visiting hut: they were not impressed. As Amery left 'he was hissed and booed', whilst those who had been forced to listen to him 'all signed a protest against having had to attend such a meeting'.[20]

This protest was echoed by the Camp Committee, the prisoners' representatives, who gave a note of protest to the Commandant and published the following notice on the camp bulletin board:

The Committee of this camp wish to place on record that they had no prior knowledge of, nor were they invited to attend, the meeting that was held in the visiting hut this morning.

They moreover wish to state that they strongly resented the presence in the camp of Mr Amery, and have since advised the Camp Commandant accordingly. We are sure that in so doing we expressed the general disapproval of all internees.

G. D. Pugh, Camp Secretary   C. F. Hadkinson, Camp Adjutant
G. Fletcher, Camp President

This was a protest that the Commandant chose to ignore. On 21 April, he allowed a consignment of Amery's recruiting literature and posters to be distributed round the camp and Plack and Amery returned the following week.

The purpose of their second visit was to interview selected prisoners who were perceived as possible candidates for member-ship of the legion. It is not clear how this sifting process was carried out, but it is possible that the selection was made – or information passed on – by Oswald John Job, a British-born builders' merchant who had been interned at St-Denis since 1940. Job, whose father was German born, acted as an interpreter between the internees and their German captors and was believed to have a very close relationship with them, a fact that was borne out by his execution for treachery in 1944 after being sent to Britain to replenish a German agent's supply of cash: unfortunately for Job, the agent in question was part of MI5's Double Cross network – DRAGON-FLY – and his refusal to admit guilt or to agree to work for MI5 was enough to ensure his trial and eventual meeting with executioner Pierrepoint.[21]

The only two who are known to have succumbed to Amery's blandishments at this stage were both young men: Jean Tunmer, the French-born son of British parents who owned a large sports shop in central Paris, and Kenneth Edward Jordan Berry, a merchant seaman, who was then aged sixteen.

Berry was a strange and isolated figure in St-Denis. He was a Cornishman from Falmouth who had left school at thirteen and, as he did not get on with his father who was an Admiralty policeman, eventually went to sea as a deck-boy on the SS *Cymbeline* in May 1940. In September of the same year, when he was still only fourteen years old, the *Cymbeline* was sunk by a German raider and Berry became a prisoner of war and was held over the next few years in several camps around France. Ill-educated and slightly dim-witted, he was soon spotted by Oswald Job who used him as a gopher around the camp, thus arousing the suspicion of other inmates and further isolating him. Berry was not invited to Amery's lecture, but he saw the posters and literature left around the camp, and a few days afterwards was told to go with Hauptmann Gillis, the camp security officer, to a private house outside the camp.

I was there introduced to Amery and Plack by Captain Gillis. Captain Gillis introduced Amery to me as 'Mr John Amery, the Foreign Secretary of England'.

Amery then said, 'I suppose you are wondering what you are doing here. I expect you have heard what I came to the camp for.' I said I had heard about it from other people and Amery then asked me, 'Do you know anything about Russia?' I said no. Amery then said, 'Do you think you are doing right by staying in a prisoner of war camp? Your duty is to fight Russia.' I asked, 'What makes you say that?' and Amery replied, 'I have been sent over especially from England to form this Legion to fight against Russia. I have my orders to ask all prisoners of war if they are willing to join in order to fight Russia.' Amery then asked if I would like to join and I said I did not know.[22]

Berry's intellectual resources had been used up by this blistering banter and Amery gave him a week to make up his mind, told him to keep his mouth shut and sent him back to the camp. Over the next few days, Gillis sent for Berry several times to see if he had decided to join, and eventually was told that he would. Berry was still just sixteen years old.

Not long after having agreed to join, Berry was removed from the camp, along with Tunmer, Logio and Job, and sent to stay with Tunmer at his apartment on the Boulevard Exelmanns. Tunmer appears to have been moderately protective of his young charge during the few days they were together – 'he took me sightseeing and gave me money to spend' – but some nine days after their arrival at Tunmer's flat, two men in civilian clothes arrived and escorted Tunmer away. According to Berry,

Later the same day Amery came to the address, and appeared to be surprised to find Tunmer had gone. Amery asked if I knew where he had gone. He then said it did not seem safe for me to remain at the address, and he then rang the Gestapo and three of them came along. They questioned me about Tunmer and I was then taken away and kept in detention for about eight weeks.[23]

The sixteen-year-old Berry was to be the only recruit ever found for the British Legion of St George, a military unit that only existed

22. John Amery: a portrait taken in the early 1930s.

23. 112 Eaton Square, John Amery's childhood home.

24. Winston Churchill as a schoolboy at Harrow, where he began a lifelong friendship with Leo Amery.

25. Leo and Florence ('Bryddie') Amery in London, October 1940.

26. Sir Samuel Hoare (*left*), John Amery's godfather and possible source of a British diplomatic passport he owned, talking with Neville Chamberlain.

27. Julian Amery (*far right*), John's younger brother, as an SOE officer in the Balkans, *c.* 1944. MI6 subsequently suggested that Julian had attempted to fabricate evidence to save John from the gallows.

28. John and Una Amery, pictured at John's house in Chelsea after their bizarre wedding in Athens in 1933.

29. John Amery (*right*) with his bigamously married third wife, Michelle, at a propaganda event in Antwerp in 1944.

30. Amery (*second from left*) meets officials of the Flemish collaborationist VNV and German officers, Antwerp, 1944.

31. Amery addresses Flemish Nazis.

32. William Joyce, the only other individual to be executed for high treason following the Second World War. The scar was acquired when he was stewarding a Conservative Party meeting in London in the 1920s.

33. Joyce about to be returned to Britain for trial, Germany, 1945.

34. Two members of the British Free Corps recruiting at the Marlag–Milag POW camp for naval prisoners in Germany, 1944. On the left is Kenneth Berry, John Amery's only recruit from the St-Denis internment camp in Paris.

35. 'Our Flag is Going Forward Too': one of the recruiting posters Amery had printed in Paris before his unauthorized and disastrous visit to St-Denis.

36. Marcel Déat, the French collaborationist leader and friend of John Amery.

37. (*Above left*) Hartley Shawcross, the Labour Attorney-General who would have led the prosecution of Amery.

38. (*Above right*) Field Marshal Jan Smuts: his appeal for clemency was ignored by Clement Attlee.

39. Caught: John and Michelle Amery in British custody in Italy, 1945.

in Amery's imagination. Job was recruited by the Abwehr; Tunmer disappeared; Logio went to Sofia. The real soldiers, the Wehrmacht and the Waffen-SS, took over, with the intention of creating a real military unit, and John had neither the suitability nor the experience for this. And, as Roy Courlander, one of the NCOs in the unit, pointed out, 'John Amery's connection with the unit was easily severed by pointing out to the SS that he was partly Jewish.'[24]

Instead, after a couple of weeks at ease in the fleshpots of Paris, John returned to Berlin.

11. 'I Thought They Were Going to Shoot Me'

The meat and potatoes of John Amery's collaboration took place over a five-month period, from November 1942 until April 1943, but from the German point of view, he hung around like a bad smell until the end of the war. Although he was used in various propaganda undertakings, his effectiveness as a propaganda star-turn rapidly decreased for one very basic reason – he was not very good at it. What he was good at was spending other people's money, and this he continued to do with considerable aplomb.

None the less, Hesse and his colleagues in the Foreign Ministry were keen to try to realize some return on their investment, and in May 1943 Hesse asked Amery whether he would consider taking on the job of news editor for a new English language broadcasting service that the German Foreign Office was about to initiate: Radio National.

Practitioners of psychological warfare identify three types of propaganda. 'White' propaganda is broadcast or published material whose origin is openly avowed, as with the BBC, or, in Germany, the Reichsrundfunk's 'Germany Calling' service and the Haw-Haw broadcasts. This kind of material normally relies for its impact on being largely truthful and checkable, and on broadly representing the actual views and intentions of its originator. 'Black' propaganda is more or less the opposite: it is broadcast or published material which falsely claims to come from some source other than its real origin, and its nature is often – if not always – deliberately misleading, downright untrue, scurrilous, seditious, offensive and/or obscene. Somewhere in between black and white propaganda is 'grey' material: propaganda which does not claim any particular origin, but leaves its audience to guess and assume where it has been derived from and what its intentions are.

Even before the start of the war, Goebbels' Propaganda Ministry was experimenting with grey propaganda alongside the Reichsrundfunk's European and Overseas services. In 1937, they began a French language programme on Radio Stuttgart, aimed at exploiting tensions and divisions within French society. After the war began this early experiment was deemed successful enough for a new organization to be set up by the Propaganda Ministry, to control and direct black propaganda on a formal and organized basis: this was the Büro Concordia.

The aim of Concordia was to broadcast subversive, divisive black propaganda as a weapon of war, and during the fall of France in 1940, it was strikingly successful. Operating three separate stations, Radio Humanité, Poste du Réveil and La Voix de la Paix, the German propagandists managed to sow the seeds of defeatism and dissension amongst the French public and armed forces, causing panicky evacuations which clogged up military supply routes and lines of communication, and encouraging pro-German and anti-war groups within the Government. It was a success that they aimed to repeat with the British.

The first 'British' Concordia station to go on air was the New British Broadcasting Station which started up in February 1940, broadcasting pro-German versions of the news in English to an English audience, supposedly from England. In fact, the broadcasters on the station were a motley crew of pro-Nazis, most of whom had been resident in Germany for some time and who were able to gain their release from internment by agreeing to work for Concordia. This was followed by three further stations which started up in the summer of 1940: Workers' Challenge, a supposedly Communist station which enjoyed a brief popularity because of its ripe language (including the first broadcast use of the word 'fuck'); Radio Caledonia, appealing to Scottish Nationalists; and the Christian Peace Movement. All these stations gained a listenership amongst people hungry for news – any news – at a time of great national emergency, but they were never used tactically, in the way the French stations had been, because there was of course no invasion: as far as the Germans were concerned however, they ensured that an anti-war message was getting through in Britain.

Radio National was to be slightly different, however. In the first place, although it used broadcasting facilities provided by Concordia and the Propaganda Ministry, it was under the control of the Foreign Ministry's broadcasting section, and was actually supervised by Peter Adami, a former journalist. Second, though purporting to be British, the station was also to be avowedly Fascist, reiterating the kind of anti-Semitic views held by Amery and pushing for the so-called reforms outlined in his book *England Faces Europe*. The problem with the whole idea turned out to be Amery himself. His version of events was that 'the whole affair having to pass through the Propaganda Ministry and Joyce's friends I accepted it only to return it without its having, with me, effected a single transmission'.[1] In fact Joyce played no part in Amery's removal from the project: he simply wasn't up to the job, having no journalistic experience and completely lacking the self-discipline and motivation to fulfil a pivotal role in such an operation. Radio National began broadcasts in July 1943, using a number of broadcasters recruited through POW camps, including Walter Purdy, Francis Maton, Railton Freeman, and Norman Baillie-Stewart, who had fallen out with the Propaganda Ministry; editorial control was left to the German Adami, and John's only task was to provide background commentaries on British press reporting, which he was able to do from his hotel or his office in the Foreign Ministry.

Nineteen forty-three was the crucial turning point in the war in Europe: on 2 February the remnants of 6th Army had finally surrendered in Stalingrad; on 13 May came the capitulation of all Axis forces in North Africa; whilst July saw the Battle of Kursk, the last German throw of the dice on the Eastern Front, and the resignation and arrest of Mussolini. These events passed Amery by; he subsequently recalled: 'In the end of September I returned to Paris. Once more much political talk and on October the 4th I remarried at the German consulate. Politically the situation remained almost unchanged.'[2]

Nothing better illustrates the delusional world in which Amery lived: 'Politically the situation remained almost unchanged' actually meant that his occasional meetings with Hesse at the Foreign Office and drunken discussions in Berlin's cafés, restaurants and bars had failed to sway the Third Reich's social policies in the occupied territories. There is no evidence from this period that Amery was involved in any other political activities, nor that he ever met any influential Nazi leaders, or even tried to do so. His political activities were confined to his self-important bustling between Paris and Berlin and his friendship with the leaders of the tiny French Fascist sects who had risen to exaggerated prominence as the result of the German occupation.

Equally, his bland statement regarding his remarriage is worth examining. At this point Amery was still married to Una: indeed, they never divorced. If he did, as he claimed, marry Jeanine Barde, then that marriage was undoubtedly bigamous. Evidence on this point is equivocal: he told people he met at the time that Jeanine was his wife, and she was indeed issued a German *Fremdenpass*★ in the name of Jeanine Amery,[3] although some witnesses, like Hesse, persist in describing her as Amery's mistress or girlfriend. But there is no question but that Amery bigamously married Michelle Thomas, as if the death of Jeanine had freed him of all previous encumbrances. This seems to echo Leo Amery's observation that once an event had taken place, John had no further interest in it: that he lived entirely in the present without any real conception of the past or future. Una is not mentioned at all in the statement that John gave to MI5, covering his activities from 1936 onwards, even though he was certainly in touch with her until 1940 and, by her own claim, last saw her in Paris shortly before the German invasion; John had simply sloughed her off.

For the next year, Hesse and the England Committee continued to make use of Amery as a propaganda celebrity, sending him to

★ A passport for foreign nationals.

make a series of speeches and visits throughout occupied Europe. The first of these took place in early November 1943, when he was invited to visit Serbia by General Milan Nedić, the leader of the Serbian collaborationist Government. Travelling with Counsellor von Losch, a German Foreign Office minder, John arrived in Belgrade on 14 November for a visit strongly reminiscent of the 'fact-finding missions' which are much in favour with modern-day politicians, although more as a means of attracting attention and publicity than anything else. Amery reported his visit to Hesse in a self-satisfied, self-serving memorandum some months later:

We remained in Belgrade five days during which time I was able to have numerous contacts with Serbian people both of the so-called aristocratic and merchant classes. I tried in so much as possible to contact persons who were either neutral or else still hypnotized with the idea that their salvation would come from London . . . in this connection we had some very notable success.

Several press conferences were held and the trip wound up with a speech made at the Belgrade University Hall before some 1,500 people. We held the headlines on the front page of all the Serbian newspapers★ on four columns as a result of this speech, which was considered one of the biggest sensations since the war.

General Nedić† who received me alone and with whom I discussed the political situation for over an hour was kind enough to declare that my action 'had been of great help to him, to forward the restoration of common sense in the minds of his countrymen'. He was also kind enough to make me several presents of Slivovic and Serbian cigarettes in souvenir of my visit.

The German authorities of Radio Belgrade and the representatives of Gesandter von Neubacher‡ were also kind enough to state their appreciation and satisfaction of our action.

★ Not entirely surprisingly, as the press was state controlled.
† Amery actually spelt his name Neditch.
‡ The German Ambassador to Serbia.

This whole affair came at a very opportune psychological moment, precisely when Mihailović was being abandoned by the allies in favour of Tito . . . it is my hope that in some small way this visit may have added a little weight in the balance of the decisions that Mihailović seems to be taking to collaborate now with Germany.[4]

What is extraordinary about this episode, and something that John Amery cannot possibly have known at this time, was that by now his brother Julian, as an officer of the Special Operations Executive, was taking part in the effort to supply, train and direct partisans in the neighbouring territory of Albania. In his lecture at the Kolerac Popular University, John had cited Julian's pre-war visits to Yugoslavia to indicate his own family involvement in the area, before going on to attack the partisan movement, inevitably, as the tool of Jews and Communists.

John's return from Belgrade to Berlin coincided exactly with the opening of British Bomber Command's strategic air offensive against the German capital. A major raid on 22 November had severely damaged the government quarter; a follow-up the next night caught up John himself.

We returned to Berlin on November the 23rd and hardly had we arrived when owing to enemy action both the office in the von der Heydt Strasse and the Kaiserhof in which we lived disappeared.

Having passed the night unsuccessfully attempting to extinguish the Kaiserhof fire, in which nevertheless I was able personally to extinguish some number of phosphorus canisters, we presented ourselves for instructions to Gesandte Schmidt at the Minister Büro the next morning around eleven o'clock.

It was agreed that in view of the housing situation caused by the bombardment, provisionally I should withdraw to Paris.

Not without considerable difficulty we managed to reach Paris on the 26th with all the articles we had managed to save of our belongings. Losses were about 30% and include all my documents.[5]

Any inference that John was running from the bombing is probably false; his behaviour during the raid was sufficiently distinguished to earn him an award for 'exceptional bravery'.* Most likely, the Foreign Ministry was happy to have him out of the way while it reorganized itself. As usual, John and Michelle took a suite at the Hôtel Bristol except that they now appeared on the register as a married couple. Meanwhile, John's fantasy political odyssey continued.

I profited of my time in Paris to conduct personal propaganda amongst different classes and persons in Paris and I also was able to address some 800 people, forming the militants of the Revolution Nationale Populaire Party [sic], of which my friend Marcel Déat is the leader.† In this speech I sought mostly to give these militants the essential arguments necessary to combat enemy propaganda. The results I am told are very satisfactory, especially at that time when finally the German authorities seemed to have imposed at least two real Frenchmen and revolutionaries in the shape of Joseph Darnand and Philip Henriot on the Vichy Government whose treasonable activities I have not in the passed [sic] ceased denouncing.[6]

Henriot, an ultra-collaborationist, had just been appointed Vichy's Minister of Information and Propaganda, whilst Darnand, a Fascistic ex-soldier, who had briefly been a POW of the Germans before escaping, became the Secretary of State for the Interior. The fact that by this time he was also Secretary-General of the Milice, a militia formed to counter the French Resistance, and an officer in the Waffen-SS, gives some indication of the state of dependence to which Vichy had been reduced by the beginning of 1944. Amery did not see it that way.

The possibilities that are open for improving the French situation since the nomination of these two men are now enormous, all the more so if

---

* It is not clear which particular award this was: possibly the War Merit Cross.
† In fact Déat's party was called the Rassemblement National Populaire.

this is the first step to bringing the French Government back to where it should be in Paris. And the placing in that Government of men like Déat and Doriot who will help to consolidate the rebirth of a real Socialist and National France.[7]

The irony that 'a real . . . National France' could only be imposed by diktat of the occupying power seems to have escaped Amery. Instead, he was more interested in the next stage of his travels: a brief trip to Prague between 5 and 11 January 1944, where he gave a speech to representatives of the Czech press and collaborationist politicians, *schmoozed* with the German occupation authorities and then returned to Paris, via a short stay in the Hotel Imperial in Vienna. Interestingly, Amery's accounts from this period survive and demonstrate the lavish level of expenses he was given by the Foreign Office and the high style in which he chose to live.

Although John had declined to take a salary from Hesse, he was none the less granted a basic allowance of RM 650 per week, equivalent to 13,000 French francs. Currency comparisons are difficult to make but RM 650 is in the region of £30, a considerable weekly stipend at the time, and more than twice what William Joyce was earning as chief commentator of the Reichsrundfunk's English section. But in addition to this allowance, Amery also received payments to cover his hotel bills, travel costs and incidental expenses, thus making his altruistic and 'unpaid' service to the cause of European unity and anti-Communism a profitable business. To put the whole matter in perspective: Europeans, including Britons, who volunteered to serve in the Waffen-SS or Wehrmacht as soldiers, and thus made a somewhat more tangible contribution to the struggle, were paid RM 1 per day as private soldiers, rising by increments of 20 pfennigs for each promotion.

Amery's next excursion, after a further two weeks in Paris, was to Norway.

The trip . . . which lasted fifteen days can only be described as most exceedingly satisfactory.

I spoke in English in the towns of Trondheim, Bergen, Stavanger, Kristiansand and finally Oslo before 2,500 persons.

The trip caused a most extraordinary sensation in this country whose multiple commercial relations attached it closely to England and where almost everybody speaks English.

Not only were we able to give heart and courage to the members of Quisling's party, the National Sammling, but the fear of Bolshevism, the fact that an Englishman of a well-known family also espoused the cause of 'the defence of civilization in collaboration with Germany', brought to our side many so far neutral persons, mainly amongst the ship owners, the herring kings and so on.

In the interview I had with President Quisling he was also kind enough to say that 'my activity was of a great help to him and the friends of Germany'. I had the impression he was a powerful, strong and tenacious man in whom one can have every confidence. Throughout our trip the halls in which I spoke were overcrowded contrary to the provisions of the organizers and in Oslo more than 600 people were unable to enter the vast hall overcrowded itself to capacity [sic]. In consequence the speech was also broadcast on the streets. This speech in English on the streets of Oslo in the fifth year of the war, naturally caused a great sensation. The newspapers gave us the whole front page in some cases the next morning, and we figured also on the newsreel in prominent position.

Dr Müller, chief of the Wehrmacht's propaganda, and I understand at the request of President Quisling, offered my wife a superb silver fox . . . all in all we left Norway in a storm of applause and enthusiasm such as I had not hoped for.[8]

Amery's delight in his apparently enthusiastic reception in Norway should also be kept in perspective. Nazi racial policy recognized the Norwegians as another element of the Germanic race and the Germans' inclination had initially been to allow a greater measure of independence for the Norwegian Government under the supervision of the military occupation authorities. Unfortunately for the Germans their man, Vidkun Quisling, was tremendously unpopular in his own country, and had never managed to gain more than 3 per cent of the popular vote in pre-war elections standing on a National Socialist platform. Amery's visit probably did arouse a certain amount of interest – once again, attempting to judge by the impact on the state-controlled newspapers is pointless – but it is fair to argue that a good deal of the interest he generated was due to simple curiosity rather than any enthusiasm for his confused and simplistic message.

Next stop on Amery's European tour was Belgium:

Here I spoke in French, with a few words of introduction in English to 1,700 people in Antwerp, 1,000 in Ghent, 700 in Liege and over 2,500 in Brussels. The result was very satisfactory, as also the numerous personal contacts we were able to make in very widely differing circles. The press gave us a good reception as also the people who attended the conferences . . .

Radio transmission was also given by Brussels in English for the Flemish population and in French for those of Wallonia.[9]

Speaking in French to members of the Flemish National Party (VNV) was somewhat tactless, although no doubt they listened to him out of politeness.

The trip to Brussels was followed during April and May by an extensive tour around France, during which Amery spoke in Dijon, Lyons, Nice, Monaco, Toulouse, Bordeaux, Poitiers, Nantes, Rennes, Rheims, Lille and finally Paris. At this point, it is worth noting that in his report to the German Foreign Ministry on his activities during the first half of 1944, he gives a tantalizing clue to some other activities in which he appears to have been involved. In this document, he is arguing that the Foreign Ministry should continue to allow him to maintain his 'headquarters' in Paris in order, among other reasons, to 'assist in the measure of my capabilities the SD* and other services concerned with the repression of terrorism, enemy activities, etc. These two later functions in no

* Sicherheitsdienst: the SS Intelligence and Security Service.

way impairing my other work, and my wife, being French, has also a whole field of activity.'[10]

This cryptic statement remained unexplained until four days before John's execution in December 1945 when MI5 officers, examining captured German Intelligence files, made an interesting discovery.

During March 1944, the III Luft officer was concerned in a plan to penetrate the Resistance organization France d'Abord through a V-Mann* of Sonderführer Nottermann (of Section IIIF, Alst Frankreich). Nottermann's V-Mann was clearly Amery since on 21.3.44 there was a meeting of the Luft III officer, Sdf. Nottermann, V-Mann Dan and V-Mann Amery to discuss Amery's penetration of the organization.

The diary gives no indication of the methods used by Amery or of the success or failure of his mission.[11]

This discovery lifts the lid on a hitherto unsuspected aspect of Amery's treason: that he was not only prepared to follow what might loosely be described as the 'logic' of his political beliefs in order to broadcast and inveigh against Jews and Communists, but was also willing to get his hands dirty as a spy, informant, call it what you will. This is a significant point: by the time this information had been filed, Amery had been hanged for high treason and it was of posthumous interest only, but had the Intelligence Services followed it up, they might have been able to prove a capital case under the Treachery Act of 1940 as well.

Amery's analysis of his achievements as an itinerant propagandist was typically ebullient:

I do wish to stress that since I did the first trip to Serbia, I have at last found my right place in this war. At last I am in something I understand and at which, I think I can claim, I excel. I have put forward time and again my advice that: My name, my person in England in propaganda to

---

* Vertrauensmann: a trusted agent.

England does not at the present moment carry any more weight than the same things said by unknown persons; but that all the credit of my name, my position, my family plays overwhelmingly in the balance of my activities in the different occupied and neutral countries . . . and there we get really positive, tangible results.

It would seem to me silly to consider that because we are an English department we should overlook the so essential work of demolishing Churchill propaganda in the different countries of Europe. On the contrary, 'No man is a prophet in his own land'. In the same way that eventually everyone will realize that a Norwegian is more interested to hear lectures by a French Doriotist than a Quisling man or vice versa we are evoluting [sic] in propaganda matters. The initiative Dr Hesse takes in organizing these trips of mine by pushing the propaganda of our ideas in a big town in mental turmoil like Paris, bears the standard of our department in the forefront of innovations. Small department but the one that has all the scoops, all the newest conceptions . . . and it's an honour for me to be in this department.[12]

Unfortunately for John, these views were not entirely shared by the German Foreign Ministry. Hesse recalled:

During his stays in France and Italy Amery caused constant trouble to the German authorities by his drunken habits and general activities. No one took him seriously. But I have no complete information in this respect because it was Plack who had charge of him, and in fact I was not interested. The only thing that worried me was the bills I had to pay.[13]

John quickly discovered this as well. On his return from his French tour he

found a pressing telegram end May asking me to return to Salzburg. I found Hesse there displeased at my activities, probably not personally but from Ribbentrop, bombarded with the protests of Abetz and most likely Monetrol, Pétain, etc. I was grieved and surprised: my other political friends having been more than contented with these results. Also it transpired after patient enquiry that in almost every instance every report was double: one favourable; one not. Depending whether it came from a revolutionary source or a reactionary one. This brought things to a standstill.

After two days Hesse asked me 'in view of the present situation of an impending [invasion] in France, to do anything I like but leave France to the military'. I returned to Paris at once where it became obvious that the 'partisan' movement which the Germans persisted in considering a police problem was a very serious political factor (we had been saying so for eighteen solid months and more). Wondering whether we would ever get to something sensible and also at the desire of my French friends who wished me once again to tackle Berlin, I returned there in June 44.[14]

This would be John's last visit to Paris. As he pointed out, the resistance was now becoming a significant factor and following the D-Day landings, on 6 June, the safety of collaborators like Amery was a real issue. To underline this point, the collaborationist Propaganda Minister, Henriot, was assassinated on 28 June by *Résistants* in front of his wife in his apartment inside his Ministry building.

Marcel Déat had finally achieved ministerial rank in Vichy in March 1944 – Jacques Doriot frightened Marshal Pétain too much ever to gain it – but the whole Vichy edifice, never more than wobbly at best, was about to collapse, and in some senses, although Amery and other collaborationists would have denied it, their political *raison d'être* was now disappearing. Germany was in the process of losing the war, and nothing that they could do would now change that. Their stance had been that with Germany as the dominant force in Europe, they should collaborate as closely as possible, although in a distinctive and nationalist way, and thus earn German respect and trust as junior partners. With Germany in terminal decline, however, they discovered that their political calculations had been wrong. This is not to suggest that their collaboration had been entirely cynical in all cases: many Vichy politicians and other collaborators throughout Europe sincerely believed that it was their duty to do what they could for their fellow countrymen by cooperating with their occupiers. But the philosophy that under-pinned the view of Amery and his French ultra-collaborationist friends – that it was right to support Germany because Germany was all that stood between European civilization and domination by Jewish–Bolshevik–Mongol hordes – was hardly tenable when Germany was collapsing in the face of the Soviet army. In reality, since the battle of Kursk in July–August 1943, Germany had com-pletely lost the ability to inflict more than occasional tactical reverses on the Soviets; it would seem self-evident under these circum-stances, if the war *was* actually all about preserving Western civiliz-ation, that the best way of preserving it would be to surrender in the west, allowing relatively strong American and British forces to garrison Germany and thus protect the west from the advancing Soviets. Of course, outside the limited circles of the German resist-ance – many of whom thought exactly that – these kinds of idea remained completely taboo.

Back in Berlin, John was no longer able to stay in his favoured luxury hotel suites because of Allied bombing: instead he was lodged at a building in the suburbs owned by the Foreign Ministry, the Haus am See in Gatow, where he continued to fill some of his time writing commentaries on the British press for Radio National but remained otherwise unemployed. It was during this period that the anti-Nazi conspirators within the Army High Command and Abwehr launched their attempted coup against Hitler.

As John sat idly in the suburbs, the drama of the attempted coup d'état passed him by. After Stauffenberg's bomb detonated in the conference hut at Hitler's field headquarters in East Prussia, just before 1 p.m. on 20 July, the government quarter of Berlin became a hive of military activity as the conspirators issued orders to confused army units to arrest elements of the Nazi Government, and these were countermanded by Propaganda Minister Goebbels who had taken control of the situation. Heinrich Himmler, the Interior Minister, Reichsführer-SS and overall chief of the German police, decided that he would arrest everyone who had even the most marginal involvement with the plot and 'was appalled to find the eventual list totalling over six thousand'.[15] With arrests taking place on this scale, the suggestion was floated in the Swedish press that Amery, who had been absent from his old haunts for some time, might now be a prisoner of the Gestapo, and thus the upshot of the Putsch, as far as John was concerned, was that he was wheeled out to write and record another series of broadcasts.

The first series had been composed and broadcast with the specific intention of suggesting the possibility of a compromise peace. The only reason for the second series was to prove that John was still a free agent and had not lost his faith in Nazism. In consequence, the content was considerably cruder and less polished, consisting mainly of simple cat-calling and insults against the British and American Governments, along with unlikely claims that Germany would still win the war. Of the seven short talks recorded between 26 July and 26 August, it appears that only the first three were actually broadcast.

Meanwhile, the Vichy regime was in its death throes. In mid-August, as the 3rd United States Army, under Patton, was approaching Paris, the Germans forcibly evacuated Pétain and his Government to Belfort, and subsequently to Simaringen on the Danube, where the last months of the war were played out as a schoolyard squabble between impotent and discredited dupes. It was not beyond the bounds of possibility that John might have followed them; instead, he received an offer of employment from a different source:

At the end of September I received an invitation from the Italian Government, telling me that Mussolini wished to see me.

I set out in the middle of October and saw him on Lake Garda at the end of that month. Contrary to what has often been said he was in the best of health and we talked for several hours.

His view was, in brief, that he had made a great mistake in 1922 in not carrying through what he was now attempting, i.e. to create a Social republic. But that he was optimistic that this could be done even with the increasing military difficulties and that once Northern Italy was going properly, he, who had after all been responsible for organizing the Peace of Munich, felt himself capable of throwing his whole person into the balance and obtaining the peace we had for long years been seeking.

In this line he asked me to assist him. I consented readily, all the more so that he was much more likely to succeed in negotiations where the Germans had so readily failed.[16]

Once more, this is evidence of the delusional world in which John lived. Mussolini was by now a spent force, and his Italian Social Republic a farcical puppet of the Germans.

In reality, Mussolini's efforts to involve Italy in the war had been disastrous. His intention had been to do just enough to earn Italy a place at the table at what he imagined would be the post-war peace conference, where he would be able to grab British and French Imperial possessions in Africa and the Mediterranean. Convinced that Germany would win – the more so after the rapid defeat of France – Mussolini committed the poorly trained and organized Italian armed forces to a series of campaigns which they proved unable to win on their own. As the Italian army was enveloped and destroyed at Stalingrad and in North Africa, leading members of Mussolini's regime realized that they had to get rid of him if Italy was to survive: after a meeting of the Fascist Grand Council on 24 July 1943, Mussolini was arrested on the orders of the king, and a government under Marshal Badoglio almost immediately opened secret negotiations with the Western allies in order to bring about an armistice. Badoglio's scheme was to make the timing of the announcement of an armistice coincide with the arrival of a large Anglo-American landing force which would hopefully prevent too much of Italy being occupied by Germany. Realizing what was happening, the Germans played for time in order to build up their forces in Italy.

The sequence of events turned out to be that Badoglio's Government announced the armistice on 7 September 1943; Mussolini was freed from Italian captivity by a daring German commando raid on 8 September; and the Allies began landings at Salerno on 9

September, by which time the Italian army had largely disintegrated. The Germans ended up in occupation of the whole of northern Italy and Mussolini was re-installed as leader of the Italian Social Republic (RSI), with its capital at Gargnano.

The RSI presented itself as a return to the republican and socialist roots of Fascism, accusing the monarchy, the generals and the industrialists who had supported Badoglio of betraying the Italian people, but in reality it was simply a tool of the German occupiers. While Mussolini continued to strut and pose, the Germans systematically looted Italy of its gold reserves, industrial output and workers, as well as annexing several provinces in the Veneto. Indeed, the mere existence of the RSI, and its attempts to conscript young Italians into its armed forces, brought to life and nurtured a largely Communist-influenced partisan movement in Axis-occupied Italy which fought a bitter campaign against the republic and its German masters. John Amery's suggestion that Mussolini had any prestige at this stage – even in the eyes of the Germans – was genuinely laughable. Nevertheless, he now had a project and a political leader who would take him seriously, and he took to the microphone once more.

In Italy I spoke in Italian to the Italians over the Republican network, uncensored, and made some speeches in Genoa, Turin, Biella, Cremona and Milan.

At last in Italy, with Mussolini's gathering efforts and his intention to set up the government in Milan, we seemed to be making some practical progress.[17]

Amery's participation in this 'progress' was interrupted at the end of January 1945 by the German Ambassador to the RSI, Rahn, who informed him that he was needed back in Germany. John departed immediately but in a phone call to Berlin from Constanz, where he was staying overnight, he discovered that the message was bogus and

simply a machination of certain people . . . and of course of Rahn. Hesse
told me to go back to Italy and tell the Embassy 'to mind their own
business'. To this effect he had me accompanied by the Ritterkreuzträger*
Dr Brenner to Italy. Brenner had some talks with Rahn which resulted
in that I could do what I liked but he, Rahn, would have nothing to do
with it.[18]

    While this small spat was taking place, John learned of the death
of his friend and mentor Jacques Doriot. Having survived service
on the Russian front with the LVF, 'Grand Jacques' had become the
leading figure among the Vichy collaborators in exile in Germany,
setting up a Committee of National Liberation and staking out his
claim as chief of the largest group of active French collaborators
still working for Germany. On 22 February 1945, after a series
of meetings with Marcel Déat and Joseph Darnand, his car was
machine-gunned on the road near Mengen where he had set up
his headquarters; hit by eleven bullets, Doriot died immediately.
The official version was that an Allied aircraft had strafed him, but
rumours abounded among the collaborators that the aircraft might
have been German, or even that there was no aircraft at all.[19] John
attended Déat's funeral at Mengen a few days later and then left
Germany for the last time.

    Things were now moving quickly. In the West, the failure of
the Ardennes offensive, which had been launched on 16 December,
had signalled the beginning of the end of German resistance there;
in the East, Soviet forces had invaded East Prussia on 14 January
and on 17 January had finally taken Warsaw; their advance towards
Berlin continued relentlessly. Meanwhile, on 9 April 1945, British
and American forces launched their final offensive in Italy. The
end was now near, as John knew very well.

Mussolini had by this time . . . moved definitely to Milan where I saw
him on April the 23rd. As is known, the military situation had so

---

* A holder of the Knight's Cross of the Iron Cross.

degenerated by this time that his view was that there remained only to betake ourselves to the mountains where a great stock of food, ammunition, radio apparatus, etc. was to be laid in. The area Como following the winding Swiss border to the Stelvio and coming down in front of Bergamo to Lecco and Como again. It was to be said to be purely defensive, to show the world that there were a sufficient number of idealists who were willing to sacrifice a great deal to obtain a general anti-Communist front, but who would never surrender unconditionally or to the local Communists.[20]

Even John was a little sceptical of this plan:

he offered me a commission in the 'Brigada Nera'. I told him that I could not accept that because such an acceptance might involve me in firing on my fellow countrymen and this I was unwilling to do, but that I would certainly go with him and dress myself in a manner that my opinions should be unmistakable. He thought the front might hold three or four weeks on the Po and seemed in no hurry to abandon Milan, although it was my opinion and that of Colombo of the Muti and others that the defence of Milan was not very practical.

In any event I decided to go over to Como to have a look round and see what was happening there. In accordance with that I left Milan on the night of the 25th and two-thirds of the way along the autostrada to Como I was surrounded by partisans and made prisoner.[21]

In a sense Amery was lucky. Two days later, a Communist partisan leader, Lieutenant Colonel Valerio, arrived at the farmhouse near Lake Como where Mussolini was being held after being detected by partisans hiding amongst a group of evacuating German soldiers. Valerio bundled Mussolini and his mistress, Clara Petacci, into a car and set off in the direction of Milan. Having travelled part of the way, Valerio stopped the car, ordered his two prisoners out and unceremoniously shot them. In contrast, John and Michelle made it to Milan, where they were imprisoned in one of the town's jails. Meanwhile the partisans put out a message announcing that:

From the general command of the Freedom Volunteers Corps: In the Novarese, a brigade of the Freedom Volunteers has arrested the British citizen John Amery – we repeat John Amery. The General Command of the Freedom Volunteers Corps orders that he should be immediately transported to Milan to be handed over to the General Command in Milan.[22]

In response to this, Captain Alan Whicker of the Intelligence Corps, later to become the celebrated television journalist, quickly made his way to Milan:

I went to the Milan radio station and told them to broadcast an announcement calling for his [Amery's] whereabouts. Within minutes a message arrived to say he was being held in one of the city jails. I drove over with Sgt Huggett and ordered the Governor to produce him.

'Thank God you're here,' said a very pale Amery when led into the Governor's office with his girlfriend, an appealing brunette in a dark trouser suit. 'I thought they were going to shoot me.'[23]

This was the beginning of the end for John Amery.

PART III

Nemesis

12. Trial and Execution

Roger Casement's end began around dawn on 21 April 1916, when he, Robert Monteith and Daniel Bailey finally floundered ashore on Banna Strand near Curraghane in County Kerry. They had had a hard row from the U-boat which had brought them from Germany to Ireland, and the tiny dinghy in which they had come ashore had overturned once in the heavy chop and then run aground on a sandbank. All three men, dressed in civilian clothes, were soaked to the skin; all were tired: Casement, who had spent the previous year in the grip of a nervous breakdown and associated psychosomatic illnesses, was virtually prostrate with exhaustion. They pulled the dinghy a little way up the beach and then looked about for the party of Irish Volunteers they had expected to come to meet them: there was nobody to be seen. They buried their kit in the dunes and headed inland in the direction of Tralee, pausing to wash the dirt from their clothes in a nearby stream.

Although it was not yet five o'clock in the morning, the local community was beginning to stir, and as the three men walked on in the early morning light, they were noticed by several people. A farmer who had gone out early, it being Good Friday, to visit a holy well, saw their boat abandoned on the beach; he fetched a neighbour to help him move it, and when he returned, found his eight-year-old daughter playing with several revolvers that she had apparently removed from a tin trunk nearby. The farmer took the weapons up to his house while his neighbour went to fetch the Royal Irish Constabulary.

Meanwhile, Casement and his two companions had come to an ancient Irish ruin, known as McKenna's Fort, where they stopped to rest and to decide what their next move should be. Casement was too tired to continue for the moment, so Monteith and Bailey decided to leave him while they pushed on to Tralee to collect transport from the Irish Volunteer group there.

By now, Curraghane and Ardfert, the adjoining village, were in as much of an uproar as it is possible for a tiny, isolated rural community to be, as the RIC began their search for the new arrivals, and around 1 p.m., Casement, who was still lying in an almost fugue-like state at McKenna's Fort, heard a noise amongst the brambles and looked up to see a policeman pointing a rifle at him.

'If you move hand or foot, I'll shoot,' warned the constable.

'That's a nice way to treat an English traveller,' was Casement's response.

A sergeant now appeared, and after a further exchange during which Casement gave his name as Richard Morten (an English friend of his), they escorted him to the main road where they found a small boy driving along in a pony and trap. He was prevailed upon to give them all a lift to the police barracks at Ardfert.

From Ardfert Casement was transferred to Tralee where he was searched and formally charged with illegally importing arms, contrary to the Defence of the Realm Act. It is clear that by now the policemen had a good idea about who they had caught. They had summoned a local doctor – who happened to be a Nationalist sympathizer – to examine him, and Casement had managed to ask him to tell the local Volunteers he was there in the hope that they might attempt a rescue. As the doctor was leaving on this errand, a police officer showed him a photograph of Casement, covered the beard with a piece of paper (Casement had shaved off his beard before leaving Germany) and asked the doctor if he thought it was the same man; the doctor told him no.

The doctor hurried to the local Volunteers but they declined to believe his story; Monteith and Bailey had only slightly more success in persuading the local Volunteer commander to go to collect Casement. By the time he had found a vehicle and they had reached the vicinity of McKenna's Fort, Casement had been under arrest for some time.

During the evening, Casement asked to see a Catholic priest and when one was summoned, requested that he pass on a warning to the Volunteers that the Rising which he knew was coming would be hopeless; the Germans would not be providing any help beyond the arms shipment. The priest was reluctant to do this but eventually agreed to pass on the warning in order to avoid bloodshed, and went to find Commandant Stack, the local Volunteer leader. He gave him the message and Stack passed it up the chain of command; it reached Professor MacNeill, the Chief of Staff of the Volunteers, who was not aware of the planned Rising, the following day.

On the Saturday morning, Casement was taken by train from Tralee to Dublin, and from there under military police escort he travelled on the night mail boat from Kingstown to Holyhead. By now he knew, from seeing a discarded newspaper, that the arms-carrying ship *Aud* had not made it either. In the early hours of the morning of Easter Sunday, Casement arrived at Euston Station and was taken to Scotland Yard where he was cautioned and given breakfast.

At about ten in the morning on Easter Sunday, Casement was seen for the first time by the Head of the CID, Basil Thomson, and Captain Reginald Hall, the Chief of Naval Intelligence at the Admiralty. It was during this interview that he came to the conclusion that there was no point in attempting to deny his actions and freely admitted what he had done and why, taking care only not to incriminate any others if possible:

What I say I must act on. Some Irishmen are afraid to act, but I was not afraid to commit high treason. I am not endeavouring to shield myself at all. I face all the consequences. All I ask you is to believe I have done nothing dishonourable, which you will one day learn. I have done nothing treacherous to my country. I have committed perhaps many follies in endeavouring to help my country according to what I thought was best, and in this last act of mine in going back to Ireland I came with my eyes wide open, knowing exactly what I was going to do, knowing that you were bound to catch me. Knowing all the circumstances, I came from a sense of duty, in which, if I dared to tell you the fact, you would be the first to agree with me.[1]

Casement was of course referring to the Rising that he knew to be imminent. In fact his arrest, and the interception and scuttling of the arms vessel *Aud* which had taken place on the day of his landing in Ireland, had persuaded the British Government that the danger of an armed revolt in Ireland, which they believed to be timed for Easter, had receded. They were wrong: when Casement's interrogation resumed the following morning, the first reports of fighting in Dublin were filtering through to London and the assumption was that Casement had been sent over to lead it.

On 24 April Casement was charged with high treason and transferred in military custody to the Tower of London while the Government made arrangements for his trial. As he faced his first week of custody and interrogation in London, the Easter Rising was played out in Dublin. The rebellion itself began at around noon on Easter Monday, 24 April 1916, when a group of a hundred or so members of the Irish Volunteers and 'Citizen Army' seized control of the General Post Office in Sackville Street, Dublin, whilst others attempted to blow up the Magazine Fort in Phoenix Park and a third group attempted to seize control of Dublin Castle. Even at this early stage, events had an air of unreality about them: the main reaction of bystanders at the GPO was bewilderment, whilst the men who had seized Dublin Castle were so unnerved to find it virtually unguarded (the garrison was on 'minimum manning' for Easter and most of the officers and senior civil servants had gone to the races at Fairyhouse) that they swiftly evacuated it and occupied some nearby buildings instead.

In fact, the rebels had seized two dozen strongpoints throughout Dublin on Easter Monday, but lacking clear strategic direction they simply sat and waited while the security forces closed in on them using the advantage of superior numbers, firepower, tactics and training. Militarily futile as this was, it was in accordance with the ideas of Patrick Pearse, the mystical and unworldly Irish-language teacher who was the military leader of the rebellion. He believed that the rebellion and the shedding of blood on Irish soil would be enough to spur the Irish people on to independence. In some respects he proved to be right.

On Saturday, 29 April, with parts of central Dublin reduced to smoking ruins by British army artillery, Pearse and his men at the GPO surrendered, and during the next twenty-four hours his orders to the rest of the rebels were passed around Dublin until the guns finally fell silent. Many Irish people had been outraged by the rebellion, coming as it did at a time when their fathers, sons and brothers were fighting and dying for Britain and Ireland on the Western Front; even so, it was recognized at the highest levels that too extreme a reaction could well prove counter-productive. Nevertheless, that is precisely what was allowed to happen: fifteen men were executed after brief and secret military courts-martial in a display of brutality which, as much as any other single factor, undermined popular support for the continuation of 'British' rule in Ireland.

It was twenty-nine years, to the day, after the Easter Rising had ended that John Amery was handed over to the British authorities by the Communist Partisans of Milan, but with Europe in the grip of the turmoil of the end of the war and the security authorities on the look-out for a list of suspected traitors and renegades that totalled nearly two hundred, there was less pressure to proceed against him, particularly as the evidence against Amery was, at this point, considerably less comprehensive than that against Casement.

Like Casement, John Amery held back very little about his activities on behalf of the Third Reich and Italian Social Republic. After freeing him from partisan custody in Milan, Alan Whicker had handed him over to Sergeant John Martin of the Intelligence Corps who took him to R Internee Camp at Terni in northern Italy where he was placed in military custody. On 22 May 1945, Major Leonard Burt, a Scotland Yard detective seconded to MI5, arrived to interview him. After a formal caution had been administered, Amery told him that as he was a journalist (a rather strange claim to make, as he wasn't) it would be best if he typed out a statement of his own. Burt arranged for a typewriter to be brought in and Amery duly produced an eleven-page document that was eventually finished the following day, in which he cheerfully described his activities as a broadcaster and recruiter for the British Free Corps, as well as his contacts with leading French collaborators. He ended up with a rather plaintive plea for his luggage and belongings to be returned to him.

By the help of the American officer of CIC Milan I managed to get back from the luggage that I possessed at the Hotel Diana, Milan a few personal belongings and the papers above mentioned, but the very great majority of my belongings, diaries (that I greatly need to prove various happenings, in the period heretofore given) and other documents, still remain in the hands of the local Liberation Committee via Piave 8 Milan. My entire luggage these people seized in the Hotel Diana during my absence and took to their office, they seem not very inclined to return it.

    Moreover, the Col commanding the Piazza di Milano who brought me from Sorrogno to Milan undertook at the time to have returned my personal property that was seized by the partisans when they arrested me. Of this nothing has so far been seen it consists of:

    1 suit case (important documents and personal effects)

    1 overcoat

    1 fur coat and two silver foxes

    A 20 liter petrol tin full

    1 Lancia Aprilia motor car No 78410 Ml C. D. I.

It remains unclear what he thought he was going to be able to do with a car in an internment camp.

    In making his statement, Amery had effectively condemned himself. To ensure that he would be convicted, it remained only to prove that the activities he had admitted to amounted to treason, and the plethora of witnesses available to the British authorities with the end of the war would provide independent evidence to back up his admissions. His future was undoubtedly bleak.

The same was true of Casement. Although he does not appear to have made a formal statement incriminating himself, he did not need to. Oddly enough, the Germans had provided the prosecution, which was to be led by F. E. Smith, the Attorney-General (and a former leader of the Ulster Volunteer Force), with all the evidence that it needed by repatriating a number of Irish POWs who were deemed too severely wounded to be of further military use. Many of these men had been held at Limburg and had seen Casement making his appeals for volunteers for the Irish Brigade: there would be little point in attempting to refute their evidence.

Casement's defence was funded by donations from a number of friends, including Alice Green and Sir Arthur Conan Doyle; $1,000 were covertly provided from Germany via the Clan na Gael in New York. His lawyer was George Gavan Duffy, a well-known Irish Nationalist solicitor who, after committal proceedings at Bow Street in May 1916, engaged as leading counsel a well-known figure from the Irish Bar. This was Serjeant A. M. Sullivan, KC, a New Yorker by birth who had come to Ireland as a young man and taken up the law. Although as a law officer of the Crown in Ireland, he could not take briefs for the defence there, his standing at the English Bar was as a junior barrister and there was no such obstacle. Sullivan was initially reluctant to take on such a hopeless and unpopular case, but Gavan Duffy, his brother-in-law, persuaded him with the offer of 150 guineas as a fee and the promise that it would considerably enhance his legal standing in England. The Attorney-General, concerned that he should be seen to be facing a barrister of equal standing, did apparently approach the Lord Chancellor to have Sullivan made a KC in England as well, but this was turned down and Sullivan remained technically a 'junior' throughout the trial.

Two possible approaches to defending Casement were considered. The first of these, favoured by Casement himself, was essentially a political argument: that he could not be tried for treason by an 'English' court because he was Irish, and that while what he had done might have been harmful to England, it was not contrary to the interests of Ireland. This was an argument that Sullivan was not prepared to entertain: in the first place it was certain to fail; in the second, it would not allow him any scope to demonstrate his legal skills at the English Bar.

Instead, Sullivan favoured a technical legal defence in which he would not challenge the prosecution's presentation of the facts of the case, but would seek to prove that they were not treasonable within the meaning of the ancient statute under which Casement had been charged. In effect, Sullivan wanted to claim that Casement did not show any intent to harm the United Kingdom but that his actions took place within the domestic political context in Ireland; that Casement was not aiding Germany, or seeking to do so, but was simply providing arms for the Irish National Volunteers in terms of a precedent established by the actions, it would no doubt be implied, of the Attorney-General himself who had undoubtedly been preparing to foment armed rebellion in Ulster. To those involved with the defence, this also seemed certain to fail.

By contrast, for a while at least there did seem to be a possibility of escape for Amery. He was brought to England on 9 July 1945 and taken to Wandsworth Prison, prior to remand proceedings that took place at Bow Street Magistrates Court the following day. It seems, however, that during the course of briefing the solicitors, Lickfold's, who had been appointed to act for him, he, or a member of his family, mentioned the story of his service in the Spanish Civil War. Somehow the idea arose that he might have become a Spanish citizen before the war and could not therefore be a traitor to Britain.

How this story had arisen can only be surmised at. John had not made this claim before, so far as we can tell, and had not mentioned it in his statement. There were also several other crucial pieces of evidence which would seem, at face value, to contradict it, including the fact that Amery had continued to travel on a British passport and had required visas on the handful of brief visits he could be shown to have made to Spain; and that he was restricted as a British citizen while in Vichy France and had been unable to travel to Spain as a result.

Undaunted by this, Julian Amery, who had spent much of the war in the Balkans as an officer in the Special Operations Executive, was sent to Spain to gather evidence. He did this very well: by the time he returned he had obtained a judicially notarized certificate showing that John had gained membership of the Spanish Legion dated 15 March 1937, and a certificate of naturalization dated 19 March of the same year. Julian Amery was able to make use of the communications facilities at the British Embassy in Madrid to report his findings without realizing that the MI6 office there would alert MI5 in London to the line that the defence were adopting.

Enquiries initiated at the behest of MI5 revealed that the certificates acquired by Julian Amery were not what they seemed, and that in any case, John had been at sea or in Italy on the two dates mentioned. As MI6 reported back to London:

Very strong suspicions exist that the whole conduct of Julian Amery's enquiries to assist his brother have involved conspiracy to manufacture evidence and documents. Certainly ample material for the cross-examination of all defence witnesses is available.[2]

On 28 November 1945, at 11.30 a.m., John Amery entered the dock at the Central Criminal Court at the Old Bailey to listen to the Clerk of the Court read out the first indictment of eight counts of high treason contrary to the Treason Act of 1351. According to Rebecca West, who was covering the trial for the *New Yorker* magazine, he looked like a 'sick little monkey'. He was then asked whether he would plead guilty or not guilty. To the astonishment of almost everyone present he replied: 'I plead guilty to all counts.'

Mr Justice Humphreys leaned forward and addressed G. O. Glade, Amery's counsel: 'I never accept a plea of guilty on a capital charge without assuring myself that the accused thoroughly understands what he is doing and what the immediate result must be, and that he is in accord with his legal advisors in the course he has taken.' Slade's reply was simple: 'I can assure you of that, my Lord. I have explained the position to my client and I am satisfied he understands it.'

The judge donned the black cloth square and pronounced sentence of death.

Casement's trial lasted longer but the result was just as inevitable. After four days of evidence and argument, Sullivan's defence was rejected and Casement was sentenced to hang. The most interesting aspect of his trial for non-lawyers was the speech in justification of his actions which Casement gave after the verdict had been announced (reproduced in full at Appendix One). Having pleaded 'Not Guilty', Casement now had the right to appeal and duly exercised it. Sullivan chose to fight the appeal on the same grounds that he had fought the original trial: namely, that the statute of 1351 could not be applied to his client's actions. This too was bound to fail and duly did so.

Casement's final appeal was to the House of Lords and for this he required the *fiat* of his prosecutor and former political opponent, the Attorney-General, F. E. Smith. In capital cases this was usually a formality but in this case it was not. Smith refused to allow leave to appeal to the House of Lords. The reason was straightforward: the appeal could not succeed. Although this has been characterized as an act of vengefulness towards a political enemy, it would probably have been much easier for Smith to allow an appeal to go forward in the knowledge that it would certainly fail.

It was at this time that the most controversial aspect of Casement's trial and execution became an important factor: the so-called 'Black Diaries'. The official version is that around the time that Casement arrived at Scotland Yard, several trunks of his possessions were seized from a house where he stayed in Ebury Street, Pimlico, and from a warehouse owned by W. J. Allisons, a company used by soldiers, colonial officials and missionaries around the world. Amongst the material that they discovered were the 'Black Diaries': three volumes of notes and jottings covering the years 1903, 1910 and 1911 when Casement had been engaged in his atrocity investigations. As we have seen, these included a good deal of material of a sexually explicit nature which, in an era when homosexuality was regarded as an abomination, would have horrified the majority of heterosexuals who read it. This is indeed what happened.

At about the time of Casement's committal hearings in May 1916, Captain Hall of Naval Intelligence held a private briefing for several journalists at which he showed them extracts from the Diaries. Word spread and soon a major whispering campaign was in process, fuelled by Hall and Thomson who had no hesitation in showing the Diaries to as many influential people as possible. It seems, although it is not explicitly clear, that Thomson and Hall intended to stifle the emergence of any campaign to prevent Casement's eventual execution. In this they had some success; the majority of those who saw the Diaries, or the extracts hawked around by Thomson, Hall and their agents, concluded that Casement was too despicable to be allowed clemency. But it is true that the majority of those who really knew Casement, and were aware of his achievements in the Congo and the Putumayo, were prepared to forgive him his homosexuality.

From the legal point of view, Casement's alleged homosexuality had no bearing on the case, or on whether he should be granted clemency, but what seemed a disgusting crime to the majority of influential members of the Government who knew about it (and those who did not think it disgusting undoubtedly kept quiet), inevitably influenced the outcome of discussions about whether Casement should be reprieved, and equally inevitably slanted opinion towards the position that he should not. In the meantime, dissemination of the Diaries in the United States had certainly muted Irish-American protest there to some extent.

A considerable debate did take place, both within and outside the Government, over whether Casement should hang, but on 29 July the decision was finally made at Cabinet level and the die was cast. Casement was given the terrible news on 2 August by the Governor of Pentonville Prison, where he was being held, but by then, although he had originally assumed after the Easter Rising – and the catastrophe of the executions of Pearse and company – that the British Government would not dare to hang him, he had become resigned to the fact. On 30 June he had been deprived of his knighthood and in the days leading up to his execution he was accepted into the Catholic faith. Executioner Ellis came for him on 3 August at 9 a.m.

For John Amery there could be no appeal. He had pleaded guilty to high treason and could only hope that he would be granted clemency. There were good grounds to encourage this hope. His behaviour over the years had been so strange that it was clear he was in the grip of some pathological disorder. In the period after the sentence was pronounced, Leo Amery took steps to see whether he could influence the Home Secretary's decision on clemency, and to this end, he asked the psychiatrist Lord Horder, a personal friend, to undertake an examination of John with a view to compiling a report on his mental state.

The main problem that Horder faced was that he was not allowed to interview John, but he skirted this by tracking down, with Leo and Julian's help, the most important figures they could find from John's past, including teachers, tutors, nannies and even Una, who had been living in a lesbian relationship with a friend in Hampshire. These witnesses universally testified to John's oddness. Horder commissioned Dr Edward Glover, a Wimpole Street psychiatrist and the founder of the Psychopathic Clinic, to compile a report which he circulated to four other senior psychiatrists, Professor Henderson and Drs Hart, Rees and MacNiven, for their views. They were all broadly in agreement: John, whilst undoubtedly not insane according to the M'Naghten rules, was incapable of appreciating the moral difference between right and wrong. Dr Glover's conclusions were summarized in the report he gave to Horder:

1. That whatever may be his existing mental state, as regards sanity, he is certainly a severe and long-standing case of psychopathic disorder of the type at one time called 'moral insanity' or 'moral imbecility'.
2. That his conduct in life is determined by diseased mental processes.
3. That even if he should prove to be aware of the nature of his actions and utterances, his behaviour is governed by these diseased processes to such an extent that he is incapable of a normal appreciation of consequences and is devoid of the moral sense by which normal people control their actions and utterances.[3]

This report was so emphatically at variance with the views of the senior medical officer at Wandsworth Prison, who would normally have played a crucial role in a decision to grant clemency on medical or psychiatric grounds, that the Home Secretary's advisors took the unusual step of commissioning a further psychiatric examination. Dr Hugh Grierson, medical officer at Wandsworth, had merely noted, on 1 December 1945, that Amery was an 'insignificant looking and weedy individual', who 'showed no signs of mental disease. He was untidy and not over-clean in his personal attention. He read the daily papers and smoked innumerable cigarettes and was generally indolent.'[4]

The report of the two Home Office doctors must have been disquieting for the Home Secretary. In the two cases of high treason following the Second World War in which the death sentence was imposed and then repealed – those of Thomas Cooper and Walter Purdy – the commutation of the sentence had followed quickly after the failure of the final legal appeals, and the fact that Amery's case was dragging out to the last few days before the execution was scheduled to take place was indicative that the Home Office was minded to let the law take its course. But then Drs East and Hopwood, the psychiatrists appointed by the Home Office, delivered their bombshell. In a report delivered both in writing and orally to the Home Secretary on 14 December – the same day that Leo Amery wrote to the Home Secretary attempting to explain his son's conduct (see Appendix Two) – with Amery's execution only five days away, they informed him of their conclusion: that Amery was a moral defective in the sense that his mind was sufficiently unsound for him to be unable to form moral judgements about his own conduct, and that therefore he should not be executed, even though he understood that his acts infringed against the law and against normally accepted social standards.[5]

The question which faced the Home Secretary was this: should such a form of mental unsoundness be sufficient grounds for inter-fering with the course of the law? In two opinions,[6] drafted on 15 December, the Permanent Secretary at the Home Office, Sir Frank Newsam, argued strongly that they should not. The most important factor from the legal point of view was that Amery had not been certified as insane, and that medical opinions were not, as a result, binding on the Home Secretary. In the first of these documents, Newsam argued that Amery had sufficient intelligence to under-stand the nature of his acts and that they were wrong, and possessed enough self-control to direct his activities: his 'mental defect' should not prevent his execution.

The second document, which appears to have been a more detailed response to the report of East and Hopwood, advances several considerably less compelling arguments for going ahead with the hanging. The first of these was that because Amery was not insane, he would have to be held in a normal convict prison, rather than Broadmoor, and that if his sentence were respited, he would not serve more than twenty years before being returned to the community.

Newsam noted:

The doctors said, in discussion with the S of S, that the moral defect in this case is so serious that it is not beyond the bounds of possibility that Amery might commit homicide. The question thus arises whether the

Secretary of State would be justified in taking any action now which (since detention for life in a convict prison is not practical) will sooner or later result in Amery's release.[7]

It must be somewhat unusual to justify executing a man for treason on the basis that he might, when released from prison, commit murder.

After a brief discussion of whether there were any further extenuating circumstances in Amery's case which might justify a reprieve – there were not – Newsam came to the issue which had been haunting the entire process of Amery's trial and execution:

There is the further consideration of the effect of a reprieve on public opinion. Capital punishment in this country is tolerated as a deterrent because the man in the street believes that the law is administered without fear or favour. If Amery were reprieved it would be difficult to convince the ordinary man that Amery had not received exceptional and privileged treatment.[8]

Over the next three days Amery said his final farewells to his family. During the evening of 18 December he was visited for the last time by the Governor of Wandsworth Prison and asked for, and was given, 'a little brandy'.[9] There was no religious conversion for John, and at nine o'clock the following morning he finally met Albert Pierrepoint.

What do the cases of Casement and Amery tell us about treason? In the first place we can see that it is a crime which is purely political in character. It is abundantly clear that neither Roger Casement nor John Amery succeeded in causing any appreciable damage to Britain and to British interests by the actions for which they were convicted and hanged (Casement's previous involvement in running guns into Ireland is more problematic but he was not tried for this and his lawyer's attempts to introduce it as an element of his defence were ruled irrelevant). During the twentieth century, those 'traitors' who actually did harm to British interests were tried under Official Secrets or emergency powers legislation (including the 1940 Treachery Act, aimed at spies and enemy agents): high treason was reserved for those who had taken a *political* stand against the state during wartime, however futile and, indeed, laughable their efforts might have been.

Casement espoused political views which, though perfectly legal, were shared by only a relatively small minority of his countrymen (in both the narrow Irish sense and the broader British one). Amery's political philosophy, combining as it did Imperialism, anti-Semitism, pan-Europeanism, Socialism and Fascism, was probably unique to him, if in fact he really understood what he was saying. What categorizes both men is a lack of moderation: Casement would argue his case, but he was not listening to the opposition: he was right and his opponents were wrong. It was this lack of moderation that led Casement to believe – uniquely amongst the Irish Republican 'leadership' – that Germany had a sincere interest in Irish independence from Britain over and above gaining a tactical advantage on the Western Front; this had previously led him to reject the compromises implicit in the Home Rule Act of 1911. The majority of Irishmen who fought in the British Armed Forces during the First World War were drawn from the mainly Catholic and broadly Nationalist community; the great majority of Fascists who were not interned as enemies of the state happily served their country.

The origins of such lack of moderation are easy to see in Amery's case, slightly less so in Casement's. Amery was the lifelong victim of a personality disorder; with Casement we must conclude that his experiences in the Congo in particular, but also subsequently in South America, played the most important part. What is evident is that Casement changed from being an Imperialist jingo with a deep interest in Irish history to a radical Irish Nationalist within the space of a year or so. This was undoubtedly the result of Casement's analysis of what he found in the Congo, almost certainly combined with some form of breakdown caused, we can speculate, by anger, stress and physical illness; perhaps also by the strain involved in living a secret life as a homosexual, and maybe also by guilt at his own role in pioneering Leopold's colony. Casement's humanitarian achievements in the Congo were considerable, but they were to cost him dear.

The crime of high treason is the legal cloak with which the British state covers the retribution it takes against anyone who offers a challenge to it, however weak that person may be. Traitors are not necessarily weak, of course, but they certainly lack the moral and social restraint which governs the way others conduct themselves. This is probably the only sense in which Casement's homosexuality is of historic interest: both Casement and Amery, like the majority of the Cambridge spy ring in the 1930s and 1940s, conducted themselves sexually in a way which was completely at variance with the *mores* of most of their contemporaries. Clearly, it would be ridiculous to suggest that homosexuality or other bizarre sexual behaviour is either a necessary or sufficient pre-condition for treason, but it may be that it is, or in the cases of Casement and Amery was, an indication of the value that an individual ultimately placed on the opinion of his peers.

It would be idle to pretend that Casement and Amery were men of equal stature, but their differing paths through life led them both to a situation in which the underlying similarities between them – self-importance and lack of restraint – caused them to throw down the gauntlet to the state which one had served faithfully for more than twenty years and the other had affected to want to save. The response in both cases was brutal and merciless.

13. Epilogue: The Casement Diaries Forgery Controversy

The most enduring aspect of the story of Roger Casement has proved to be the continuing controversy over whether the three diaries and two cash ledgers which were supposedly found at the time of his arrest and were subsequently used to deter potential campaigners for clemency were, in fact, forgeries.

The reasons that this should be the case are quite straightforward; those people who admired Casement as a humanitarian were uncomfortable that he should be revealed to have been paying poor, young native men and boys for sex; whilst those who admired him as an Irish Republican revolutionary hero have, for the most part, shared the morally conservative Catholicism which has traditionally underpinned mainstream Republicanism, in which the practice of homosexuality is widely regarded as aberrant if not an abomination. The revelations of Casement's sexuality which the diaries presented do not sit well with either standpoint and, over time, partisans of both of these essentially positive views of Casement have tended to look for evidence which would exonerate 'their' man.

This has not, however, been a necessarily intellectually dishonest process. The most important single piece of evidence which would suggest that the diaries were forged is the fact that few, if any, of Casement's close friends and collaborators either knew or, as far as we can tell, suspected that he might be homosexual. The example of the disgrace of Oscar Wilde is enough to show how serious the implications of exposure as a homosexual were at that time. When details of what the diaries contained began to be circulated in 1916, many people who knew Casement were astounded and horrified. Opinion was divided among his friends over whether to accept the diaries at face value, and several of his closest friends, as well as members of his family, could not bring themselves to believe that they were genuine. This, combined with the disgraceful use that was made of the diaries – as a means of muting protest at Casement's execution – led to the first forgery theories emerging among those who could not accept that their hero was homosexual.

Early theories regarding the forgery of the diaries were not refuted, because although the transcripts and some pages from an original diary were widely shown around – chiefly by Captain Reginald 'Blinker' Hall of Naval Intelligence and Basil Thomson of the CID – in the period leading up to Casement's execution, the diaries themselves were kept firmly in the custody of the British authorities; and once the execution had taken place any copies that had been made were quickly removed from circulation, although by then knowledge of their contents was widespread. Inevitably this tended to suggest that the Government had something to hide and this was compounded by the refusal of successive Home Secretaries to confirm or deny whether the diaries still existed and were in the possession of the Government.

Confusion was added to the story of the diaries by Thomson himself. Between 1921 and 1939 he published several different versions of how the diaries had come into the possession of the police. The first of these, printed in an article in *The Times* in November 1921, suggested that Casement's London lodgings, in Ebury Street, Pimlico, had been searched around the time of his arrival in London in 1916, and that the trunks had been opened and the diaries found more or less simultaneously with the interviews conducted by Hall and Thomson. This rather unlikely tale was superseded by a second version, the following year, in which Thomson suggested that the trunks had been found some months earlier but that they had not been opened and searched. Thomson describes the moment when 'Towards the end of the interview a policeman entered the room and whispered to me that Casement might have the key of the trunks. I asked him, and with a magnificent gesture he said, "Break them open; there is nothing in them but clothing, and I shall not want them again." "[1] Whilst Casement's response is supported by the transcript of the interview in his MI5 file,[2] again it seems unlikely that the police had not taken the opportunity to search Casement's luggage before this point. In a third version, which appeared in 1925 in the magazine *English Life*, Thomson suggested that the trunks which contained the diaries had been brought to Scotland Yard by Casement's landlord; and finally, in 1939, when Thomson's own diaries were published, it was simply stated that Casement's luggage 'was lying in the Special Branch Office'.[3]

Complications were added to the story by a journalist, Peter Singleton-Gates, who had been given a typescript copy of the diaries by Thomson – who used Singleton-Gates to plant stories in the press – in 1922. Singleton-Gates decided that he wanted to write a book based on the diaries, but when this was announced, he was threatened with prosecution under the Official Secrets Act and his flat was covertly searched, in an apparent attempt to seize his copy of the diaries (he had hidden them elsewhere). Again, although this was evidence of nothing more than a desire to suppress publication of the diaries at a time when relations between Britain and the fledgling Irish Free State were somewhat delicate, it was certainly suggestive of the supposition that the British Government felt it had something to hide.

Even so, the forgery theory was not formally stated until 1936, when an Irish American, Dr William J. Maloney, published a book, *The Forged Casement Diaries*, in which he argued that the diaries were indeed the work of a British Government forger, and that they had been accomplished by using material from a diary which Casement had retrieved from Armando Normand, one of the section chiefs working for the Peruvian Amazon Company in the Putumayo, who had been noted by Casement and members of the commission as a considerable sexual predator.

Until this time, it had been generally accepted, outside a small circle of Casement's family, friends and admirers, that the diaries were genuine, but the publication of Maloney's book began to change this. Maloney's theory was deeply flawed. It relied for the most part on the recollections of several of Casement's friends that Roger had told them of an obscene diary which he had obtained from Normand and which he was sending to the Foreign Office in support of his Putumayo report. Maloney argued that it was Casement's handwritten copy of the Normand diary, with dates suitably altered, which had been used to discredit him. This was supported by the claim of Michael Doyle, an American lawyer who had served in Casement's defence team at his trial, that Casement had repeatedly reiterated that he had never written a homosexual diary. In fact there is no external evidence to support the Normand diary theory. None of Casement's correspondence makes any reference to such a document; it was not used in the Putumayo report and, in any case, it fails to explain the existence of the 1903 Congo diary. It is also worth pointing out that Normand's reported sexual exploits were entirely heterosexual in character.

Doyle's claim that Casement denied his homosexuality is more problematic, not least because it is directly contradicted by Serjeant Sullivan, leader of the defence team, who also claims to have discussed the issue with his client. As we have seen, a typescript of the diaries was given to the defence by F. E. Smith, who had suggested it might facilitate a plea of guilty but insane. Sullivan was not prepared to do this: he believed that the court would not accept such a 'plea bargain' between prosecution and defence and that he would have to attempt to prove Casement's insanity by using the diaries, which would inevitably bring extreme discredit on everything Casement had done dating back to at least 1903. In any case, to prove insanity, as John Amery later discovered, is not so easy: the defence need to establish that the accused could not understand the difference between right and wrong, not just that he was in the grip of a sexual obsession. Casement supposedly raised the issue of the diaries with Sullivan because he was concerned that they would be introduced as evidence into the trial and would not accept Sullivan's assurance that they would not: 'He instructed me to explain to the jury that the filthy and disreputable practices and the rhapsodical glorification of them were inseparable from true genius; moreover, I was to cite a list of all truly great men to prove it.'[4]

Maloney's book, which suffered from the fact that the author had not seen or read the diaries, was soon discredited by most interested parties, but its effect was to bring the diary forgery conspiracy theory into the mainstream. Alfred Noyes, a Princeton professor, who had denounced Casement in the United States in 1917 on the basis of having read the typescripts, subsequently came to believe that he had been deceived as part of a British propaganda measure and took up the cudgels to promote the forgery argument.

Noyes refined the Maloney theory by arguing in *The Accusing Ghost, or Justice for Roger Casement*, published in 1957, that the diaries were genuine but the homosexual material had been interpolated into them by a forger, working on behalf of Thomson, Hall and Smith. This idea was taken up by Dr Herbert Mackey who also pointed to apparent internal contradictions in the text. One of the most famous of these relates to a sexual encounter with a friend called 'Millar' which supposedly took place on 28 May 1910.

The diary entry reads: 'Left for Warrenpoint with *Millar*. Boated & *Huge* Enjoyment. Both Enjoyed. He came to lunch at G Central Hotel. Rode gloriously – splendid steed. Huge – told of many – *Grand*'. This is followed by a marginal entry describing their sexual activities that evening.

Mackey pointed out that there was no Grand Central Hotel in Warrenpoint, nor had there ever been one, and suggested that the sexual material had been inserted into what was probably a description of a meeting between Casement and his friend and political associate, Bulmer Hobson, who was certainly not homosexual.

In 1959 the question of the authenticity of the diaries was once again brought into focus, this time by the publication in Paris, by Peter Singleton-Gates and Maurice Girodias, of an edition of the diaries based on Singleton-Gates's typescript and called 'The Black

Diaries'. The response of the British Home Secretary, R. A. Butler, at the prompting of a number of Members of Parliament, was to release the diaries from the Home Office to the Public Records Office where they could finally be inspected by bona fide researchers who could demonstrate a legitimate interest in them.

Study of the diaries by anyone who is not a specialist in forensic document examination suggests that if they are forgeries, then they are very sophisticated indeed. There are no obvious signs of significant alterations above and beyond those one would expect the author of a jotted notebook to make and, although the hand-writing does tend to differ, depending on what type of medium was being used, it is reasonably consistent throughout. Since their release, however, the diaries have, on at least two occasions, been subjected to examination by handwriting and document specialists. Both Dr Wilson Harrison, of the South Wales Forensic Science laboratory in 1959, and Dr David Baxendale, who examined the diaries for the BBC in 1994, concluded that they were the work of one hand and have not been significantly altered, and that they are consistent with other examples of Casement's handwriting. This is not in itself conclusive: a highly competent forger might well be able to produce a convincing imitation of Casement's handwriting at length, but it is indicative of the amount of trouble that a forger would have to have taken in perpetrating the forgery.

More recent advocates of forgery theories have tended to point towards techniques of textual analysis as indicators, if not proof, that all three Black Diaries were produced by someone other than Casement. Patterns, phrasing, key words and expression have been analysed and apparently tend to contrast with Casement's other writings, thus suggesting that he may not have been the author at all.

So have the forgery theorists made a convincing case? The answer is no. The British Government has now released all the material that has been held in the archives, including police, Home Office and MI5 files, and not a single shred of positive information, evidence or even suggestion has emerged which would indicate that the diaries are Government-directed forgeries. Of course, one might expect this to be the case: it could well be argued that no Government would care to leave 'smoking-gun' evidence lying around in its archives to be leaked or uncovered at an inopportune moment; yet the fact remains that the diaries themselves have survived to be argued over by successive generations. If they are forgeries, the perpetrators would have to be very confident of their quality to leave them for subsequent forensic examination.

In fact it is not difficult to refute most, if not all, of the claims made by the forgery school. Maloney's argument can be discounted because he was refuting rumours: he did not know in detail what was in the diaries and was simply basing his argument on the claim that Casement was not homosexual. Mackey's critique of internal inconsistencies and contradictions is more interesting but can equally be refuted. For example, in the case of the tryst at the supposed Grand Central Hotel in Warrenpoint he was wrong. The Grand Central Hotel mentioned in the diary is in Belfast,★ where Casement and 'Millar' lunched before leaving for their weekend in Warrenpoint. Moreover, the War Office Intelligence Department had actually succeeded in identifying 'Millar' as Joseph Millar Gordon of Belfast.

This last point is interesting: the British Government also investigated the diaries to ascertain whether they were genuine. Mostly this consisted of checking them against Foreign Office records but attempts were also made to identify any sexual partners that Casement had had. The only success in this direction seems to have been identifying 'Millar' as Gordon, which was achieved because, on 3 June 1911, Casement recorded in his cash ledger that he had given 'Millar' a motorcycle, and the transaction was recorded by the vehicle licensing department.[5]

Other apparent inconsistencies in the text include the remarks made by Casement regarding the suicide of Sir Hector MacDonald

★ And has, ironically, more recently been used as a British army patrol base during the Northern Irish troubles.

and the 'terrible disease' which had led to it and another, gleefully picked up by one of the more recent forgery theorists, Angus Mitchell, in his introduction to his annotated edition of Casement's Putumayo journal for 1910 (the so-called 'White Diary'). Part of the entry for 29 September 1910 reads:

I swear to God, I'd hang every one of the band of wretches with my own hands if I had the power, and do it with the greatest pleasure. I have never shot game with any pleasure, have indeed abandoned all shooting for that reason, that I dislike the thought of taking life. I have never given life to anyone myself, and my celibacy makes me frugal of human life, but I'd shoot or exterminate these infamous scoundrels more gladly than I should shoot a crocodile or kill a snake.

Mitchell's comment on this passage is to note: 'Exactly why Casement should have made such a direct statement about his "celibacy" while keeping a parallel sex diary has yet to be satisfactorily explained.'[6]

There are actually two obvious answers to this: first, if Casement did indeed write in 'clear and succinct English prose and show his grasp of language',[7] as Mitchell suggests, he would have known that to be celibate is to be unmarried, and that its extension to mean abstention from sex is a more recent usage.

The second answer is that the Black Diaries were obviously written with a completely different intention to any of Casement's other surviving prose. As we have seen, the Black Diary for 1910 is mirrored for the three months of Casement's Amazon expedition by the so-called White Diary. Whilst the Black Diary is a series of disjointed notes and jottings, the White Diary is a more fluent and composed narrative which Casement allowed to be read by others in order to give them a context in which to set the facts of his Putumayo report; it is unthinkable that he would allow anyone else to read the Black Diary for the same period, nor would there be much point in doing so as much of it is explicable only to the author. Forgery theorists have tended to argue that the forger must have based his work on the White Diary for the same period; the only extant evidence is that the opposite was true. The Black Diary makes several references to the White, indicating broadly that the White was written up from time to time when Casement paused in his travels. This evidence is ignored by, for example, Mitchell who argues *inter alia* that it is unrealistic to imagine Casement spending long periods each day writing up two diaries (at a period when he was also suffering problems with his eyes): '. . . it forced him to be as economic as possible with his writing and avoid unnecessary strain. Why then he would have bothered to keep two diaries repeating the same information is hard to explain.'[8] In fact, of course, he didn't: he kept a private diary in which he jotted down facts, figures and notes and every few days expanded into a narrative journal of his work, as he describes in the Black diary on, for example, Friday, 21 October: 'I am writing up my diary since Monday . . .'.

In reality, the forgery theories represent wishful thinking on the part of admirers of Casement. The truth is that the British Government had no real need to forge the diaries: Casement was, by his own admission, a traitor and his 'Not Guilty' plea and defence were essentially a formality. There were indeed a number of petitions for clemency for him and under certain circumstances these might have been effective; but not in the midst of the most bloody war Britain had ever fought. Casement was convicted and sentenced to death for his treason on 29 June 1916. Two days later, on the first day of the battle of the Somme, 60,000 soldiers, many of them Irish, were lost. These were the brothers, fathers and sons of the people who would be electing the next Government and they were unlikely to tolerate a Government which failed to exact retribution against such a flagrant traitor.

The only serious public opinion problem which the Government faced in executing Casement was in the United States and in its attempts to mute this, Asquith's Cabinet did indeed authorize the use of the diaries. But this was only possible because the Government had found them, not because it had had time to have them manufactured. If we accept that the British Government had had little or no warning that Casement, whom it had probably assumed would stay in Germany or possibly return to the United States, was actually coming to Ireland, then the diaries must have been faked between the end of April and the beginning of June when a copy of them was passed to the defence team by F. E. Smith. It is highly unlikely that such an intricately detailed task – involving, as it inevitably would, considerable research as well as the physical task of the forgery – could have been so successfully accomplished in such a short time. It is possible that the forgery might have been done before this period, but it would be difficult to see why the Government would have bothered, unless it was to use the diaries as part of a propaganda campaign, and there is no evidence to support this view (indeed, the evidence of Casement's MI5 file, which is essentially negative, is that British Intelligence did little more than collect whatever fragments of information turned up on Casement prior to his sudden reappearance: it certainly didn't launch any active operations against him).

Even if the British Government had indeed managed to contrive a forgery in the short time available, it is unimaginable that it would then have given a copy of the diaries to the defence team. If they were forgeries, they would have immediately been exposed and denounced as such by Casement and his legal advisors, and as we know, they weren't. Michael Doyle's claim that Casement had denied authorship of the diaries sits uneasily with his failure to mention this until questioned in the 1930s.

The Casement diary forgery theories are a conspiracy theory which is no more plausible than, for example, John F. Kennedy assassination conspiracy theories and, because they are based on suppositions rather than evidence, equally difficult to refute. Every time evidence is used to lop the head off the conspiracy, another one grows to replace it. The controversy over the diaries is a dead end because, ultimately, neither side will concede the argument. In reality, Casement's homosexuality is historically trivial: he was a great humanitarian and, to Irish republicans, a patriot and hero. His homosexuality does not alter that: there is no evidence in the diaries that he did anything worse than have paid sexual intercourse with willing young men. This was scandalous and disgusting to many of his contemporaries but in this more tolerant time does not actually matter very much except to those who seek to sanctify Casement: he was an idealist and patriot, though a traitor, but he was certainly no saint.

Appendix 1 Casement's Speech from the Dock 29 June 1916

My Lord Chief Justice, as I wish to reach a much wider audience than I see before me here, I intend to read all that I propose to say. What I read now is something I wrote more than twenty days ago. I may say, my Lord, at once, that I protest against the jurisdiction of this Court in my case on this charge, and the argument that I am now going to read is addressed not to this Court, but to my own countrymen.

There is an objection, possibly not good in law, but surely good on moral grounds, against the application to me here of this old English statute, 565 years old, that seeks to deprive an Irishman today of life and honour, not for 'adhering to the King's enemies', but for adhering to his own people.

When this statute was passed in 1351, what was the state of men's minds on the question of a far higher allegiance – that of a man to God and His Kingdom? The law of that day did not permit a man to forsake his church or deny his God save with his life. The 'heretic' then had the same doom as the 'traitor'.

Today a man may forswear God and His heavenly kingdom without fear or penalty, all earlier statutes having gone the way of Nero's edicts against the Christians; but that Constitutional phantom, 'The King', can still dig up from the dungeons and torture chambers of the Dark Ages a law that takes a man's life and limb for an exercise of conscience.

If true religion rests on love it is equally true that loyalty rests on love. The law I am charged under has no parentage in love and claims the allegiance of today on the ignorance and blindness of the past.

I am being tried, in truth, not by my peers of the live present, but by the peers of the dead past; not by the civilization of the twentieth century, but by the brutality of the fourteenth; not even by a statute framed in the language of an enemy land – so antiquated is the law that must be sought today to slay an Irishman, whose offence is that he puts Ireland first.

Loyalty is a sentiment, not a law. It rests on love, not on restraint. The Government of Ireland by England rests on restraint and not on law; and since it demands no love, it can evoke no loyalty.

But this statute is more absurd even than it is antiquated, and if it is potent to hang one Irishman, it is still more potent to gibbet all Englishmen.

Edward III was King not only of the realm of England, but also of the realm of France, and he was not King of Ireland. Yet his dead hand today may pull the noose around the Irishman's neck whose Sovereign he was not, but it can strain no strand around the Frenchman's throat whose Sovereign he was. For centuries the successors of Edward III claimed to be Kings of France, and quartered the arms of France on their royal shield down to the Union with Ireland on 1 January 1801. Throughout these hundreds of years these 'Kings of France' were constantly at war with their realm of France and their French subjects, who should have gone from birth to death with an obvious fear of treason before their eyes. But did they? Did the 'Kings of France' resident here at Windsor or in the Tower of London, hang, draw and quarter as a traitor every Frenchman for 400 years who fell into their hands with arms in his hand? On the contrary, they received embassies of these traitors, presents from these traitors, even knighthood itself at the hands of these traitors, feasted with them, tilted with them, fought with them – but did not assassinate them by law. Judicial assassination today is reserved only for one race of the King's subjects, for Irishmen; for those who cannot forget their allegiance to the realm of Ireland.

The Kings of England as such had no rights in Ireland up to the time of Henry VIII, save such as rested on compact and mutual obligation entered between them and certain princes, chiefs, and lords of Ireland. This form of legal right, such as it was, gave no King of England lawful power to impeach an Irishman for high treason under this statute of King Edward III of England until an Irish Act, known as Poyning's Law, the 10th of Henry VII, was passed in 1494 in Drogheda, by the Parliament of the Pale in Ireland, and enacted as law in that part of Ireland. But if by

Poyning's Law an Irishman of the Pale could be indicted for high treason under this Act, he could be indicted only in one way and before one tribunal – by the laws of the realm of Ireland and in Ireland. The very law of Poyning's, which, I believe, applies this statute of Edward III to Ireland, enacted also for the Irishman's defence, 'All those laws by which England claims her liberty'. And what is the fundamental charter of an Englishman's liberty? That he shall be tried by his peers. With my peers to try me in this vital issue, for it is patent to every man of conscience that I have a right, an indefeasible right, if tried at all, under this statute of high treason, to be tried in Ireland, before an Irish Court and by an Irish jury. This Court, this jury, the public opinion of this country, England, cannot but be prejudiced in varying degree against me, most of all in time of war. I did not land in England; I landed in Ireland. It was to Ireland that I came; to Ireland I wanted to come; and the last place I desired to land was in England. But for the Attorney-General of England there is only 'England' – there is no Ireland, there is only the law of England – no right of Ireland; the liberty of Ireland and Irishmen is to be judged by the power of England. Yet for me, the Irish outlaw, there is a land of Ireland, a right of resort, a charter that even the very statutes of England itself cannot deprive us of – nay, more, a charter that Englishmen themselves assert as the fundamental bond of law that connects the two kingdoms. This charge of high treason involves a moral responsibility as the very terms of the indictment against myself recite, inasmuch as I committed the acts I am charged with to the 'evil example of others in the like case'. What was this 'evil example' I set to others in the 'like case', and who were these others? The 'evil example' charged is that I asserted the rights of my own country, and the 'others' I appealed to to aid my endeavour were my own countrymen. The example was given not to Englishmen, but to Irishmen, and the 'like case' can never arise in England, but only in Ireland. To Englishmen I set no evil example, for I made no appeal to them. I asked no Englishman to help me. I asked Irishmen to fight for their rights. The 'evil example' was only to other Irishmen who might come after me and 'like case' seek to do as I did. How, then, since neither my example or my appeal was addressed to Englishmen, can I be rightfully tried by them?

If I did wrong in making that appeal to Irishmen to join with me in an effort to fight for Ireland, it is by Irishmen, and by them alone, I can be rightfully judged. From the Court and its jurisdiction I appeal to those I am alleged to have wronged, and to those I am alleged to have injured by my 'evil example', and claim that they alone are competent to decide my guilt or my innocence. If they find me guilty, the statute may affix the penalty, but the statute does not override or annul my right to seek judgment at their hands.

This is so fundamental a right, so natural a right, so obvious a right, that it is clear the Crown were aware of it when they brought me by force and by stealth from Ireland to this country. It was not I who landed in England, but the Crown who dragged me here, away from my own country to which I had turned with a price upon my head, away from my own countrymen whose loyalty is not in doubt, and safe from the judgment of my peers whose judgment I did not shrink from. I admit no other judgment but theirs. I accept no verdict save at their hands. I assert from this dock that I am being tried here, not because it is just, but because it is unjust. Place me before a jury of my own countrymen, be it Protestant or Catholic, Unionist or Nationalist, *Sinn Feineach* or Orangemen, and I shall accept the verdict and bow to the statute and all its penalties. But I shall accept no meaner finding against me than that of those whose loyalty I endanger by my example, and to whom alone I made appeal. If they adjudge me guilty, then guilty I am. It is not I who am afraid of their verdict; it is the Crown. If this be not so, why fear the test? I fear it not. I demand it as my right.

That, my lord, is the condemnation of English rule, of English-made law, of English Government in Ireland, that it dare not rest on the will of the Irish people, but it exists in defiance of their will – that it is a rule derived not from right, but from conquest. Conquest, my lord, gives no title, and if it exists over the body, it fails over the mind. It can exert no empire over men's reason and judgment and affections; and it is from this law of conquest without title to the reason, judgment, and affection of my own countrymen that I appeal.

My lord, I beg to say a few more words. As I say, that was my opinion arrived at many days ago while I was a prisoner. I have no hesitation in re-affirming it here, and I hope that the gentlemen of the press who did not hear me yesterday may have heard me distinctly today. I wish my words to go much beyond this court.

I would add that the generous expressions of sympathy extended me from many quarters, particularly from America, have touched me very much. In that country, as in my own, I am sure my motives are understood and not misjudged – for the achievement of their liberties has been an abiding inspiration to Irishmen and to all men elsewhere rightly struggling to be free in like cause.

My Lord Chief Justice, if I may continue, I am not called upon, I conceive, to say anything in answer to the enquiry your lordship has addressed to me why sentence should not be passed upon me. Since I do not admit any verdict in this Court, I cannot, my lord, admit the fitness of the sentence that of necessity must follow it from this Court. I hope I shall be acquitted of presumption if I say that the Court I see before me now is not this High Court of Justice of England, but a far greater, a far higher, a far older assemblage of justices – that of the people of Ireland I sought to serve – and them alone – I leave my judgment and my sentence in their hands.

Let me pass from myself and my own fate to a far more pressing, as it is a far more urgent theme – not the fate of the individual Irishman who may have tried and failed, but the claims and the fate of the country that has not failed. Ireland has outlived the failure of all her hopes – and yet she still hopes. Ireland has seen her sons – aye, and her daughters too – suffer from generation to generation always for the same cause, meeting always the same fate, and always at the hands of the same power; and always a fresh generation has passed on to withstand the same oppression. For if English authority be omnipotent – a power, as Mr Gladstone phrased it, that reached to the very ends of the earth – Irish hope exceeds the dimensions of that power, excels its authority, and renews with each generation the claims of the last. The cause that begets this indomitable persistency, the faculty of preserving through centuries of misery the remembrance of lost liberty, this surely is the noblest cause men ever strove for, ever lived for, ever died for. If this be the case, I stand here today indicted for, and convicted of sustaining, then I stand in a goodly company and a right noble succession.

My counsel has referred to the Ulster Volunteer movement, and I will not touch at length upon that ground save only to say this, that neither I nor any of the leaders of the Irish Volunteers who were founded in Dublin in November, 1913, had quarrels with the Ulster Volunteers, as such, who were born a year earlier. Our movement was not directed against them, but against the men who misused and misdirected the courage, the sincerity, and the local patriotism of the men of the North of Ireland. On the contrary, we welcomed the coming of the Ulster Volunteers, even while we deprecated the aims and intentions of those Englishmen who sought to pervert to an English party use – to the mean purpose of their own bid for place and power in England – the armed activities of simple Irishmen. We aimed at winning the Ulster Volunteers to the cause of a united Ireland. We aimed at uniting all Irishmen in a natural and national bond of cohesion based on mutual self-respect. Our hope was a natural one, and if left to ourselves, not hard to accomplish. If external influences of disintegration would but leave us alone, we were sure that Nature itself must bring us together. It was not we, the Irish Volunteers, who broke the law, but a British party. The Government had permitted the Ulster Volunteers to be armed by Englishmen, to threaten not merely an English party in its hold on office, but to threaten that party through the lives and blood of Irishmen. The battle was to be fought in Ireland in order that the political 'outs' of today should be the 'ins' of tomorrow in Great Britain. A law designed for the benefit of Ireland was to be met, not on the floor of Parliament, where the fight had indeed been won, but on the field of battle much nearer home, where the armies would be composed of Irishmen slaying each other for some English party gain; and the British navy would be chartered 'transports' that were to bring to our shores a numerous assemblage of military and ex-military experts in the congenial and profitable business of holding down subject populations abroad.

Our choice lay in submitting to foreign lawlessness or resisting it, and we did not hesitate to choose. But while the law breakers had armed their would-be agents openly, and had been permitted to arm them openly, we were met within a few days of the founding of our movement, that aimed at uniting Ireland from within, by Government action from without, directed against our obtaining any arms at all. The manifesto of the Irish Volunteers, promulgated at a public meeting in Dublin on 25 November 1913, stated with sincerity the aims of the organization as I have outlined them. If the aims contained in that manifesto were a threat to the unity of the British Empire, then so much the worse for the Empire. An Empire that can only be held together by one section of its governing population perpetually holding down and sowing dissension among a smaller but none the less governing section, must have some canker at its heart, some ruin at its root.

The Government that permitted the arming of those whose leaders declared that Irish national unity was a thing that should be opposed by force of arms, within nine days of the issue of our manifesto of goodwill to Irishmen of every creed and class, took steps to nullify our effort by prohibiting the import of all arms into Ireland as if it had been a hostile and blockaded coast. And this proclamation of 4 December 1913, known as the Arms Proclamation, was itself based on an illegal interpretation of the law, as the Chief Secretary has now publicly confessed. The proclamation was met by the loyalists of Great Britain with an act of still more lawless defiance – an act of widespread gun-running into Ulster that was denounced by the Lord Chancellor of England as 'grossly illegal and utterly unconstitutional'. How did the Irish Volunteers meet the incitements of civil war that were uttered by the party of law and order in England when they saw the prospect of deriving political profit to themselves from bloodshed among Irishmen?

I can answer for my own acts and speeches. While one English party was responsible for preaching a doctrine of hatred designed to bring about civil war in Ireland, the other, and that the party in power, took no active steps to restrain a propaganda that found its advocates in the army, navy, and Privy Council – in the Houses of Parliament and in the State Church – a propaganda the methods of whose expression were so 'grossly illegal and utterly unconstitutional' that even the Lord Chancellor of England could find only words and no repressive action to apply to them. Since lawlessness sat in high places in England and laughed at the law as at the custodians of the law, what wonder was it that Irishmen should refuse to accept the verbal protestations of an English Lord Chancellor as a sufficient safeguard for their lives and their liberties? I know not how all my colleagues on the Volunteer Committee in Dublin reviewed the growing menace, but those with whom I was in closest cooperation redoubled, in face of these threats from without, our efforts to unite all Irishmen from within. Our appeals were made to Protestant and Unionist as much almost to Catholic and Nationalist Irishmen. We hoped that by the exhibition of affection and goodwill on our part towards our political opponents in Ireland we should yet succeed in winning them from the side of an English party whose sole interest in our country lay in its oppression in the past, and in the present in its degradation to the mean and narrow needs of their political animosities. It is true that they based their actions, so they averred, on 'fears for the Empire', and on a very diffuse loyalty that took in all the peoples of the Empire, save only the Irish. That blessed word 'Empire' that bears so paradoxical a resemblance to charity! For if charity begins at home, 'Empire' begins in other men's homes, and both may cover a multitude of sins. I for one was determined that Ireland was much more to me than 'Empire', and that if charity begins at home so must loyalty. Since arms were so necessary to make our organization a reality, and to give to the minds of Irishmen menaced with the most outrageous threats a sense of security, it was our bounden duty to get arms before all else. I decided with this end in view to go to America, with surely a better right to appeal to Irishmen there for help in an hour of great national trial than those envoys of 'Empire' could assert for their weekend descents upon Ireland, on their appeals to Germany. If, as the right honourable gentleman, the present Attorney-General, asserted in a speech at Manchester, Nationalists would neither fight for Home Rule nor pay for it, it was our duty to show him that we knew how to do both. Within a few weeks of my arrival in the States the fund that had been opened to secure arms for the Volunteers of Ireland amounted to many thousands of pounds. In every case the money subscribed, whether it came from the purse of the wealthy man or the still readier pocket of the poor man, was Irish gold.

Then came the war. As Mr Birrell said in his evidence recently laid before the commission of enquiry into the cause of the late rebellion in Ireland, 'the war upset all our calculations'. It upset mine no less than Mr

Birrell's, and put an end to my mission of peaceful effort in America. War between Great Britain and Germany meant, as I believed, ruin for all the hopes we had founded on the enrolment of the Irish Volunteers. A constitutional movement in Ireland is never far from a breach of the constitution, as the Loyalists of Ulster had been so eager to show us. The cause is not far to seek. A constitution to be maintained intact must be the achievement and the pride of the people themselves; must rest on their own free will and on their own determination to sustain it, instead of being something resident in another land whose chief representative is an armed force − armed not to protect the population, but to hold it down. We had seen the working of the Irish constitution in the refusal of the army of occupation at the Curragh to obey the orders of the Crown. And now that we were told the first duty of an Irishman was to enter that army, in return for a promissory note, payable after death − a scrap of paper that might or might not be redeemed − I felt over there in America, that my first duty was to keep Irishmen at home in the only army that could safeguard our national existence. If small nationalities were to be the pawns in this game of embattled giants, I saw no reason why Ireland should shed her blood in any cause but her own, and if that be treason beyond the seas I am not ashamed to avow it or to answer for it here with my life. And when we had the doctrine of Unionist loyalty at last − 'Mausers and Kaisers and any King you like', and I have heard that at Hamburg, not far from Limburg on the Lahn − I felt I needed no other warrant than that the word conveyed − to go forth and do likewise. The difference between us was that the Unionist champions chose a path they felt would lead to the Woolsack; while I went a road I knew must lead to the dock. And the event proves we were both right. The difference between us was that my 'treason' was based on a ruthless sincerity that forced me to attempt in time and season to carry out in action what I said in word − whereas their treason lay in verbal incitements that they knew need never be made good in their bodies. And so, I am prouder to stand here today in the traitor's dock to answer this impeachment than to fill the place of my right honourable accusers.

We have been told, we have been asked to hope, that after this war Ireland will get Home Rule, as a reward for the life-blood shed in a cause which whoever else its success may benefit can surely not benefit Ireland. And what will Home Rule be in return for what its vague promise has taken and still hopes to take away from Ireland? It is not necessary to climb the painful stairs of Irish history – that treadmill of a nation whose labours are as vain for her own uplifting as the convict's exertions are for his redemption – to review the long list of British promises made only to be broken – of Irish hopes raised only to be dashed to the ground. Home Rule, when it comes, if come it does, will find an Ireland drained of all that is vital to its very existence – unless it be that unquenchable hope we build of the graves of the dead. We are told that if Irishmen go by the thousand to die, not for Ireland, but for Flanders, for Belgium, for a patch of sand on the deserts of Mesopotamia, or a rocky trench on the heights of Gallipoli, they are winning self-government for Ireland. But if they dare to lay down their lives on their native soil, if they dare to dream even that freedom can be won only at home by men resolved to fight for it there, then they are traitors to their country, and their dream and their deaths alike are phases of a dishonourable phantasy. But history is not so recorded in other lands. In Ireland alone in this twentieth century is loyalty held to be a crime. If loyalty be something less than love and more than law, then we have had enough of such loyalty for Ireland or Irishmen. If we are to be indicted as criminals, to be shot as murderers, to be imprisoned as convicts because our offence is that we love Ireland more than we value our lives, then I know not what virtue resides in any offer of self-government held out to brave men on such terms. Self-government is our right, a thing born in us at birth; a thing no more to be doled out to us or withheld from us by another people than the right to life itself – than the right to feel the sun or smell the flowers, or to love our kind. It is only from the convict these things are withheld for crimes committed and proven – and Ireland, that has wronged no man, that has injured no land, that has sought no dominion over others – Ireland is treated today among the nations of the world as if she was a convicted criminal. If it be treason to fight against such unnatural fate as this, then I am proud to be a rebel, and shall cling to my 'rebellion' with the last drop of my blood. If there be no right of rebellion against a state of things that no savage tribe would endure without resistance, then I am sure that it is better for men to fight and die without right than to live in such a state of right as this. Where all your rights become only an accumulated wrong; where men must beg with bated breath for leave to subsist in their own land, to think their own thoughts, to sing their own songs, to garner the fruits of their own labours – and even while they beg, to see things inexorably withdrawn from them – then surely it is braver, a saner and a truer thing to be a rebel in act and deed against such circumstances as these than tamely to accept it as the natural lot of men.

My Lord, I have done. Gentlemen of the jury, I wish to thank you for your verdict. I hope you will not take amiss what I said or think that I made any imputation upon your truthfulness or your integrity when I spoke and said that this was not a trial by my peers. I maintain that I have a natural right to be tried in that natural jurisdiction, Ireland, my own country, and I would put it to you, how would you feel in the converse case, or rather how would all men here feel in the converse case, if an Englishman had landed here in England and the Crown or the Government, for its own purposes, had conveyed him secretly from England to Ireland under a false name, committed him to prison under a false name, and brought him before a tribunal in Ireland under a statute which they knew involved a trial before an Irish jury? How should you feel yourselves as Englishmen if that man was to be submitted to trial by jury in a land inflamed against him and believing him to be a criminal, when his only crime was that he had cared for England more than for Ireland?

Appendix 2 Leo Amery's Explanation to the Home Secretary of His Son's Conduct 14 December 1945

My son's lawyers have asked for an enquiry into his mental condition. I am fully satisfied that such an enquiry is necessary and am prepared to give all the information in my possession to whatever medical tribunal may be appointed by the Home Office.

At the same time I feel that, apart from the issue of mental instability, the Home Secretary, in considering the general question of the granting or refusal of a reprieve should have before him the main facts bearing upon my son's temperament and antecedent history and upon the environment in which he took his decisions. These could not afford a valid defence in law as he was advised that adherence to the King's enemies against the King's allies amounted to adherence against the Sovereign himself. It was in view of this legal advice and in order to spare his family further distress that he determined to plead guilty.

The consequence, however, of this decision is that the Home Secretary, in reviewing the case, will have had before him not only the incontrovertible facts on which legal guilt was admitted, but also the assumptions and inferences with regard to motive and intention which would naturally accompany the case for the prosecution. He will not have had any statement of those elements of the case which would, in that respect, put a very different complexion on his conduct. Taken in conjunction with those abnormal features of his character which are the object of enquiry, they afford, I submit, not indeed a justification, but an intelligible explanation of his sincere, if misguided, conviction that his action was in no sense directed against his country, but was inspired by a desire to save the British Empire as well as Europe from a danger which he felt the British Government of the day refused to realize.

I need not dwell further on those serious issues affecting his mental stability and moral judgement which are under investigation, beyond saying that he was, in any case, by nature given to strong obsessions and curiously unable to appreciate the consequences of his actions or the light in which they would be seen by others. But they should be borne in mind in estimating the effect upon him of the influences to which he was submitted and of the circumstances in which he found himself.

He was largely brought up by a French governess, to whom he was devoted, and not only spoke, but thought, as readily in French as in English. He travelled much while young and lived abroad most of the time from the age of twenty onwards. He was thus particularly susceptible to the continental political environment and almost inevitably drawn into that ideological conflict which has convulsed Europe.

He was unhappy at school, no doubt as a result of his abnormal temperament, but that experience accentuated the tendency to disregard or revolt against generally accepted standards. His rash premature venture into business, his precipitate marriage and subsequent bankruptcy, all prevented his settling down to any normal career at home. He consequently decided in 1936 to settle abroad and make a new start.

He was at that time already of a more European, as distinct from a purely British, outlook, on political questions, strongly anti-Communist – as, indeed, were most people of all parties in this country – and, no doubt, pre-disposed to Fascism. His failure in the film world and his unfortunate experience with money-lenders similarly inclined him to the current Nazi and Fascist doctrine of the Jews as the prime instigators of Communism as well as of the evils of international high finance.

These tendencies were intensified by contact, soon after his arrival in France in 1936 with the forceful and eloquent personality of Doriot. This former Communist leader had recently revolted against Moscow control and become the head of a violent anti-Communist popular organization in France, and was in close touch with corresponding movements in other countries. My son was thus drawn, almost at the outset, into the Spanish Civil War, both working for France's cause outside Spain, but also as a combatant officer serving with the Italian troops. That Civil War was accompanied by atrocities on both sides, and it seems that what my son saw, at the taking of Barcelona, of the Communist torture chambers

there, greatly intensified his horror of the prospect of the spread of
Communism in Europe. He was demobilized from the Spanish service
in July 1939.

He was in Spain when the war broke out in September. Conscription
was not, at that time, applicable to British subjects outside the United
Kingdom. But we corresponded on the subject of his moral duty to report
for service. I have a letter of his written from Lisbon in February 1940 in
which he asked for my advice as to whether he should try to qualify for
the Air Force or apply to the Intelligence Service in view of his knowledge
of languages. It was about the same time, or earlier, that he sent his name
to the Finnish legation in Paris offering to serve in one of the volunteer
corps then being formed to help the Finns against Russia, but without
receiving a reply. In March 1940, he came to see me in Paris and told me
that he was willing to serve. He hoped that he might be allowed to join
our forces directly in France without having to go home first, and I
remember making some enquiry on the point from our Military Attaché
in Paris. But he asked if his joining up could be deferred to June, as
he had secured a contract for the completion of three short films at
Nice which would enable him to clear off his outstanding obligations.
In May he had a breakdown and was found to be suffering from tuberculosis, sufficiently serious to compel him to stop all work and to take a
cottage near a sanatorium at Thorenc, in the mountains above Nice. The
collapse of France left him unmolested for over a year and, in view of
the state of his health and of the physical difficulties of travel, there
seemed at the time no special reason for any attempt to get away. In
November 1941, the Vichy authorities interned him for a short time in
reprisal for our arrest of certain Vichy officials in Syria. He was then
released but obliged to stay at or near Grenoble. In February 1942 he
appealed to the French authorities for repatriation to England in view of
his state of health. This was refused, after a medical examination, by the
Vichy authorities on the ground that he might still be fit enough for
'auxiliary service'. After that, escape from France was no longer even a
possibility.

It is essential to have clearly in mind the situation when, with the
collapse of France, the 'iron curtain' came down and my son was finally

cut off from all English newspapers and from all contact with the political outlook at home. Russia, by her unprovoked aggression on Poland, our ally, was morally our enemy (on the very principle on which my son's propaganda campaign against Russia has been regarded in law as treason against the King), and only prudential considerations restrained us from being actually at war. But so far were we from regarding her in any other light that the British and French Governments had not only sanctioned volunteer forces to fight with the Finns but had actually organized a large-scale expedition for that purpose. Both Governments, too, had been seriously studying plans for bombing the Caspian oilfields in order to deny the oil to Germany. In France itself, for a year after the collapse, the Communists were still regarded by all parties, including the Resistance, as traitors who had sabotaged France's war effort. Their leader, Thorez, now a minister in the de Gaulle Government, had, when called to the colours, escaped to Russia where he was engaged in broadcasting against the French war effort. He had been condemned as a deserter and deprived of his rights as a citizen. In this country too, the *Daily Worker* had to be suspended. Is it altogether to be wondered at that my son, in his French environment and cut off from home influences, should have failed to readjust his outlook, when Hitler attacked his former confederates, with the same wholehearted promptitude that we did fighting for our lives at home?

I gather from him that for the next few months he watched the struggle between Germany and Russia as one between forces both of which were enemies of his country, looking forward to the eventual exhaustion of both, and assuming, in his hopeless ignorance of our outlook and temper here at home, that the British Government would take the same view and find a convenient opportunity of making a compromise peace with Germany. It was at that point, in the summer of 1942, that Doriot, back from the Russian front, visited him in order to say that the Germans had shot their bolt in Russia and that, unless the British Government made a compromise peace with Germany, the whole of Europe would be overwhelmed and come under Communist domination. That this was the greatest of all possible catastrophes was a view widely held at that time by our friends in all the occupied countries, and not least strongly by men like Mihailović in Yugoslavia, or many of the Polish leaders, who had staked all in the fight against Germany. My son at any rate shared that point of view, a fact which presumably became known through Doriot, and led to his being persuaded by a German emissary that Germany genuinely desired peace and to take seriously the, to us, fantastic notion that, even if Mr Churchill's Government rejected it, the British public could be brought round to it by propaganda. He claims that it was with this object in view that he went to Berlin in November 1942, after Stalingrad and El Alamein had justified Doriot's predictions, and delivered his broadcasts. It was with the same purpose, he insists, of impressing the British public with the idea that there were Englishmen ready to put the war against Communism above all other considerations, that he lent himself to what was undoubtedly his most heinous offence, the attempt to create a British anti-Russian unit. For the rest, his chief efforts were given to lecturing on the Communist danger in the occupied countries. He seems throughout these transactions to have demanded and received, from the Germans, a considerable measure of independence, more particularly as regards censorship of his utterances. The frankness of his criticisms of German official policy, in fact, led to an attempt by the German authorities to intern him when in Italy in 1945, an attempt stopped by Italian intervention.

I know that none of the facts above related could amount to a justification or excuse for his conduct. But they do afford a coherent explanation of a course of action consistent with itself in its obsession with the Communist danger, and not incompatible, especially in one of his abnormal temperament and in his environment, with a sincere belief that he was acting in the best interest of his country. Events in Eastern Europe, in Persia and in China might suggest that such a view, however exaggerated, was not based on a merely disloyal anti-British or pro-German partisanship.

I have written this statement because the relevant background of facts is necessarily better known to myself as his father than to anyone else. But apart from that I feel a certain responsibility for the position in which he finds himself, because it was the fact that he was my son that made it worthwhile for the Germans to approach him, and subsequently to give his utterances and actions a prominence which they would not otherwise have received.

Notes

While writing and researching *Patriot Traitors* I consulted and made use of a wide range of books, newspapers and other publications, ranging from *The Times* to Nazi propaganda leaflets. In the Select Bibliography I have listed the most useful books which readers may care to consult if they wish to read more widely into the subject of Roger Casement or examine issues concerning other British renegades in the Second World War. Full details of all works cited by short title only in the Notes will be found in the Bibliography.

Documents relating to Roger Casement's life and career have been picked over at great length by his many biographers but a sense of reality may be restored by examining his Consular despatches in the Public Records Office in FO369, and by reading the Black Diaries on microfiche in HO161 (the originals may be inspected by arrangement with the Public Records Office (PRO)). Casement's MI5 file (KV2) reveals nothing new which is not covered at greater length in his extensive Home Office file in HO144: this is perhaps significant in itself, bearing in mind the supposed machinations of British Intelligence in the forgery conspiracy theories.

The sections of *Patriot Traitors* which deal with John Amery have been derived almost entirely from primary sources. Principally these are held in the Public Records Office in London and comprise his MI5 personal file (KV2), his Home Office 'Renegade' file (HO45), a general Home Office file dealing with his arrest, sentence and execution (HO144) and the file created by the Prison Commissioner relating to his imprisonment and execution at Wandsworth (PCOM9). In addition I made extensive use of the collections of the German Federal Archives in Koblenz and the United States' National Archives in Washington. The diaries of Leo Amery, and John Amery's brother Julian, remain closed to researchers at present until a decision on their disposal is taken by the British Government.

INTRODUCTION

1 Karl Marx, *The 18th Brumaire of Louis Napoleon*, Progress Publishers, Moscow, 1978.
2 Howard Engel, *Lord High Executioner*, Robson Books, London, 1997.
3 PRO: PCOM 9/1117.
4 V. A. C. Gatrell, *The Hanging Tree*, Oxford University Press, Oxford, 1996, p. 306.
5 Ibid., p. 307.
6 Ibid., p. 306.
7 Ibid., p. 316.
8 J. Bellamy, *The Tudor Law of Treason: An Introduction*, Oxford University Press, Oxford, 1979, p. 204.

CHAPTER 1: THE CASEMENTS OF COUNTY ANTRIM

1 Sawyer, *Casement*, p. 10.
2 Ibid., p. 9.
3 Ibid., p. 10.
4 Ibid., p. 12.
5 Ibid., p. 19.
6 Ibid., p. 14.
7 Ibid., p. 17.
8 Elizabeth Bannister, quoted in Inglis, *Roger Casement*, p. 23.
9 Robert Kee, *The Green Flag*, Penguin Books, Harmondsworth, 1989, p. 9.
10 Ibid., p. 11.
11 Gertrude Bannister, quoted in Inglis, *Roger Casement*, p. 24.

CHAPTER 2: A GOOD MAN IN AFRICA

1 Hochschild, *King Leopold's Ghost*, p. 7.
2 Ascherson, *The King Incorporated*, p. 89.
3 Ibid., p. 28.
4 Ibid., p. 47.
5 Leopold II, quoted in Hochschild, *King Leopold's Ghost*, p. 45.
6 Burton, quoted in ibid., p. 50.
7 Stanley, quoted in Ascherson, *The King Incorporated*, p. 118.
8 Sawyer, *Casement*, p. 21.
9 Quoted in Hochschild, *King Leopold's Ghost*, p. 81.
10 Quoted in Inglis, *Roger Casement*, p. 27.
11 Stanley, quoted in Hochschild, *King Leopold's Ghost*, p. 97.
12 Casement, quoted in Inglis, *Roger Casement*, p. 29.
13 Bentley, quoted in ibid., p. 30.
14 Joseph Conrad, *Heart of Darkness*, Penguin Books, Harmondsworth, 1989, p. 43.
15 Hochschild, *King Leopold's Ghost*, p. 72.
16 Joseph Conrad, quoted in Inglis, *Roger Casement*, p. 32.

CHAPTER 3: HER MAJESTY'S CONSUL CASEMENT

1 Quoted in Sawyer, *Casement*, p. 26.
2 PRO: HO161; 1903 diary, 17 April.
3 Inglis, *Roger Casement*, p. 67.

CHAPTER 4: FROM IMPERIALIST JINGO TO REPUBLICAN REBEL

1 Sawyer, *Casement*, p. 47.
2 Casement to Gertrude Bannister, quoted in Inglis, *Roger Casement*, p. 163.

3 Sawyer, *Casement*, p. 81.
4 Ibid., p. 97.

CHAPTER 5: ENGLAND'S DIFFICULTY IS IRELAND'S OPPORTUNITY

1 PRO: HO144/1637.
2 Handwritten note by Sir Roger Casement in BA [Bundesarchiv]/ PA, AA, WK 11k secr: Vol. 1.
3 PRO: KV2/10.
4 1914 diary, 6 December.
5 BA/PA, AA, WK 11k secr: Vol. 1.
6 Ibid.
7 Ibid.
8 PRO: KV2/10.

CHAPTER 6: 'I'M A LUCKY BOY'

1 W. D. Rubinstein, 'The Secret of Leopold Amery', *History Today*, vol. 49, no. 2, February 1999: my account of L. S. Amery's ethnic background relies in large measure on this article.
2 Ibid.
3 Winston Churchill, *My Early Life*, Eland Books, London, 2000, p. 18.
4 William Roger Louis, *In the Name of God, Go!*, Yale University Press, 1979, p. 35.
5 PRO: HO144/22823/227.
6 Ibid.
7 Ibid.
8 PRO: HO144/22823/235.
9 Ibid.
10 Louis, *In the Name of God, Go!*, p. 61.
11 Ibid., p. 73.
12 PRO: HO144/22823/242.

13 PRO: HO144/22823/235.

14 PRO: HO144/22823/231.

15 Ibid. This is a marginal note in a psychiatric report commissioned by Leo Amery in an effort to prevent John's execution.

16 PRO: HO144/22823/228.

17 PRO: HO144/22823/235.

18 PRO: HO144/22823/264.

19 Ibid.

20 PRO: HO144/22823/235.

21 PRO: HO144/22823/265.

22 PRO: HO144/22823/236.

23 PRO: HO144/22823/160.

24 Ibid.

25 PRO: HO144/22823/425.

26 PRO: HO144/22823/244.

27 Ibid.

28 Ibid.

29 Ibid. Presumably, these girls were of the least desirable type from Jameson's point of view, not Amery's.

30 PRO: HO144/22823/249.

31 PRO: HO144/22823/250.

32 PRO: HO144/22823/236.

33 PRO: HO144/22823/161.

34 PRO: HO144/22823/157.

35 PRO: HO144/22823/162.

36 PRO: HO144/22823/236.

37 PRO: HO144/22823/239.

38 Ibid.

39 PRO: HO144/22823/241.

40 PRO: HO144/22823/237.

41 Ibid.

42 PRO: HO144/22823/253.

43 Ibid.

44 Ibid.

45 Una's account of John's sexual preferences was given to the

psychiatrist Dr Glover in December 1945. It is in PRO: HO144/
22823/255–6.

46 PRO: KV2/78.

47 PRO: KV2/80.

48 Christopher Andrew and Vassily Mitrokhin, *The Mitrokhin Archive*,
Allen Lane, London, 1999, pp. 91–2.

49 PRO: HO144/22823/238.

50 PRO: HO45/25773.

CHAPTER 7: 'KEEP YOUR CHIN UP, BABY BEAR'

1 PRO: KV2/81.

2 PRO: HO45/25773.

3 Ibid.

4 PRO: KV2/81.

5 Ibid.

6 Ibid.

7 Ibid.

8 Ibid.

9 Leo Amery, *Diaries* (2 vols), ed. John Barnes and David Nicholson,
vol. II, *The Empire at Bay*, Hutchinson, London, 1988, p. 397.

10 W. D. Rubinstein, 'The Secret of Leopold Amery', *History Today*,
vol. 49, no. 2, February 1999.

11 Quoted in Louis, *In the Name of God, Go!*, pp. 121–2.

12 Winston Churchill, *The Hinge of Fate*, Penguin Books, Harmondsworth, 1985.

13 PRO: KV2/81.

14 Ibid.

15 Weale, *Renegades*, p. 40.

16 Churchill, *The Hinge of Fate*.

17 Ian Ousby, *Occupation*, John Murray, London, 1997, p. 35.

18 Ibid., p. 89.

19 PRO: HO45/25773.

20 PRO: PCOM9/1117.

21 PRO: HO45/25773.

22 PRO: CX/10000/1341 dated 5 August 1942, quoted in KV2/79.

23 Ousby, op. cit., p. 89.

24 Ibid.

25 PRO: HO45/25773.

26 PRO: KV2/79.

27 PRO: HO45/25773.

28 OKH Directive 21: quoted in *The Oxford Companion to the Second World War*, p. 109.

29 PRO: KV2/81.

30 John Amery, *England Faces Europe*, Berlin, 1943, p. 36.

31 PRO: KV2/81.

32 Ibid.

33 Ibid.

34 CX/10000/1341, op. cit.

35 PRO: KV2/81.

36 CX/10000/1341, op. cit.

37 PRO: CX. Report dated 22 February 1942 quoted in KV2/79.

38 PRO: KV2/81.

39 Ibid.

40 Ibid.

41 Ibid.

42 PRO: KV2/79.

43 Ibid.

44 Ibid.

45 Ibid.

46 PRO: KV2/81.

47 Ibid.

48 Ibid.

49 Ibid.

50 Ibid.

CHAPTER 8: RATHER A SENSATION

1 Interrogation of Dr Hesse in PRO: KV2/81.

2 Ibid.

3 Haferkorn in PRO: KV2/81.

4 PRO: KV2/81.

5 Ibid.

6 Ibid.

7 Ralf George Reuth, *Goebbels*, Constable, London, 1993, p. 257.

8 PRO: KV2/81. Dr Hesse saw the order which decreed this only once: 'It was a lengthy paper, stipulating that Goebbels was solely responsible for executing propaganda, and that Ribbentrop was limited to giving advice.'

9 Ibid.

10 Ibid.

11 See particularly K. Hildebrand, *The Foreign Policy of the Third Reich*, Batsford, London, 1973, but most historians of the Third Reich would agree that Hitler was not particularly antagonistic towards Britain; in *Hitler's War*, David Irving has argued, very plausibly, that 'Operation Sealion', the projected invasion of Britain in 1940, was a strategic deception rather than a real plan.

12 PRO: KV2/81.

13 Reuth, *Goebbels*, p. 257.

14 PRO: KV2/81.

15 Ibid.

16 Antony Beevor, *Stalingrad*, Viking, London, 1998, p. 31.

17 *The Oxford Companion to the Second World War*, p. 113.

18 PRO: KV2/81.

19 Ibid.

20 Ibid.

21 Ibid.

22 Ibid.

23 Ibid.

24 Ibid.

25 Ibid.

26 Ibid.

27 Ibid.

28 Ibid.

29 Ibid.

30 Ibid.

31 Ibid.

32 Ibid.

33 PRO: KV2/79.

34 Ibid.

35 Ibid.

36 PRO: HO45/25773.

37 Ibid.

38 Ibid.

39 Ibid.

40 Ibid.

41 Ibid.

42 Trevor-Roper, *Hitler's Table Talk*, p. 687.

43 PRO: HO45/25773.

44 Ibid.

45 PRO: KV2/80.

46 PRO: KV2/78.

47 PRO: HO45/25773.

48 Ibid.

49 Ibid.

50 Ibid.

51 Ibid.

52 Ibid.

53 Ibid.

54 Ibid.

55 PRO: KV2/81.

56 Ibid.

57 Ibid.

58 PRO: KV2/80.

CHAPTER 9: 'I PERSONALLY HAVE NO GREAT BELIEF IN THIS UNIT'

1 David Littlejohn, *Foreign Legions of the Third Reich*, vol. 1, R. J. Bender Publishing, Mountain View, California, 1979, p. 146.
2 PRO: KV2/81.
3 Ibid.
4 John Warburton (John 'Christian')/Friends of Oswald Mosley: Letter to author. I should emphasize that Warburton explicitly distanced himself from anti-Semitism; nevertheless, it was undoubtedly an aspect of British Union policy at this time.
5 J. H. O. Brown, *In Durance Vile*.
6 Warburton, op. cit.
7 Weale, *Renegades*, p. 105.
8 Ibid.
9 USNA: T-175/105/2627701-3.
10 PRO: WO71/1117.
11 USNA: T-120/1168/715/327969.

CHAPTER 10: ENGLAND FACES EUROPE

1 PRO: KV2/80.
2 PRO: KV2/81.
3 Ibid.
4 PRO: KV2/79. *England Faces Europe*, p. 7.
5 *England Faces Europe*, p. 8.
6 Ibid., p. 79.
7 PRO: KV2/81.
8 PRO: KV2/80.
9 PRO: KV2/84.
10 PRO: KV2/81.
11 PRO: KV2/80.
12 PRO: KV2/81.

13 PRO: HO45/25773/95.

14 PRO: HO45/25773/98.

15 PRO: HO45/25773/96.

16 PRO: HO45/25773/91.

17 Ibid.

18 PRO: HO45/25773/89.

19 PRO: KV2/80.

20 Ibid.

21 Full details of the Job case are in his MI5 files in the PRO: KV2/50 and 51.

22 PRO: CRIM1/485.

23 Ibid.

24 PRO: KV2/79.

CHAPTER 11: 'I THOUGHT THEY WERE GOING TO SHOOT ME'

1 PRO: KV2/81.

2 Ibid.

3 PRO: KV2/84.

4 PRO: KV2/81.

5 Ibid.

6 Ibid.

7 Ibid.

8 Ibid.

9 Ibid.

10 Ibid.

11 PRO: KV2/84.

12 PRO: KV2/81.

13 Ibid.

14 Ibid.

15 Irving, *Hitler's War*, p. 673.

16 KV2/81.

17 Ibid.

18 Ibid.

19 Jean-Paul Cointet, *Marcel Déat*, Editions Académiques Perrin, Paris, 1998, p. 321.

20 PRO: KV2/81.

21 Ibid.

22 PRO: KV2/79.

23 Alan Whicker, *Within Whicker's World*, John Murray, London, 1994, p. 45.

CHAPTER 12: TRIAL AND EXECUTION

1 PRO: KV2/7.

2 PRO: HO144/22822 (CX/10,000/1341 of 22.11.45).

3 PRO: HO144/22823.

4 PRO: PCOM9/1117.

5 Ibid.

6 Ibid.

7 PRO: HO144/2283.

8 Ibid.

9 PRO: PCOM9/1117.

CHAPTER 13: EPILOGUE: THE CASEMENT DIARIES FORGERY CONTROVERSY

1 Basil Thomson, *Queer People*, Hodder & Stoughton, London, 1922, p. 90.

2 PRO: KV2/8.

3 Basil Thomson, *The Scene Changes*, Collins, London, 1939, p. 276.

4 MacColl, *Roger Casement*, p. 228.

5 PRO: HO144/1637.

6 Mitchell, *The Amazon Journal of Roger Casement*, p. 45.

7 Ibid., p. 42.

8 Ibid., p. 44.

Select Bibliography

Ascherson, Neal, *The King Incorporated*, George Allen & Unwin, London, 1963

Brown, J. H. O., *In Durance Vile*, Robert Hale, London, 1981

Burleigh, Michael, *The Third Reich: A New History*, Macmillan, London, 2000

Cole, J. A., *Lord Haw-Haw and William Joyce: The Full Story*, Faber and Faber, London, 1964

Dear, I. C. B., and Foot, M. R. D., *The Oxford Companion to the Second World War*, Oxford University Press, Oxford, 1995

Doerries, Reinhard R., *Prelude to the Easter Rising*, Frank Cass, London, 2000

Hochschild, Adam, *King Leopold's Ghost*, Macmillan, London, 1999

Höhne, Heinz, *The Order of the Death's Head*, Secker and Warburg, London, 1969

Inglis, Brian, *Roger Casement*, Hodder and Stoughton, London, 1973

Irving, David, *Hitler's War*, Macmillan, London, 1977

Kershaw, Ian, *Hitler 1936–1945: Nemesis*, Allen Lane, The Penguin Press, London, 2000

Kershaw, Ian, *The Nazi Dictatorship*, Arnold, London, 2000

MacColl, R., *Roger Casement: A New Judgement*, Hamish Hamilton, London, 1956

Mackey, H. O., *The Life and Times of Roger Casement*, C. J. Fallon, Dublin, 1954

Mackey, H. O., *Roger Casement: The Truth about the Forged Diaries*, C. J. Fallon, Dublin, 1966

Mitchell, Angus, *The Amazon Journey of Roger Casement*, Anaconda, London, 1997

Montgomery Hyde, H., *The Trial of Roger Casement*, William Hodge, London, 1960

Reid, B. L., *The Lives of Roger Casement*, Yale University Press, New Haven and London, 1976

Rolf, David, *Prisoners of the Reich: Germany's Captives 1939–1945*, Leo Cooper, London, 1988

Sawyer, R., *Casement: The Flawed Hero*, Routledge & Kegan Paul, London, 1984

Sawyer, R., *Roger Casement's Diaries: 1910, The Black and the White*, Pimlico, London, 1997

Selwyn, Francis, *Hitler's Englishman: The Crime of Lord Haw-Haw*, Routledge & Kegan Paul, London, 1987

Spitzy, Reinhard, *How We Squandered the Reich*, Michael Russell, Norwich, 1999

Tieke, Wilhelm, *Tragödie um die Treue*, Munin Verlag, Osnabrück, 1971

Trevor-Roper, Hugh, *Hitler's Table Talk 1941–44*, Phoenix, London, 2000

Weale, Adrian, *Renegades: Hitler's Englishmen*, Weidenfeld and Nicolson, London, 1994

West, Rebecca, *The Meaning of Treason*, Macmillan, London, 1949

Index